ARLO J. NAU

The Impact of Context on Content in Matthew

Fairway Press, Lima, Ohio

THE IMPACT OF CONTEXT ON CONTENT IN MATTHEW

FIRST EDITION
Copyright © 1999 by
Arlo J. Nau

ISBN 0-7880-1467-6   PRINTED IN U.S.A.

Dedications

To Lynn, my loved, loving and long-suffering wife of 40 years;

To Mr. Erdal Çenel, tour-guide extraordinaire, who led me on the most exciting days of discovery in my life.

All biblical quotations in the English language in this book are taken from *The New Oxford Annotated BIBLE with the Aprocryphal / Deutero-canonical Books, The New Revised Standard Version*. Eds. Bruce M. Metzger and Roland E. Murphy. Oxford University Press, New York, 1991.

TABLE OF CONTENTS

THE IMPACT OF CONTENT ON CONTEXT IN MATTHEW

PREFACE

A Preface is intended to put a *pre-face* on the subsequent book. I find the task of Preface composition for this particular volume more uncomfortable than difficult. In a way, this book, paradoxically, represents a scholarly attempt to be unscholarly, a religious quest to redress contemporary religiosity, and an apparently audacious effort to desacralize at least one portion of the sacred scriptures — the Gospel of St. Matthew. Such going-against-the-grain of one's own upbringing, training and traditional commitments is personally unnerving, but, I believe, necessary nonetheless. My intentions are entirely positive — to make the import and impact of this *First* Gospel more accessible to all readers.

Perhaps an initial word of autobiographical explanation would help. As a relatively young Lutheran campus pastor at the State University of New York at Buffalo in the late 1960s I decided that I needed something which could make my curriculum vitae more academically respectable. Where better could one in my position begin than with Matthew, the *first* Gospel listed in the New Testament. I read it...and reread it...and then read everything at hand about it. Thanks to a very generous church and home community I pursued graduate study at the Toronto School of Theology and the University of Toronto, Canada, fulfilling Doctor of Theology degree requirements by writing a dissertation, and eventually a book, on ***PETER IN MATTHEW: Discipleship, Diplomacy and Dispraise.***[1]

Through it all, I found myself increasingly at odds with my heritage. Matthew, the Gospel, did not walk in lock-step syncopation with my Pauline/Lutheran traditions, and trying to rationalize ways to make it do so proved an exercise in futility. For example, instead of *"faith, hope and charity,"* I Cor. 13:13, the *first* evangelist promoted *"justice, mercy and faith,"* Mt. 23:23, marking a reorientation in moral perspective and emphasis. In places, *Matthew* made Paul look like an irresponsible antinomian, removing not only *"one letter, or one stroke of a letter"* from the law, Mt. 5:18, but obviating the law itself (cf. Gal. 3:10-12). In contrast, *Matthew* seemed totally ignorant of Paul's favorite word "grace," χαρις. In sum, I found my whole theological landscape strewn with the still writhing remains of numerous *theologoumena*, i.e., doctrines, practices and arguments which may once have served a positive purpose, but which now seem devoid of any real support in the biblical texts themselves. *

Something had to be done. The angels of sentimental devotionalism, easy traditionalism and pious ignorance which still fluttered about this Gospel had to be dispersed. Some degree of *Matthean* humanness needed to be restored to its hallowed pages. If we were going to understand it, and identify with it, this Gospel which speaks so uniquely about the *"kingdom of heaven"* begged to be brought down to earth and re-anchored in the quagmire that is history. In short, Matthew needed a controlling context, enabling the reader once again to feel at home in its milieu. I decided by way of this book to attempt to provide that kind of ambiance and perspective.

As part of my preparation, I undertook a brief trip to the city of Antakya, the ancient Syrian Antioch, located today in extreme south-central Turkey. I wanted to "rub shoulders" with the culture, the flora and fauna, the climate and the archeological vestiges of that area where the vast majority of scholars believe Matthew was originally written. It proved to be the experience of a lifetime.

Here due recognition must be given to my personal companion and guide, Mr. Erdal Çenel of Mersin, Turkey. As a former wildcat oil driller in South America, salmon fisherman in Alaska, deep-sea diver, mountain climber, Turkish patriot and historian, he has to be numbered among the two or three most extraordinary human beings whom it has been my privilege in life to know. You will meet him, too, in the pages to follow.

My gratitude must be expressed also to my two closest and most empathetic local friends, both clergymen: Bernie Backman, who as a man with more raw talent than life provides opportunity to implement, keeps my literary juices flowing; and Dr. Charles Emerson, who as a Professor in New Testament Studies at Arizona State University, patiently, meticulously and yet graciously critiques my efforts and encourages their continuation. In an Arizona environment that is on average as arid exegetically as the host Sonoran Desert is geologically the thoughtful contributions of such friends are invaluable.

If the *first* evangelist needed assistance in publishing his *First* Gospel (cf. pp. 108-112), I certainly did in authoring this book. My sincere thanks, therefore, to Mr. Thomas W. Lentz, Acquisitions Editor at CSS Publication Co., and Mr. Terry Heminger, Director of Fairway Press, and to their corps of caring and capable associates, Teresa Rhoads, Managing Editor; Renee Brooks and Laurie Byer, Project Coordinators.

A few preliminary aids to understanding the literary strategies employed in this book are also apropos. "Gospel" is capitalized to indicate the literary text. A lower case "g" is employed when referring to the proclaimed "good news." Again, the designation, "Matthew," as we have already experienced, can either be the title of the Gospel or the name of the author. I make a clarifying distinction by placing the latter in italics, and, for reasons which will soon become apparent, by trying to use the author's traditional name, *Matthew,* as infrequently as possible. Furthermore, as you will learn in

Chapter Four of this book, I have given the evangelist a *nom-de-plume*, "Ben Grammateus", to accurately disassociate him from the traditional disciple, *Matthew, the tax collector,* Mt. 10:3. Similarly, I consistently put *"first"* in italics when referring to the *First* Gospel, or the *first* evangelist, to remind the reader of the limited sense in which this designation is true. Matthew, indeed, heads the list of New Testament books, but, according to the Two Source Hypothesis in resolution of the "Synoptic Problem," Matthew was not the first Gospel written, but was in large measure a rewrite of Mark. All biblical quotations in the text are also italicized for easy identification. Finally, the spelling, "Antiochene," as the adjectival cognate of Antioch, is used here as apparently preferred by current commentators, although "Antiochian" and "Antiochan" at times appear in the literature.

Introducing each chapter of the book are brief poetic quotes or vignettes of personal experiences. They are designed and intended to assist you to identify with me as the author of this book, and perhaps, through me, with the author of the *First* Gospel.

As we shall see, the *first* evangelist was a very resourceful editor and author, employing a wide range of rhetorical tactics to retain his readers' interest and promote understanding — anecdotes, double entendres, plays-on-words, repetitions, exaggerations, paradoxes, and esoteric hints which only the initiated could comprehend. I have attempted to use similar approaches, on occasion, to make your reading experience of this book match that of any sensitive reader, or hearer, of the *First* Gospel. The *first* evangelist, it seems to me, wrote in a very personal vein. I try to do the same.

Surely Matthew was meant to be understood on its own terms, without devotional harmonizing designed to remove its discordant uniquenesses. I hope you will be equally patient and forgiving with me and the several loose ends undoubtedly left dangling in this exploratory study.

Since this work is intended to be "popular scholarship," aimed at the broad spectrum of interested laity, clergy, theology students and faculty, every effort will be made to limit the use of technical language and the number of distracting footnotes. Some of each, of course, will be unavoidable. I attempt early in each chapter, or important subsection, to introduce either in the text or in endnotes those general authorities on whose work much of the subsequent material is based. The serious student is encouraged to research these works because references to further individual details taken from them will not be credited.

While I am deeply indebted to many scholars for much of the basic information found here, the approach, organization and conclusions are my own and I take full responsibility for any deficiencies in the finished product.

Arlo J. Nau
Phoenix, Arizona, U.S.A.

[1] Published by The Liturgical Press, Collegeville, Minnesota, 1992
* Nevertheless, I remain a Lutheran, but no doubt now more of a Matthean one.

PART I

CONTEXT

Prologue to Part I

Double Exposure

Imagine that you and I are tourists standing on the crest of Habib (Mount) Neccar overlooking the modern city of Antakya, Turkey, located some twenty miles inland and seventy-five miles south of the extreme northeast corner of the Mediterranean Sea. This is not your usual crowded coastal tourist haven, such as Istanbul, Antalya or Izmir. Nevertheless, the setting is itself impressively imposing. Besides, it's April — springtime on the lush Hatay peninsula dangling down like an umbilical cord from the underbelly of present day Turkey (cf. Maps 1 & 2, pp.6& 7). In the distance, to the northwest, are the final eruptions of the Nur Daglari mountain range still vainly clawing at the morning skies before helplessly plunging into the teal waters of the Mediterranean pit. Coming closer, in mid-view, is the Amik plain, unbelievably green at this time of year with its vast fields of barley, parsley and onions. And then, finally, in the valley immediately below, the city itself, bisected by the silver thread of the Asi Nehri (River) and punctured with the needles of a hundred Islamic minarets. This is Antakya! And what a pleasant place to be! (cf. cover photo)

But as we momentarily put aside our normal tourist haste to watch and wonder, a curious sight trips the circuitry of our memories. Amid the twisted tangle of this typical Middle-Eastern, Turkish-Syrian town, where extended family lines and ethnic loyalties are often more important than convenience or aesthetic orderliness, there is one abnormally straight street coming directly toward us from the river's edge (cf. the cover

3

photo of this book and Map 3, p. 7). Could this still be the one thoroughfare that Glanville Downey, writing in 1961 and recalling the Princeton University archeological digs of 1932-39, described as covering and retracing one branch of the celebrated double colonnaded avenue of Roman times?[1] If so, then this is not only twentieth century Antakya, Turkey, which we are viewing, but also first century C.E. Antioch, capital of the Roman province of Syria. The Asi Nehri is in fact the famed Orontes River and the precipice upon which we are standing is none other than Mount Silpius, frequently mentioned in ancient Greek and Latin accounts of Roman/Syrian and Arab/Byzantine wars. That road down there, on the left, reaching out to the south, must then lead to Daphne, the notable, and sometimes notorious, garden retreat of the ancient world's rich and famous, where even Anthony and Cleopatra chose to honeymoon.   And that bridge crossing the Orontes to the southwest must similarly head toward what is left of Seleucia Pieria, the once prosperous port town which satiated the capital city's immense appetite.

This Syrian Antioch, then, is where Barnabas and Saul/Paul ministered to early followers of Jesus in Diaspora, Acts 11:19-26, 13:1-3; where Jew and Gentile disciples were first called Christians according to Acts 11:26; where Peter and Paul argued divisively as recounted in Galatians 2; and where most contemporary biblical scholars believe the Gospel of Matthew was written sometime around 85 C.E. What we are experiencing, then, is truly an historic, if not inspirational, sight!

But wait a minute. Perhaps we had better come down from our mountain lookout for a while. We are getting too far ahead of our story and actually pre-empting the purpose of this book which is to provide the reader with some fresh, alternative and perhaps even corrective insights into the *First* Gospel when viewed in the context of its original setting in time and place. So please, let us momentarily retrace our steps and begin again.

4

Endnote

[1] Cf. Glanville Downey, A HISTORY OF ANTIOCH IN SYRIA FROM
SELEUCUS TO THE ARAB CONQUEST; Princeton University Press,
Princeton, N.J., 1961. Also: Glanville Downey, ANCIENT ANTIOCH;
Princeton University Press, Princeton, N.J., 1963.

Map 1:
The Hatay Province as it is known today with its Provincial Captial city
of Antakya

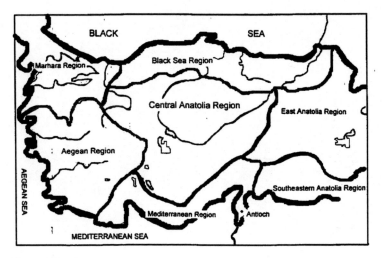

Above: Map 2:
The seven geographic regions of modern Turkey with the Hatay Peninsula pointing south from the Mediterranean Region.

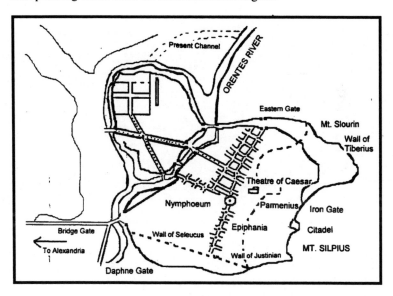

Above: Map 3:
Topographical line-drawing of ancient Antioch showing the Orontes River, the island, the route of the colonnaded cardo (street) and the protective walls of the city circling the crest of Mt. Silpius.

Chapter 1

Context or Pretext?

Faith and credulity....
Identical twins with conflicting personalities;
Sugar and salt; Pill and placebo;
Strangers occupying the same pew.
How do they differ? How can we tell?
Which is which? And which are we?[1]

Like me, many of you readers of this book will remember the traditional seminary truism: "A text without a context soon becomes a pretext." Certainly, context in its various modes adds perspective, color and credibility to the content of any literary work. What, for example, would be our American estimate of **The Gettysburg Address** if we did not know that Abraham Lincoln, our honored 16th President, delivered it in person at the dedication of a military cemetery on the site of the decisive battle of the Civil War with many wounded veterans looking on? Would it still rank with the **Declaration of Independence**, the **Constitution** and the **Bill of Rights** as one of the definitive statements of our identity and integrity as a nation? Probably not. Historians would more likely relegate it to the back pages of their books theorizing that it represented nothing more than an exemplary patriotic speech delivered, no doubt, by some Philadelphia lawyer at a banquet in Independence Hall for a group of 19th century morticians. Content, minus reliable context, equals pretext.

Here, then, is the locus of this study, particularly this PART I. I hope to expand our horizons for understanding the Gospel of Matthew by giving its composition a home, its narrative a neighborhood, its plot a time-line, its cast a personality, its author a name and its audience a face...and all this, I would argue, with more justification, breadth and reliable supportive evidence than has been previously attempted in a single volume.

The Rise of Context I

The tragedy, if I may so speak of this enterprise, is that the Gospel of Matthew once enjoyed a comprehensive context, but in time lost it.

The original concept began to build already in the first half of the second century, C.E., when Papias, Bishop of Hieropolis in Asia Minor, wrote: "Matthew composed his history in the Hebrew dialect, and everyone translated it as he was able."[2] Seemingly, just that suddenly, the Gospel had a compositional language, Hebrew; a name, The Gospel According to St. Matthew; and an author, the tax-collector/disciple called "Levi, the Son of Alphaeus," in Mark 2:14 and Luke 5:27, but significantly re-named "Matthew" in Mt. 9:9.

While this ascription of the Gospel to *Matthew* probably represented only a pious opinion on the part of the venerable bishop, it was approvingly picked up and popularized by his eminent successors, Irenaeus of Lyon, Origen of Alexandria, and in the fourth century C.E., by Eusebius, the first great church historian living in Caesarea Maretima.

St. Augustine, 354-430 C.E., the celebrated Bishop of Hippo in North Africa, added the further authoritative opinion: "Mark follows him (i.e., Matthew) closely and looks like his attendant and epitomizer."[3] This was enough to guarantee Matthew the prominent first place in subsequent codices of the canonical gospels, with the much shorter Marcan "epitome," or abbreviation, relegated to the second position sandwiched between Matthew and Luke. Matthew, now the *First* Gospel, thus became also the foremost Gospel of the church, particularly in the early and medieval periods of the church's history.

The choice was made-to-order for subsequent systematic theological development. With its more than one hundred quotations from and allusions to the Old Testament, Matthew, as the *First* Gospel, formed a natural bridge to the New Testament. As a proposed translation into the Greek from a "Hebrew dialect" it performed a similar function linguistically. More importantly, *Matthew*, the disciple, had been an active participant in, and an eye and ear witness to Jesus' entire ministry — privileges even Mark and Luke did not enjoy. What better credentials could an author have for the role of an inspired evangelist whose every word could be trusted?

Popular supportive commentators even enthusiastically noted evidences of a tax collector's hand in the *First* Gospel's preference for larger monetary amounts, e.g., talents instead of minas in the Parable of the Talents, cf. Mt. 25:14-30 vs. Luke 19:11-27.[4] The content and the context were thus a perfect fit. For the religiously circumspect, Matthew, along with the other canonical Gospels, had become a divinely inspired, totally consistent, inerrant deposit of truth for all time and every situation. Obviously, it deserved its place at the head of its class.

The Demise of Context I

This comfortable rapport lasted for more than a millennium until the period of the Enlightenment in the late 17th century. Then, with the emergence of large European universities and renewed interest in classical languages it was only natural that the Holy Scriptures, too, would be subjected to critical review — hesitant and faithfully well-intended at first, but forced by the evidence inexorably toward increased skepticism over time. The age of historical criticism in biblical study had arrived.

11

The obvious omission and/or addition of isolated pericopes within the three Synoptic Gospels were now noted and questioned. When, why and how did these independent stories originate and presume to weave their way into the sacred text? The long acknowledged irregularities in sequence, location, vocabulary, narrative detail and even theological emphasis between parallel Synoptic accounts were also accorded added weight as evidence of individual editing.

The most devastating blow to Matthean inviolability in particular, however, resulted from the debate over the priority of authorship of the Synoptic Gospels, i.e., the so-called Synoptic Problem. It was obvious from the large amount of shared, almost verbatim, material found in Matthew, Mark and Luke that a common source, or sources, had been employed, or that the evangelists had unabashedly copied from one another in some unknown sequence. The eventual, generally accepted solution to this quandary in the mid-19th century was that the authors of Matthew and Luke, in addition to materials uniquely their own, had independently used Mark as their primary source, but then also shared another set of written *logia,* or sayings of Jesus, referred to simply as "Q."[5] This solution is known as the "Two Source Hypothesis" and remains predominant among biblical scholars today.

The effect of these discoveries upon the traditional concept of Matthean priority and supremacy, however, has been disastrous. Obviously, Matthew was not the *First* Gospel written after all, but the second or perhaps even the third (explaining our use of italics when referring to the *First* Gospel or the *first* evangelist to indicate the limited nature of the Gospel's primacy and the questionable identity of its authorship). Mark was not an "epitome" of Matthew, as St. Augustine had opined, but, conversely, Matthew was a secondary expansion of Mark. Furthermore, the author could not have been *Matthew*, the disciple. Why would a direct, eye-witness companion of Jesus defer to an account composed by an uninvolved bystander, such as Mark, cf. Mk. 14:51-52, whose information about Jesus' life and ministry would have to have been at the very best second hand? Then, too, it soon became clear to 19th century linguists that, except for some Old Testament quotations and isolated Jewish-Christian traditions, this Gospel was not written in "translation Greek" based on some unidentified "Hebrew dialect," as Papias had surmised, but was originally composed in authentic, fluent, idiomatic Greek of its own time and place. True, this Gospel displayed an interest in taxes and finance, but the amounts as noted in the parable referred to above were exorbitant and unrealistic, obviously serving more of a literary than any historical purpose. Further, the excision here in the *First* Gospel of the winsome story of the Widow's Mite, Mark 12:41-44, argues against authorship by someone preoccupied with attitudes about finances. The proposed discovery of a tax collector's hand in the authorship of the work, thus, was also left unsubstantiated. In short, the once neat context of this Gospel as long perceived had split apart at the seams.

The contextual vacuum thus created was unbearable, especially for Matthew which unlike Luke 1:1-4, for example, seemed to lack any internal vestige of "publication facts." As a consequence, a feverish quest for answers to questions of context was initiated in various fields and down diverse methodological paths: Textual Criticism sought a purer original biblical text free from the corruptions which had accrued over time as the result of primitive transmission processes. Archeology went searching for literary and material artifacts in Bible lands hoping to confirm biblical dates, descriptions and itineraries. Form Criticism worked to identify the literary forms of individual pericopes and their "situations-in-life" accounting for their origin and development. Patristic studies attempted to gauge the fluctuating winds of theological

13

discourse in the early church. Finally, a wide variety of schools and methodologies, among them the Tübingen School of F.C. Bauer, the History-of-Religions and the Historical Jesus schools, all tried to "position" each of the New Testament writings, including the *First* Gospel, in such a way as to provide reliable perspectives for interpretation and evaluation.

The Triumph of Pretext

Sadly, the initial result of all these pursuits was frustration, leading for the most part to applications which fall under the general category of pretext. While most research efforts were initially well intended and undertaken with the aim of reaffirming cherished positions, their success was limited. Every positive answer generated several more troublesome questions, and, unfortunately, the solutions arrived at by following the various strategies did not uniformly coincide. Traditionalists, with some justification, now scoffed at all attempts at new learning labeling it "negative criticism."

The general effect on church life over the past one hundred years can only be described as one of malaise accounting at least in part for what one astute observer has called "the strange silence of the Bible in the church."[6] The laity has either retreated into the seemingly safe arms of the old traditions which, while although unsupported by the facts, at least exude a satisfying sense of piety, or they are content to simply defer to the clergy for answers to questions about such biblical niceties as who really authored the *First* Gospel and where. Church school lesson materials have been reduced largely to moralizations, and so-called Adult Bible Studies are more often topical than textual. Preachers, while introduced to contemporary investigative approaches and insights in seminary, find it impossible to keep up with new fashions in biblical scholarship, much less explain them to their constituencies. Expository preaching, consequently, has given way to bombast or theatrics, especially on television. Denominations, similarly, refuse to make liturgical changes that might confuse members. The Feast of St. Matthew, Apostle and Evangelist, for example, continues to be observed each September 21st even though few serious theologians today still believe that one and the same *Matthew* filled both roles.

Even "objective" biblical scholars are not immune to the inertia of traditionalism. Though aware of the fact that most, if not all, New Testament Gospels, Letters and Apocalypses were initially written in the Greek language and in Diaspora, quasi Hellenistic, situations these academicians in their intertextuality, social science and literary research continue to focus almost exclusively on Hebrew, Jewish and Palestinian provenances.[7]

Finally, we now find that even the sacrosanct domain of Bible translation is influenced not only by what the text actually records but also by considerations of what the present day consumer will tolerate and purchase. The translations of the various biblical texts, accordingly, have been homogenized making Matthew sound almost exactly like Mark, or even Moses, obviating most distinctive differences in authorial style, literary quality or personal perspective.

Add all of these negatives together and we are confronted with a plague of pretext, everything from pious demagoguery to irreverent jokes, conducive to credulity, but all ultimately injurious to honest, mature faith.

The Reconstruction of Context II

Yet, there are signs of hope. Over time a residue of generally accepted clues to a new and supposedly true context of the *First* Gospel has accumulated, gleaned from the many fields of study. Redaction Criticism, for example, has been a major contributor. The careful analysis of additions, omissions and transpositions in Matthew as compared with its

15

sources in Mark and Q, plus patterned, consistent, changes in vocabulary, emphasis and nuance, have exposed hints of the redactor/author's personal characteristics, preferences, orientation, training and convictions, as well as something of his environment and opposition.

Studies in classical rhetoric have further illuminated the literary strategies employed in the text. One technique of particular interest is that of "transparency," involving a kind of "reading-between-the-lines" exercise. By noting the *first* evangelist's choice of subject matter, extensive use of direct speech, double entendre, repetitions, and incidental references to "local color," scholars now recognize that often, while quoting Jesus addressing his disciples in the basic narrative, the evangelist has so nuanced Jesus' words that they simultaneously speak to *Matthew's* own contemporary community and situation. It is a case of a double horizon, one narrative artfully superimposed on the other. To understand the full import of much of the *First* Gospel, then, requires skill in reading it, as it were, through bifocal lenses with one eye on the past, the time of Jesus, and the other on the immediate situation and place of the Gospel's actual composition.

Another scholarly approach, Narrative Criticism, has freed us from a long-standing preoccupation with individual pericopes, micro-analyzing single parables, miracles or sayings, by reminding us that the Gospel, despite its initial appearance as a series of independent vignettes, is after all a unified story with a continuous plot, developing various characters and interweaving an assortment of themes on its way to a cohesive conclusion. The interpreter, therefore, must beware premature, incomplete theological deductions based on individual passages or anecdotes discovered along the way. The import of this Gospel is dependent more on how it ends than how it begins. The significance of each part, therefore, must be determined by the ultimate perspective of the whole.

Add to these investigations insights from parallel written materials, the other Gospels and the Book of Acts, from pseudepigrapha, church and secular historians, and contemporaneous philosophers, plus the discoveries of archeology and the personal observation of local flora and fauna and we have grounds for the reconstruction of a formidable context for the First Gospel. We may refer to it as Context II and will attempt to define its parameters in more detail in the chapters to follow.

Ours is not a totally new endeavor. One of the earliest and most delightful attempts at pulling the scattered pieces of the Matthean context together is the little book by R.E.O. White published in 1979 and politely entitled in the United States THE MIND OF MATTHEW, but known in Britain less pretentiously as MATTHEW LAYS IT ON THE LINE.[8] Eschewing most semblances of academic pedantry, White shows how patently practical the author of the *First* Gospel was in addressing every-day issues in his own congregation located in Syrian Antioch.

This work was followed in 1983 by ANTIOCH AND ROME: NEW TESTAMENT CRADLES of CATHOLIC CHRISTIANITY, [9] co-authored by Raymond E. Brown and John P. Meier. In the first half of the book, Meier traces the probable vagaries of Antiochene theology during the first three generations of the church's history in that Syrian city as represented by St. Paul, St. Matthew and St. Ignatius, respectively.

Along similar lines, a three day conference featuring internationally known scholars discussing "The Social History of the Matthean Community in Roman Syria" was held at Southern Methodist University in Dallas, Texas, in October of 1989. The wide variety of topics chosen included the archeology and climate of ancient Antioch, the role and relation of Ignatius to

Matthew and the Jewish community, as well as the social mores and scribal culture of the city.[10]

Meanwhile, J. Andrew Overman took a different tack. In his 1990 book, MATTHEW'S GOSPEL AND FORMATIVE JUDAISM,[11] Overman suggests Sepphoris or Tiberias in southern Galilee as prime candidates for the site of the *First* Gospel's publication. He feels that Matthean Christianity and Formative Judaism, although antagonistic, still had so much in common that their conflict must have been of an intramural nature, i.e., "within the walls" of Palestinian Judaism in the 70's or 80's of the first century C.E. Both, of course, were eventually superseded by Rabbinical Judaism in succeeding decades.

Finally, a very recent publication by Warren Carter, MATTHEW: STORYTELLER, INTERPRETER, EVANGELIST, agrees with Overman that the Matthean congregation remains anchored within Judaism, but with Meier and others, Carter locates it in Roman/Syrian Antioch in late first century C.E. There it leads a marginal existence as an "alternate, inclusive community reconciling its own divisions and the divisions of its society."[12]

Inference Criticism

This present work is intended as the next step, filtering out academic anomalies while building as much as possible upon basic consensus, or near consensus, scholarship, flavoring antiseptic objectivity with a tinge of informed imagination and illustration drawn from contemporaneous, late first century C.E. thought and experience. Its orientation is thus the reverse of that found in most modern commentaries. Here we prefer, somewhat experimentally, to view the Gospel from the perspective of a Greco-Roman Diaspora point of origin rather than from that of an exclusively Jewish or Palestinian provenance. The dominant language and cultural milieu,

18

therefore, is Greek, similarly reorienting our linguistic and social compasses.

This book, accordingly, represents "popular scholarship," employing macro- rather than micro-analyses, favoring the big picture over minute detail. I sometimes refer to this operative methodology as "Inference Criticism," i.e., a rather unsightly bricolage of Redaction, Reader Response and Narrative Criticisms minus most technical jargon about "implied" readers, audiences and authors, but plus a modicum of archeological, rhetorical and historical insight. Inference in the form of logical deductions mixed with some germane possibilities has always been a respected part of scholarly theory, inquiry and practice.

Admittedly, the potential for some error and "pretext" of our own design remains. Inevitably, the evidence garnered in any research will be in direct proportion to the scope of the methodology employed. Put another way, the exegete will invariably discover only those details that the methodology he has selected is designed to find. As one Matthean commentator pertinently complains:

> "One should not spin off some hypothetical context and then read it into the interpretation of the text or assume that the Gospel was drafted solely to address burning issues for a limited group. It is conceivable, if not likely, that Matthew was intended for broad circulation in a variety of Christian communities with a variety of needs and issues and that it was motivated simply by a general desire to tell others about Jesus, who he was, what he did and what happened to him in the end."[13]

This warning is well taken, but I don't believe we are guilty of the exegetical aberrations the writer describes. In fact, in terms of the task at hand, I could hardly agree less with the author. First of all, our proposed context is not entirely hypothetical, as suggested, but is backed up by considerable supportive evidence — historical, geological and rhetorical — inferential though some of it may be. Secondly, the commentator's "conceivable" notion of the evangelist's indefinite and indistinct intentions is itself extremely hypothetical and subjective as several subsequent acknowledgments in his own commentary reveal. And finally, his attempt to universalize this Gospel, seeking to interpret its message only diachronically, is patently misguided. How can anyone possibly consider such vitriolic redactional explosions as *"Scribes, Pharisees, hypocrites!...blind guides!...You snakes, you brood of vipers!"* found in Mt. 23:13, 16 & 33, as anything but personal affronts denoting an immediate, local and specific confrontational situation? No, our chosen, composite methodology may be somewhat cumbersome, but it is comprehensive enough to detect and explain most, if not all, the variables imbedded in the *First* Gospel.

What really makes palatable the risk of such apparent "controlled recklessness" as we may be thought to employ in our analysis, however, is the realization that the ultimate goal of this study is not merely to accumulate more arid facts about Matthew — whether Systematically orthodox or not — but to engender an existential and responsible sense of empathy with the evangelist and his community. Our aim is to enter into dialog with them, to share a bit of their first century experience, their hopes and fears, thus making the reading of the *First* Gospel not only spiritually invigorating but personally captivating once again.

As a further consequence, my purpose in this study is not to present a comprehensive verse-by-verse analysis of *Matthew's* Gospel, reviewing every exegetical detail or the catalogue of scholarly opinion on every topic. In brief, it is not at all to refute or replace what others have said or done, but, hopefully, only to supplement their insights with some alternative ones of my own, based on the commitment to understand this Gospel from the vantage point of the time and place of its original composition rather than that of its storyline in the life and ministry of Jesus.

Whether the Matthean context, i.e., Context II, as developed in the following chapters is responsible enough to accomplish these purposes will be up to you to decide. Gratefully, this approach has proved sufficiently vital to have made reading and studying the *First* Gospel engaging, exciting, and even fun for me once more.

Chapter 1 Endnotes

[1] From "Faith and Credulity," #33 in PRACTICALLY POETRY, privately published by the author.

[2] Cf. Eusebius, ECCLESIASTICAL HISTORY, Bk. III, Ch. XXXIX, p. 127.

[3] St. Augustine, *"The Harmony of the Gospels"* in NICENE AND POST-NICENE FATHERS, First Series; Ed. Philip Schaff, 6.78

[4] NRSV footnotes here observe that a *talent* is the equivalent of 15 years' wages compared to a *mina,* translated "pound," which equaled one person's wages for only three months.

[5] Apparently short for the German *Quelle,* "source."

[6] Smart. James D., THE STRANGE SILENCE OF THE BIBLE IN THE CHURCH; Westminster Press, Philadelphia,1974.

[7] As Robert Gundry in his chapter on *"The Matthean Community in Roman Syria"* in SOCIAL HISTORY OF THE MATTHEAN COMMUNITY, David L. Balch, ed., Fortress Press, Minneapolis, 1991, p. 66, admits: "We are too fixated on the relation of Matthew's community to Judaism."

[8] White, R.E.O., THE MIND OF MATTHEW: Unique Insights for Living Today; The Westminster Press, Philadelphia, 1979.

[9] Raymond E. Brown and John P. Meier, ANTIOCH & ROME, NewTestament Cradles of Catholic Christianity; Paulist Press, New York/Ramsey, 1983, especially pp. 28-86.

[10] Conference papers were published in book form as SOCIAL HISTORY OF THE MATTHEAN COMMUNITY; David L. Balch, ed., Fortress Press, Minneapolis, Other relevant works: THE INTERPRETATION OF MATTHEW; Graham N.Stanton, ed., T &T Clark, Edinburgh, 1983, 1995. David B. Howell. MATTHEW'S INCLUSIVE STORY: A Study in the Narrative Rhetoric of the First Gospel; JSOT Press, Sheffield,

1990, and TREASURES NEW AND OLD: Recent Contributions to Matthean Studies; David R. Bauer & Mark Allen Powell, eds., Scholars Press, Atlanta, 1996.

[11] Sub-titled: The Social World of the Matthean Community; Fortress Press, Minneapolis, 1990. Cf. also Anthony J. Saldarini, MATTHEW'S CHRISTIAN-JEWISH COMMUNITY; University of Chicago Press, Chicago & London, 1994.

[12] Warren Carter, MATTHEW: STORYTELLER, INTERPRETER, EVANGELIST; Hendrickson Publishers, Inc., Peabody, MA., 1996, p. 100. Additional reference works consulted and recommended: GREEKS, ROMANS AND CHRISTIANS, Essays in Honor of Abraham J. Malherbe; David L. Balch, Everett Ferguson, Wayne Meeks, eds., Fortress Press, Minneapolis, 1990. Gerd Theissen, THE GOSPELS IN CONTEXT: Social and Political History in the Synoptic Tradition; Trans. Linda M. Maloney; Fortress Press, Minneapolis, 1991. THE BOOK OF ACTS IN ITS FIRST CENTURY SETTING, Vol. 2; Eds.: David W.J. Gill & Conrad Gempf; William Eerdmans Publishing Company, Grand Rapids, 1994. Helmut Koester, HISTORY, CULTURE, AND RELIGION OF THE HELLENISTIC AGE; 2nd edition, Walter De Gruyter, New York, Berlin, 1995. Another recent work, closely paralleling this book, is FROM JERUSALEM TO ANTIOCH; authored by Jerome Crowe C.P., and published posthumously by The Liturgical Press, Collegeville, MN, 1997. Unfortunately — and from my perspective, irresponsibly — this book relies almost exclusively on Paul's Letters and Acts for pertinent evidence, ignoring Matthew for all practical purposes.

[13] David E. Garland, READING MATTHEW: A Literary and Theological Commentary on the First Gospel. Crossroad Publishing Company, New York, 1993, p. 5.

Chapter 2

Where Even the Gods are Want to Dwell

Erdal, my guide, and I had just driven south from Iskenderun, across the Nur mountains, and through the Belen Pass[1] over-looking the Amik plain when I became suddenly ill. The world was whirling about me. I was dizzy, disoriented. Finally, I asked Erdal: "What's happening?" "Oh," he calmly replied: "The storks are honoring their ancestral home." Sure enough! Tens of thousands of White Storks which had wintered in Africa and India had met at this migratory staging area on their way to the chimneys and roof tops of Holland and Germany. Here they celebrated their integrity as a species with one gigantic aerial parade - a swirling column of flecked white, black and gray reaching into the clouds — a spiral "Jacob's Ladder" staircase ascending into heaven. I had been caught in the vortex. It was the most awesome natural phenomenon I had ever witnessed.

The memory reminds me that the First Gospel had an ancestral home and staging area as well...and one not far away.

The five "Journalistic Ws:" Who, What, Where, When, Why and sometimes one H, How, encompass the dimensions of context and content, also in our analysis of the Gospel of Matthew. This chapter, accordingly, will speak to the question of Where — the next to When. Chapter Four will discuss Who, both in terms of the writer's identity and that of his readership. Finally in this PART I, Chapter Five will treat the fascinating details of How and Why, leaving the question of What, i.e., "What is this *First* Gospel all about?" to occupy us throughout PART II of this book, focusing on content.

The reason we have chosen to begin with the subject of where this *First* Gospel was written is that a conclusion here promises to be the easiest to attain, with the greatest amount of supportive evidence and the highest level of consensus among scholars. But there is an even better reason. When thinking in terms of context, location is fundamental. It anchors the quest, providing an orientation, a physical milieu, a visible locus. Being able to picture the author and his readers on their own turf enables us to identify more personally with them and to gauge the impact this Gospel's message had upon them.

As you have already guessed, the confident conclusion of our research in this chapter and in this book to the question of Where is **Antioch-on-the-Orontes**, known today as Antakya, Turkey.

The Evidence

Unfortunately, the *First* Gospel itself comes to us anonymously, without title page, table of contents, or list of publication facts. On the surface, at least, it speaks to us only of the life and ministry of Jesus and his disciples in Judea in the early decades of first century C.E. Without any direct internal evidence, therefore, absolute certainty on the question of Where from this distance in time and space is, of course, impossible. Our commitment to Antioch, nevertheless, remains founded on three probative sets of clues: (1) substantial external evidence, (2) close intra-biblical concurrence, and (3) the more general evidentiary category of internal "fit."

1) As for the external evidence, most decisive is the fact that the earliest quotations from, and allusions to, Matthew

26

so far discovered have been found in the vicinity of Antioch in northwestern Syria. The seven letters written by Ignatius, Bishop of Antioch, to as many churches and bishops of Asia Minor and Rome in the first decade of the second century provide the earliest clues.

For example, in counseling his contemporary bishop, Polycarp of Smyrna, Ignatius admonishes him in words almost identical to Mt. 10:16: "Be prudent as the serpent in all things and pure as the dove forever."[2] Again, in his letter to the Ephesians, 19.2, he speaks somewhat enigmatically of "a star that shone in heaven" indicating at least some familiarity with the story of the Wise Men as recorded only in Matthew 2:2-12. Similarly in Smyrnians 8:2, Ignatius seems to echo Mt. 18:20, *"For where two or three are gathered together in my name, I am there among them,"* observing poignantly: "Just as wherever Jesus Christ is, there is the whole church." Finally, but of particular interest, is the shared preoccupation with the issue of church leadership found in both the *First* Gospel and Ignatius' letters, with Ignatius championing the role of the bishop while *Matthew*, as we shall discuss in Chapter Nine, tends to minimize all pretensions toward ecclesiastical authority and privilege as represented by the *"first"* disciple, Peter. Cf. Mt. 10:2 versus 16:23. Clearly, Ignatius in Antioch was heir to shared local Matthean traditions, if not to the *First* Gospel itself.

Further lateral support comes from the close conceptual and literary affinity of Matthew with portions of the *"Didache,"* also called *"The Teachings of the Twelve Apostles."* This primitive book of church orders is similarly associated with Syrian Antioch and is believed to have been composed there around 110-120 C.E. Book III, 7, of this work, for instance, quotes the third beatitude in Mt. 5:5: "Be thou meek, for the meek shall inherit the earth."[3] In like fashion, the Trinitarian baptismal formula given in Book VII,

27

1, repeats Mt. 28:20, and the rendition of the Lord's Prayer in Book VIII, 2, is likewise closer to that in Mt. 6:9-13 than to the abbreviated Lukan version in Lk. 11:2-4.[4] Obviously, the *First* Gospel was already known and appreciated in northern Syria early in the second century C.E.

While some circular reasoning is undoubtedly involved in this conclusion, no other location for the publication of this gospel beside Antioch is as well documented or attested.

2) Weighty, too, is the intra-biblical correspondence between the testimony given us in Acts and Galatians when compared to the situation evidenced in Matthew. Acts 11 and 13 describe the first extra-Israel Christian mission and congregation in Antioch as urbanized as well as ethnically and culturally mixed. *Matthew* displays the same characteristics in his gospel, first by redactionally inserting *"city,"* πολις, eighteen times into his text and then by including unique accounts of adoring Gentile Wise Men from the East, Mt. 2:1-12, a Canaanite woman from *"the district of Tyre and Sidon,"* 15:21-28, and two Roman centurions, 8:13, 27:54. Additionally, there is the unmistakable call to universal mission in 28:19: *"Go therefore and make disciples of all nations,"* a concept almost unthinkable in an exclusively Jewish environment. Surely the *First* Gospel originated in some city existing in a Diaspora context.

Matthew's extraordinary interest in Peter, adding three major Petrine accounts to his narrative, Mt. 14:28-31, 16:17-19, 17:24-27, is likewise foreshadowed in Galatians 2 where Paul threateningly reports: *"When Cephas* (Aramaic for "Peter") *came to Antioch, I opposed him to his face."* There are similar signs in Matthew of a continuing ambivalence toward Peter. We think, for example, of Jesus' redactional curse of the "first" disciple: *"Get behind me, Satan! You are a stumbling block to me,"* in 16:23. These, and other related topics, however, will be discussed more fully in a later chapter.[5] For

28

now it is enough to say that the Peter/Antioch nexus was characteristic of both Galatians and Matthew, suggesting some concurrence of information and/or experience.

3) Less conclusive, but all the more fascinating, are the examples of "fit" between what we know, or, with the help of a little informed speculation and hindsight, can reconstruct of the geography, history and day-to-day life of Antioch and its inhabitants, and what we actually read in the *First* Gospel. Needed first, however, is a brief review of this nearly forgotten metropolis of the ancient, classical world, once the third largest city in the Roman empire following Rome and Alexandria: **Antioch-on-the-Orontes.**

Antioch-on-the-Orontes[6]

One of Antioch's most illustrious sons, the Sophistic orator/teacher Libanius, living in the fourth century C.E., offered a public encomium of the city to introduce the Antiochene Olympic Games in 356 or 360 C.E. With understandable pride, he praised his home town as "the fairest under heaven" and a place where even the gods are want to dwell.[7]

The gods, according to Greek mythology, were indeed in large part responsible for discovering the site. As the story goes, Zeus became enamored of a human maiden named Io. This liaison angered Zeus' wife, Hera. To protect Io from Hera, Zeus changed the girl into a cow. Hera retaliated by infecting Io with a gadfly which drove the poor "bossy" to wander over all the then known world. (The name of the strait separating Europe from Asia Minor at Istanbul, the Bosporus, meaning "cow path," is an extant remnant of this ancient myth.) Zeus sent a detachment of sailors to find Io. After looking everywhere unsuccessfully for years these sailors finally came to Mt. Silpius and found the area so accommodating that they never left, salving their consciences by simply naming the location Iopolis, i.e., Io's city.

History now takes over. After defeating Darius III of Persia at the decisive battle of Issus on the Mediterranean coast near present day Iskenderun (cf. Map 1. p.6) in 333 B.C.E., Alexander the Great moved south with his Macedonian army across the Amanus (Nur) Mountains and the Amik plain to the Orontes River. There at Iopolis, according to tradition, Alexander drank of the clear spring water and found it "as sweet as my mother's milk." He built a fountain and named it Olympia after his (not so sweet) mother, and consecrated the rest of the area with a shrine dedicated to Zeus who ever after was the region's titular deity.

Alexander never returned to Iopolis, but one of his surviving elder advisors, Seleucus I Nicator, 321-281 B.C.E., did, a decade later, ca. 321B.C.E. He developed the area along the classic philosophical and architectural lines of a Greek πολις, "city," employing the Hippodamian plan with remarkably modern straight streets and rectangular "blocks" situated to take full advantage of the morning sun and the cool afternoon breezes for which the Orontes escarpment was famous. He called the town Antioch (Αντιοχια) either in honor of his father, Antiochus, or his son, Antiochus I Soter.

Seleucus I, however, also built a port city at the mouth of the Orontes on the Mediterranean coast and named it after himself, Seleucia Pieria. He made it the capital of his Seleucid Kingdom which at one time encompassed nearly three-fourths of Alexander's vast empire and stretched from the Aegean Sea to the borders of India.

Seleucus's son, Antiochus I Soter, 281-261 B.C.E., however, soon changed all that. In need of room to grow and attracted by abundant water, the fertile Amik plain, and the comfortable climate, he decided to relocate his capital at Antioch, some twenty miles inland.

To be truthful, Antioch was probably not his first choice. Five miles south of the city, on an elevated plateau, is found one of the world's supreme beauty spots, a shimmering jewel of clear, cool waters — pools, springs, falls and fountains — nurturing a natural park of verdant Laurel trees. The area became known as Daphne, or today, Harbiye. Again, according to Greek mythology, it was here that Apollo amorously pursued a beautiful young nymph named Daphne. To avoid the impending scandal, Zeus changed her into a Laurel tree. In Greek Daphne (Δαφνη) means "laurel," referring to the more commonly known Bay tree. In despair, we are told, Apollo, who was also the Greek god of music, fashioned a wreath from the tree's leaves and placed it on his head in tribute to his lost love, giving rise to the common practice ever after of acknowledging excellence in the arts with laurel crowns. Henceforth, Daphne was dedicated to Apollo. Too small for a capital city, however, it became a favorite playground of Greek and Roman elites, unfortunately also retaining its endemic penchant for pleasure, eroticism and excess.

As the Seleucid capital, Antioch-on-the-Orontes now prospered.[8] Shining white classical structures of limestone and marble with columnar facades began to crowd the city's center: official residences, courts, a mint, archives (which doubled as the public library), also temples, theaters and a large *agora*, or marketplace, near the river's edge. Surrounding the city on three sides was the fertile and well watered Amik[9] plain whose abundant harvests insured the areas' general economic stability, commercial vibrancy and cultural vitality.

A century of peace and prosperity followed, even through the reign of Antiochus IV Epiphanes, 175-163 B.C.E., who was derogatorily renamed Antiochus Epimanes, i.e., "the Mad," by his opponents and disparaged in the biblical book of Daniel, 11:21, as the "contemptible person" and as the "sinful root" of 1 Maccabees 1:10.

After Antiochus Epiphanes, however, decline did in fact set in for nearly a century with the Seleucid kings becoming little more than puppets of invading Cilician and Armenian rulers.

The period of Roman domination, of primary concern to us, began with the conquest of Syria by Pompey in 64 B.C.E. The Antiochene citizenry apparently hardly noticed the difference, except for the omnipresent Roman Legions headquartered on the "Campus Martius" across the Orontes from the city. Culturally, Antioch remained predominantly Hellenistic, continuing to prefer Attic Greek to Latin and complimenting itself as a "new Athens."

The situation began to change in 48 B.C.E., however, when Pompey was defeated by his former ally, Julius Caesar, and was subsequently murdered in Egypt. Caesar immediately undertook the task to rebuild Antioch along more traditional Roman lines, adding a royal residence and temple. Unfortunately, Caesar was himself soon dramatically assassinated on the Ides of March, 44 B.C.E.

Mark Anthony, in effect, then replaced Pompey as the titular leader in the East while Octavian, Caesar's grand nephew and the second member of the "First Triumvirate," tried to establish himself in Rome. The decisive naval Battle at Actium in 31 B.C.E. between the rival forces finally put an end to Anthony and Cleopatra's claims and restored unity to the empire.

Octavian was named emperor in 29 B.C.E. and elevated to "Augustus," the final step before deification, in 27 B.C.E. He decided to establish a permanent imperial presence in Antioch as capital of his eastern provinces by constructing a palace with nearby hippodrome, baths, theaters, a second marketplace in a new inland area known as Epiphania, and especially by developing the city's renowned double colonnaded street extending it for over two miles across the heart of the city. Herod the Great, 37-4 B.C.E., the ghoulish king of Judah, but grand builder and friend of Rome, also added his compliments to Antioch during this time by paving this celebrated cardo with solid marble. Imagine the grandeur: a two mile long promenade, thirty feet wide, milk white and smooth as silk, with a roof supported by 3200 gleaming columns protecting all revelers from the Mediterranean sun. Here and there the street was decorated with majestic palms, fountains and statues. Orators and jugglers entertained, and delights of every kind were available for purchase at small curbside shops. Royalty and tourists from all over the ancient world annually came by the thousands just to be seen, dressed in their best, strolling leisurely along this most celebrated avenue in Antioch-on-the-Orontes.

Emperor Tiberius, 14-27 CE, picked up where Augustus left off, repairing the city's infrastructure: aqueducts, walls, gates and drainage systems, and adding numerous refinements. Antioch's population multiplied proportionately to an estimated half million residents in the city's "glory years."

Not everything, however, was "peace and prosperity" in Roman Antioch.[10] The city was extremely vulnerable, especially to enemy attack. The problem was the topography of 1660 foot high Mt. Silpius, sloping, and easily accessible on the southeast side, opposite the city, but presenting a very steep and indefensible wall on the northwest side facing Antioch. The capital, once besieged by its enemies, was thus impossible to defend. Later historians, in dour humor, even boasted that Antioch was never attacked in a war it didn't lose. The task of the Roman legions, consequently, was to keep all enemies at a safe distance.

Another frequent problem, also associated with Mt. Silpius, was a deep cleft separating the southern two-thirds of the mountain from its northern extension which later in the Byzantine period became independently known as Mt. Staurin, or Mt. Cross. This crevice flooded annually during the Winter rainy season. This perennial torrent, officially

33

known as the Parmenius, (possibly so named after another of Alexander's generals, Parmenion) was more popularly, and pejoratively, labeled Ονοπνικτος, "the Donkey-drowner," describing a common experience when flash floods overtook unsuspecting caravans entering or exiting the city. Considerable engineering skill was required to thwart the ravages of such frequent deluges. A dam, which doubled as a gate during the dry season, was eventually erected. Ruins of a later edition of this "Iron Gate" are still visible. Despite heroic architectural measures designed to domesticate the Parmenius, it remained a permanent threat to the city and its teeming population.

Earthquakes, however, were the most feared tragedy of all, becoming more frequent as the centuries passed. One occurred in 37 C.E. shortly after Tiberius had completed his renovations. Another hit in 115 C.E. about the same time as Ignatius' martyrdom. Devastating fires often accompanied these earthquakes. On average, Antioch suffered from some major catastrophe once every fifteen years. Casualties numbering in the hundreds of thousands, resulting from such disasters, were reported on more than one occasion.

In addition, there were the normal discomforts of everyday life in the ancient world: crowded living conditions, foul odors, epidemics, plagues of insects, especially gnats, occasional droughts and famines such as occurred in 46/7 C.E., cf. Acts 11:28-30.

Still, the population continued to grow. One scholar has counted the presence of eighteen different nationalities resident in the city, as mentioned in the literature.[11] Each was recognized as an independent political unit (πολιτευμα) with its own governing council (βουλη). Macedonians, Romans, Syrians and Jews, however, constituted the bulk of the permanent residents, making the city a "tetrapolis" with four clearly defined ethnic quadrants.

Some of the Jews apparently dated their ancestry to the very beginnings of the city when their fathers returned from serving in Alexander's victorious armies and settled at Antioch. No doubt Herod's involvement in completing the colonnaded central avenue added to the Jewish population, estimated at one time from 22,000 to 45,000. Jews occupied the entire southern quarter of the city, the *Kerateion*.[12] One large and beautiful synagogue was built there, another in the pricey southern suburb of Daphne. Jewish wealth, power and influence were not to be trifled with in Antioch, although, as we shall see, many tried.

It was either late in the reign of Tiberius, during the brief tenure of Caligula, 37-41 C.E., or early in the emperorship of Claudius, 41-54 C.E., that the Christian era in Antioch, as recounted in Acts 11, began. Only a few individual names of members of this first Christian congregation are known to us, but they comprise a surprisingly cosmopolitan and wealthy group. According to Acts 6:5, an Antiochene proselyte named Nicolaus was among the first set of Deacons chosen by the Jerusalem congregation. An early prophet, Agabus, is also mentioned in Acts 11:28 as visiting Antioch from Jerusalem. Barnabas, a Cypriot; Simon Niger, perhaps an African; Lucius of Cyrene; and Manaen, a member of Herod's court, are introduced as resident "clergy" in Acts 13:1. Saul of nearby Tarsus, interestingly, seems to have been the only local representative. Cilician Tarsus, then as now, was located only approximately seventy-five miles northwest of Antioch, as the crow flies, across the gulf known today as the Iskenderun Korfezi.

John Malalas, a not-too-highly-regarded monk/historian of the 6th century C.E., provides us with the further detail that Barnabas and Saul/Paul preached on Singon, or Siagon, i.e., "Jawbone" Street,[13] in Antioch, possibly so named (if not totally imaginary) because of its unusual crescent shape in this Roman city of blocks and squares.

Nicephoros, another early Church historian, recalls one other possibly significant name bridging the gap between Paul and Ignatius, a supposed leader of the Antiochene Christian community for twenty-nine years named Evodius, or Euodos.[14] Eusebius, somewhat anachronistically, even refers to him as the first "Bishop" of Antioch.[15] Not much more is known of him except that he apparently authored a book entitled Φως, "LIGHT," dealing with Peter's apostolic supremacy. Malalas, with doubtful authority, even credits him with being the first to actually call the Antiochene faithful "Christians" as noted in Acts 11:26. Whether Evodius was himself a Gentile, as his name suggests, is again a matter of conjecture.

If various other traditions can be believed, Luke, the third evangelist, also had a home here and his addressee, the *most excellent Theophilus,*" Luke 1:3, was a local Antiochene dignitary.[16]

At any rate, the growth of the Christian community, both within the Jewish quarter and in the larger Gentile portions of the city in these early years, must have been substantial, although still small compared to the estimated 150,000 to 500,000 total population of the metropolitan area at different times in the city's history. If there were as few as 1500 to 2000 Christians in Antioch, we might imagine as many as thirty scattered "house churches" with fifty members each meeting in larger residences, in rented halls, on the stair-step rooftops of common Roman tenement buildings, or out in the open on the lower slopes of Mt. Silpius. Antioch provided an extraordinary point of embarkation for the impending Christian Diaspora and missionary enterprise.

Somewhere in this mix of high-stakes politics, ethnic diversity, geological threats, social clamor, hedonistic pursuit, economic competition and religious controversy the Gospel of Matthew is believed to have been painstakingly edited, published and disseminated. One hears the echoes of these conditions in its pages. The reverberations are many and varied. Here, however, we shall listen only to those that speak to the question of Where.

Internal Echoes, Evidences of "Fit"

First, the account of the Visit of the Wise Men, found only in Mt. 2:1-12, when viewed from the perspective of Antioch-on-the-Orontes, suggests several curious but intriguing correspondences in nomenclature. Consider, initially, that the Greek word for east is Ανατολη, a cognate of "Anatolia," the ancient Greek name for present day Turkey. Where, then, would be the first place a reader in ancient Antioch would think of when reading of Wise Men from the East? Surely, neighboring Anatolia — those vast interior uplands of Asia Minor which constituted the territories to the east from the vantage point of ancient Greece, located farther to the west. Anatolia, in fact, is still the name applied to these regions in Turkey today (cf. Map 2, p.7).

These were also "Bible lands." Haran, the temporary home of that *"wandering Aramean,"* Abraham, Deut. 26:5, is located only a few hundred miles northeast of Antioch. The suggestion is at least possible, then, that these Wise Men, heirs of an ancient tradition, were seen by Antiochene Christians as coming from a location not far from their own home town, allowing for some sense of ethnic and cultural identification.

And that is not all. Consider, too, the three gifts offered to the Christ-child by the Wise Men: gold, χρυσος, or "Croesus;" frankincense, λιβανος, or "Lebanon;" and myrrh, σμυρνα, or "Smyrna." Croesus was the legendary king of Lydia in northwest Anatolia who was actually credited with creating money to replace barter as the common medium of exchange. Lebanon was the rich neighboring country to the South of Syria, and Smyrna was the fabulously wealthy commercial center to the west on the Aegean Sea, known today as Izmir. Antioch, then, was located in the center of them all. Such associations may at first seem radically strange to us, if not irresponsibly "off-the-wall." However, if we take into consideration the frequent use of paronomasia in the *First* Gospel as well as the failure of even the most clever commentators to explain the symbolism of these gifts in the Matthean narrative where they are never mentioned again, then our seeing them simply as puns involving some of the most prosperous areas of the original readers' own corner of the world has a very definite and credible appeal. Anatolia and Antioch, then, even before there were Antiochene Christians, in effect, had already been involved in the adoration of the Christ-child sending him some of their most precious gifts. Here, surely, was a portent of significant things to come as Antioch and Anatolia eventually came to know and appreciate this noble infant of Bethlehem.

Add to these observances the further historical memory, as told by the historians Dio Casius, Suetonius and Josephus, of a procession across all of Anatolia by the Armenian king Tiridates with an entourage of magi to pay homage to the youthful emperor Nero in 66 C.E.[17] and you have the basic scenario for this highly redacted account of the Wise Men in Matthew, chapter two. From the very beginning of his Gospel the evangelist was apparently intent on including Gentiles from his own general area in the story of Jesus' life and ministry, even if it meant that Wise Men from the East — from the perspective of Bethlehem in Judea to the south — actually arrived there coming from the north.

Another incidental hint that the *first* evangelist is attempting to make his own readers feel a part of the Gospel narrative is found in 4:24 where he alone among the Synoptic evangelists adds the observation: *"So his* (i.e., Jesus') *fame spread throughout all Syria."* Why the gratuitous expansion of Jesus' notoriety to the totality of this northern Roman province if the notation were not assumed to be of some interest to *Matthew's* readers? Mark never extended Jesus' influence farther north than Tyre and Sidon in Phoenicia, Mk. 3:8.

The seventh chapter of Matthew also has two possible, if not probable, reflections of local color. The saying of "The Two Ways" in 7:13-14 was undoubtedly inspired by the Q parallel in Luke 13:23-24. However, the Q source, as far as we know, really only spoke of one way, the *"narrow door."* *Matthew*, somewhat uncharacteristically, expands the metaphor comparing a *"wide gate"* and *"broad way"* with a *"narrow gate"* and a *"hard,"* (NRSV) or "confining," τεθλιμενη, way. Clarification was undoubtedly the evangelist's general goal, but, perhaps, it was clarification by local illustration because Antioch was famous for its broad and beautiful gates at either end of its renowned double colonnaded street (cf. Map 3, p. 7). On the other hand, it also boasted one very narrow passageway, the Iron Gate, mentioned above, which guarded the steep crevice separating Mt. Silpius from the smaller Mt. Staurin to the north. That Donkey-drowner path was certainly "confining," very rocky and uneven. Antiochene readers, we can be sure, would have understood the analogy better than anyone else.

The Parable of the House Built Upon the Rock, which soon follows at 7:24-27, shares the same general setting. As previously mentioned, the Iron Gate functioned not only as an entrance/exit but also as a dam, occasionally resisting invading armies but more frequently the annual Winter torrent, the Parmenius. Construction in its flood plain with anything but stone was to invite disaster. It is interesting, however, to note the emphasis of the evangelist's editing. He omits Q's careful detail about digging deeply and laying the foundation. Instead,

Matthew focuses on the poetic fury of the storm when *"the rain fell, the floods came, and the winds blew"* as the generally more familiar and dramatic aspect of Antiochene experience with Winter storms.

Being sensitive to the Antiochene scene and environment may also provide answers to many minor redactional alterations in Matthew which have long puzzled scholars and too often invited preachers' flights of inordinate fancy. A few examples:

a) Why does the *first* evangelist change Q's singular *"marketplace"* in Luke 7:32, to the plural *"marketplaces"* in Mt. 11:16? Obviously, there is no significant change in meaning. Does it, then, reflect a simple case of stylistic preference? Maybe. *Matthew,* at times, does seem to have a penchant for expansion, if not actual exaggeration. But it is fascinating, and perhaps more insightful, to realize that Roman Antioch was one of the few cities in ancient times to boast of two large marketplaces, or *agoras,* one near the Orontes River in the old Greek center city and a newer Roman one built by Augustus in an area named Epiphania located close to the foothills of Mt. Silpius.

b) In the account of Jesus' Triumphal Entry into Jerusalem, Mt. 21:1-9, *Matthew* states that the people *"cut branches from the trees"* (κλαδους απο των δενδρων) while the predecessor account in Mark 11:8 had them spreading *"leafy branches* (στιβαδας, "bushes") *that they had cut in the fields."* What difference does it make? Possibly none, and yet it is just such natural reflections of local flora which would have made the story more credible for Antiochene readers. Antioch, and especially Daphne, unlike Jerusalem, were famous for their many trees.

c) In the pericope describing Jesus being mocked by the soldiers in Mt. 27:27-31a, *Matthew* says the soldiers placed a *"scarlet,"* κοκκινην, robe on Jesus where Mark 15:17 described it as "purple," πορφυραν. While both colors are used interchangeably in the literature for royal as well as military garments, the scarlet of the Roman army uniform would certainly have been the more dominant on the streets of Antioch where at least one Roman Legion was headquartered and on display for much of that city's history.

d) As the concluding example of internal "fit" we might mention the evangelist's special preference for certain words and concepts of local relevance. *"Mountain"* (ορος), for example, is added redactionally six times.[18] As a particularly fascinating case in point, note the reference in Mt. 17:20 to *"this mountain"* replacing *"mulberry tree"* in the Luke 17:6 parallel. Surely, the use of the demonstrative pronoun, *"this,"* τουτω, here functions as an explicit invitation to Antiochene readers to think in terms of Mt. Silpius looming directly overhead.

"Shakings" and "quakings" (σειω & σεισμος), also added six times in the *First* Gospel, as well as the explicit designation of the *"deep"* sea, cf. Mt. 18:6/Mk.9:42, are similarly very appropriate references for persons living in fear of all too common earthquakes and almost within sight of the Mediterranean's teal-colored depths.

When the reader or researcher once becomes sensitive to the presence of such local indicators in the text they seem to surface with surprising frequency.

Flash Forward

As a final thought, and as a way of finishing the story, it is instructive to review the later history of Antioch, i.e., the post-Matthean period, as a reflection of the on-going religious vitality

41

of the city. In the succeeding decades and centuries the traditions established by Barnabas, Paul and *Matthew* continued to energize the community. We can only mention significant names here: Ignatius, Tatian, Lucian, Arius, John Chrysostom, the three Cappadocian fathers, Nestorius and Simon Stylites — saints and heretics alike. At one time they all called Antioch home. Collectively, they constituted the famed "Antiochene School" of biblical scholarship, rivaled only by that of Alexandria. In many ways, these early Antiochene scholars even anticipated modern critical methods. On the anti-Christian side, the names of Libanius and Julian the Philosopher — known in Christian circles as "the Apostate" — are also associated with Antioch, the first as an outstanding orator, the second as a fourth century C.E. emperor who tried valiantly to obliterate Christianity from Roman Syria only to fail ignominiously.

For a while in the fourth century, Antioch, for all practical purposes, served as the capital of the entire Roman Empire while the capital city designate, Byzantium, straddling the Bosporus, was being developed into Constatinople, now Istanbul.

The end of the glory years came swiftly and tragically in the sixth century C.E. A series of earthquakes and fires in 525, 526 and 528 took an estimated 360,000 lives and destroyed most of the city. The Byzantine Emperor Justinian, 527-565, tried to rebuild its ramparts. Vestiges of his attempts are still visible, especially fragments of the defensive wall atop Mt. Silpius and the "Iron Gate." But all efforts were in vain. In 540, the Persians invaded and took control. The city soon slipped into anonymity, its classic stones crushed and burned for the lime they contained, leaving hardly a hint of the glory that once was. In 638 Arab Moslems conquered the area, then briefly the Seljuke Turks in 1094 C.E. A devastating "respite" began in 1098 with the First Crusade, but ended in 1268 when the Turkish/Egyptian Mamelukes re-established Moslem control. The turn of the Ottoman Turks began in 1517 and lasted until the close of World War I. Turkey achieved its independence as a secular, democratic state in 1923. The Hatay "peninsula," however, remained a French Protectorate for another two decades.

Between 1932 and 1939, Princeton University was allowed to make several archeological digs in and around the remaining humble village of Antakya. Foremost among their discoveries were remnants of the colonnaded street and numerous tiled floors giving evidence of the splendor of old. The scholarly world owes a huge debt of gratitude to the industry of these scholars and especially the literary achievements of Glanville Downey who brought these few artifacts back to life by recording the grand history of Antioch-on-the-Orontes. My own inquiries about the possibility of more recent archeological digs were answered in the negative. One can only wonder what surprises may still lie buried there.

By way of a plebiscite, Antakya returned to Turkish control in 1939, although this solution is still peacefully contested by Syria. Today, the city with a population of approximately 130,000 has regained some of its luster as a commercial and communications center and as the capital of the Hatay Province. On some recent maps, in fact, even the name of the city itself has now been changed to Hatay.

Only two external vestiges of its Christian past remain, a Grotto of St. Peter and the name of the mountain on which the grotto is located, Mt. Staurin. The grotto is of ancient origin but it became a modern Christian shrine only in the 19th century when Ottoman authorities in a gesture of friendship gave the site to the German Kaiser who, in turn, entrusted it to Capuchin monks. The name of the mountain, according to tradition, goes back to the terrifying final days of Antioch as a Christian city. It was then that desperate believers claimed to see a sign of the cross in the clouds above this northern extension of Mt. Silpius. The Latin name, Mt. Staurin, or Mt. Cross, has stuck in western literature ever since.

Clearly, in view of the numerous, major contributions Antioch has made to the history of world Christianity, the entire locale deserves to be remembered and celebrated much more than it is today.

A hurried review of the thirty-eight commentaries and larger monographs on Matthean subjects occupying my deskside bookcase reveals that while ten of them, because of methodological limitations, did not deal at all with the question of the location of the *First* Gospel's initial publication, only one mentioned Syria generally, while two opted for Phoenicia and three for somewhere in Galilee leaving twenty-two with more or less certainty nominating Syrian Antioch specifically. That is as close to consensus as seems possible among New Testament scholars.

All evidence considered, then, whether internal or external, probative or imaginative, circumstantial or only inferential, from foresight or hindsight, everything combines to suggest that Roman/Syrian Antioch is the logical site for the initial publication of the *First* Gospel. In terms of influence, wealth, education, ethnic composition and spiritual commitment it must be considered the leading, if not the only, candidate for such honor. As far as we can determine, it alone enjoys all the credentials.

From now on in our study and in this book, therefore, beautiful Antioch-on-the-Orontes, where even the gods were want to dwell, shall be assumed and accepted as the confirmed location for the *First* Gospel's composition.

Chapter 2 Endnotes

[1] Cf. Map #1, p. 6.

[2] Cf. *"Ignatius to Polycarp,"* II, 2, in APOSTOLIC FATHERS, I, *Loeb Classical Library;* Trans. Kirsopp Lake; Harvard University Press, 1912, p. 269. Cf. also the Hermeneia Commentary on IGNATIUS OF ANTIOCH by Wm. R. Schoedel, Fortress Press, Philadelphia, 1985.

[3] Cf. Ibid., p. 315

[4] Ibid., p. 321.

[5] Cf. Chapter Nine.

[6] Most of the material in this section is gleaned from Glanville Downey, A HISTORY OF ANTIOCH IN SYRIA FROM SELEUCUS TO THE ARAB CONQUEST; Princeton University Press, 1961. For related material see Merrill C. Tenney, NEW TESTAMENT TIMES; Wm. B. Eerdmans Publishing Company, Grand Rapids, 1965; Wayne A. Meeks and Robert L. Wilken, JEWS AND CHRISTIANS IN ANTIOCH IN THE FIRST FOUR CENTURIES OF THE COMMON ERA; Scholars Press, Missoula, Montana, 1978; Fergus Millar, THE ROMAN NEAR EAST, 31BC - AD 337; Harvard University Press, Cambridge, MA., 1993; and Everett Ferguson, BACKGROUNDS OF EARLY CHRISTIANITY, 2nd ed.; Wm. B.Eerdmans Publishing Company, Grand Rapids, 1993.

[7] *"Libanius' Oration in Praise of Antioch " (Oration XI).* Trans. Glanville Downey in the Proceedings of the American Philosophical Society, Vol. 103, no. 5, October,1959, p. 665.

[8] Seleucus I and succeeding members of his dynasty built at least twelve other "Antiochs" throughout the Seleucid empire, necessitating the distinguishing "on-the-Orontes" designation for the particular Antioch under study.

[9] Amik means "a hollow." For a time its low, central area was flooded and named "The Sea of Antioch," rendering the surrounding lands fertile not

only for crops but also for insects, animals and fowl. In modern times the Sea has been drained and the entire plain transformed into a nature preserve.

[10] For an exceptionally bleak view of life in Roman cities see Rodney Stark, *"Antioch as the Social Situation for Matthew's Gospel"* in Balch, ed., SOCIAL HISTORY OF THE MATTHEAN COMMUNITY, op. cit., pp. 189- 210.

[11] Ibid., p. 196.

[12] Cf. C. Kraeling, *"The Jewish Community at Antioch,"* JBL 51, 1932, pp. 130- 160.

[13] Cf. Downey, HISTORY, p. 275, quoting the CHRONICLE OF JOHN MALALAS, Books VIII-XVIII. Trans. Matthew Spinka and Glanville Downey, Chicago, 1940.

[14] Referred to in Downey, op. cit., pp. 284-287, n.. 44; Cf. also Excursus 3, pp. 584-586.

[15] Eusebius, ECCLESIASTICAL HISTORY, III, xxii, p. 104.

[16] Cf. Merrill C. Tenney, NEW TESTAMENT TIMES, Eerdmans, Grand Rapids, p. 216; Also Eusebius, ECCLESIASTICAL HISTORY, III, iv, p. 85.

[17] Cf. references in Ulrich Luz, MATTHEW *1-7,* trans. Wilhelm C. Linss, Augsburg Press, Minneapolis, 1989, p. 131, n. 19.

[18] Statistics taken from Robert Gundry, MATTHEW: A Commentary on His Literary and Theological Art. William B. Eerdmans Publishing Company, Grand Rapids, 1982, pp. 641-649.

Chapter 3

Then is Now[1]

In the hills just north of the circular parsley field that once was the busy harbor of Seleucia Pieria is a long and deep crevasse carved out of solid rock and designed to divert the Winter rains and accompanying sediment past the ancient port directly into the Mediterranean Sea. The idea was to keep the harbor from silting up, a goal ultimately lost. At the higher end of this imposing cloaca one comes to a rectangular tunnel 150 yards long. It is known as the "Tunnel of Titus"[2] because somewhere within its depths is a Latin inscription indicating that the work was authorized by the emperors Vespasian and his illustrious son, Titus. I was determined to identify with that genuine first century artifact and to photograph it as a piece of indisputable existential evidence. Unfortunately, there was running water on the canal floor. Erdel, the experienced mountain climber, scampered along its sheer walls like a lizard on a ledge, but I, clinging by my fingernails, choked by the straps of dangling cameras and binoculars, and hampered by a protruding midsection which refused to ignore gravity, stayed erect for no more than fifteen steps and surrendered.

Titus and Vespasian will have to wait a little longer.

The question of When may not provide answers as basic, visible or tangible as Where but it leads to discoveries about the *First* Gospel, its situation and setting, every bit as consequential.

The first difference one notes when comparing the Gospel of Matthew with its predecessor, the Gospel of Mark, is that *Matthew* frequently changes Mark's habit of linking sentences and paragraphs with *"and"* to some temporal adverb or preposition: *"when..." "then..." "while..." "at that time..."* or *"after that..."* These alterations were not simply a matter of stylistic preference on the editor's part. Rather, as any careful, sensitive reader will soon realize, the *first* evangelist was fundamentally time conscious and situation oriented. He was concerned with sequence and plot, not so much to insure historical accuracy or to demonstrate cause and effect relationships, but to maintain reader interest in a narrative that was immediately relevant and progressively intense. Of course, all the while that he was recalling events that occurred in previous decades in Judea he was simultaneously toying with his contemporary readers' minds, hearts, consciences and daily lives in Antioch, and perhaps our own today as well. The principle of transparency obtains here in the temporal sphere equally as much as it did in the geographic dimension detailed in the previous chapter.

Consider *Matthew's* repeated use of the phrase: *"to this day"* in 11:23, 27:8 and 28:15, denoting conditions which had remained unchanged over an unexpectedly long period of time. The proverbial evil of Sodom, accordingly, persisted for *Matthew "to this day,"* and Judas' tragic *"Field of Blood"* was likewise still remembered by that name *"to this day."* Obviously, while the evangelist-narrator was actively describing circumstances which pertained long ago, he was consciously, yet subtly, detaching himself from those early days and identifying with a later period, his own.

Another indicator is his eight-fold use of *"this generation"* (11:16, 12:39, 41, 42, 45c, 16:4, 23:36, 24:34), at least one time redactionally, 12:45c. While this expression is usually included in a statement attributed to Jesus addressing his disciples and contemporaries, the added redactional description of the particular generation in question as *"evil and adulterous"* in three instances, 12:39, 45c and 16:4, suggests that the first evangelist also had his own community particularly in mind. At least his readers, with notorious Daphne so close by, would certainly recognize themselves as sharing in this indictment.

Then there are those bold attention-getters, usually redactional: *"Let everyone with ears, listen!"* (Cf. 11:15, 13:9, 43). Why would the evangelist have added these imperatives to Jesus' statements spoken years earlier unless he wanted them to serve as wake-up calls for his own contemporary readers and audience?

More elusive, but perhaps also more illuminating is Jesus' cryptic comment in 11:12: *"From the days of John the Baptist until now the kingdom of heaven has suffered violence, and the violent take it by force."* The puzzling question is: What is meant by *"until now,"* εως αρτι? In the narrative context of Jesus' discussion with his disciples about the role of John the Baptist this observation makes little sense. After all, according to Luke's nativity account, Jesus and John were contemporaries, born within months of each other. Furthermore, *Matthew* had not even recorded John's tragic death yet at this point in his narrative, Mt. 14:1-12. The proposed intervening time span referred to between Jesus and John the Baptist, therefore, was not only very brief but also relatively uneventful, if not totally figurative.

Adding to the dilemma is the further realization that *Matthew* here uncharacteristically obfuscates the much clearer statement of his Q source in Luke 16:16. There the temporal parameters are quite different and the import of the message almost reversed: *"The law and the prophets were in effect until John came; since then the good news of the kingdom of God is proclaimed, and everyone tries to enter it by force,"* βιαζεται, or, as a proposed alternate NRSV sense translation puts it: *"...and everyone is strongly urged to enter it."* Here a sequence of two distinct historical "dispensations" is referred to, the first the time characterized by *"the Law and the Prophets"* and the other by the *"good news of the kingdom,"* with John the Baptist simply occupying the central, pivotal position. The emphasis in Matthew, on the other hand, is exclusively on the second half of the equation and the general perspective is much more negative. Accordingly, the experience of the kingdom of heaven from its beginning with John the Baptist right up to the present moment, i.e., *"until now,"* has been one of extended and increasingly intensive struggle as *"the violent take it by force"* (αρπαζουσιν). Obviously, this is the evangelist-narrator speaking to his Antiochene correspondents in his own day even though the words are heard to issue from the lips of Jesus as purportedly spoken fifty or more years earlier in Palestine.

We cannot know for sure what specific circumstances *Matthew* had in mind when speaking of those who over the intervening years had tried to take the kingdom *"by force,"* but most likely he was thinking of the martyrdoms of John the Baptist and of Jesus in the late 20s or early 30s, of Peter and Paul in connection with the burning of Rome in 64 C.E. and of the persecution of the Christians which followed. Perhaps included, too, was the memory of the ruthless murder of James, the "Lord's brother" and first "Bishop" of Jerusalem, in 62 C.E. Finally, of course, there was the destruction of Jerusalem in 70 C.E. together with the subsequent flight of the Christian community to Pella,[3] and no doubt to Antioch, Alexandria and Rome as well. This transparent understanding of *Matthean* redaction surely makes better sense.

If we are correct, we have here another case of double entendre, of temporal echoing, in the *First* Gospel. The story of Jesus in Matthew, consequently, is written in different frequencies and is to be heard stereophonically, as simultaneously reflecting both the time of Jesus and that of *Matthew*. The words are those of the Lord, the implications those of the evangelist. In the *First* Gospel, **_then_** is frequently telescoped to **_now_** as the title of this chapter suggests.

Salvation History scholars,[4] of course, have a somewhat different slant on the *first* evangelist's editorial strategy regarding time. They see him describing two or three epochs in God's saving activity, usually including an age of prophecy and an age of Jesus' ministry, but omitting any significant appreciation of the editor's transparency tactic or motif focusing on developments in the post-resurrection church. The latter emphasis, obviously, is the gap our study aims to fill.

The Date of Composition

The question presently challenging us, therefore, is: When exactly was *"now?"* When did *Matthew* actually live and write? And what were the prevailing circumstances — politically, culturally, economically and in terms of religion — which might have impinged on *Matthew's* presentation?

Methodological considerations provide us with some broad parameters. Since we have agreed that according to the Two Source Hypothesis *Matthew* used Mark as a source, the *ab quo* (from when) for the composition of the *First* Gospel must have been around the year 70 C.E. when Mark is generally believed to have been written, versus the *ad quem* (to when) approximately 110 C.E. when Ignatius, Bishop of Antioch, first quoted Matthew. Allowing some years for the mass production and dissemination of Mark, it was most likely somewhere within the intervening twenty to twenty-five year window, 75-100 C.E., that *Matthew* took pen in hand.

Consistent and confirming, too, are the detailed references to the destruction of Jerusalem in the Parable of the Wedding Banquet, Mt. 22:1-10, especially v. 7. The description there that *"the king sent his troops, destroyed those murderers, and burned their city"* has about it an undeniable degree of historical realism, recounting the havoc the Roman legions, under Vespasian and Titus, wracked upon the holy city. The evangelist, then, clearly redacted this parable from an after-the-fact perspective, that is, after 70 C.E. For his readers, this parable constituted an already fulfilled prophecy.

Can we be still more precise? Possibly. While a difference of opinion among scholars continues to exist over whether or not the church and synagogue were independent of each other at the time when Matthew was written, the consensus certainly favors separation and independence. After all, at least thirty years had passed since Barnabas had begun the Antiochene mission, Acts 11:19ff., around 40 C.E., giving plenty of time for some degree of independent identity to have emerged. Furthermore, it is clear that this Antiochene missionary enterprise had already developed a rather mature polity and cult with prescribed prayers such as the Lord's Prayer, Mt. 6:9-13, rules of discipline, 18:15-18, and recognized leadership in the proposed mold of Peter, 16:16-19. All such conventions take considerable time to develop and mature. The evangelist, in fact, appears to want to emphasize this advanced level of maturity and independence by anachronistically placing the word *"church,"* εκκλησια, on Jesus' lips three times, 16:18 and 18:17a & b, the only evangelist to do so. The real antagonists, then, were church vs. synagogue, Christian scribes vs. rabbis, disciples vs. Jews. We will have much more to say about the nature of Christian/Jewish interaction in Antioch in Chapter Ten, below.

Although some uncertainty remains about the exact date and impact of a much discussed Rabbinical Council of Jamnia, or Javneh, around 85 C.E. with its possible promulgation of a "12th Benediction" ostensibly ostracizing non-Jews, including Christians, from the synagogue, it cannot be doubted that some such defining tension was certainly "in the air" around that time. There was definitely enough confrontation to infuriate the *first* evangelist, as is obvious in Matthew 23, with its redacted tirade directed at *"Scribes and Pharisees, hypocrites!"* We cannot be far wrong, then, if we settle on 85 C.E. as the approximate date for the composition of the *First* Gospel.

We may locate another defining clue in the political developments of this ninth decade of the first century, C.E. As we shall discuss in greater detail later in this chapter, the Roman emperor Domitian began his reign in 81 C.E. For a number of years he was kept busy trying to shore up the foundations of his rule in northern Europe. After a successful conclusion to the campaign there in 89 C.E., however, he seemed to feel secure enough to entertain delusions of his own grandeur, demanding to be addressed as *Dominus et Deus*, "Lord and God." The absence of any direct response to this blasphemous challenge, or clear reference to any current official persecution in the *First* Gospel, therefore, argues against proposing a date later in the 80s or early in the 90s for this Gospel's composition.

On the other hand, internal church politics may also preclude a date much earlier than 85 C.E. While the traditions outlining the succession of early church leadership in Antioch are sketchy and often appear contrived there does seem to be a general agreement among such authorities as Origen, Jerome and Eusebius that after the departures of Paul and Barnabas from Antioch, Peter exerted some influence there for several years. If our information is correct, Peter was then followed by an otherwise relatively unknown figure named Evodius, or Euodos, who "ruled" for twenty-nine years until succeeded by Ignatius. Accepting this sequence as at least plausible, Glanville Downey[5] reconstructs a time-line which places the "elevation" of Ignatius at 83 C.E. Now, recalling a further tradition that Evodius had previously authored a book entitled Φως, "LIGHT," dealing with the role of Peter in the

Antiochene and Roman churches, and remembering also Ignatius' insistence upon monarchical episcopacy as the only proper form of ecclesial authority, plus simultaneously sensing the delicate way that *Matthew* treats the question of church leadership with reference to Peter in the *First* Gospel, one is led to conclude that all these claims and counter-claims were being debated at about the same time.[6] In other words, *Matthew* must have written his Gospel somewhere within the 80-85 C.E. time-frame when this issue of ecclesiastical succession and authority was in dispute. We shall accept this date of 85 C.E., as so variously attested, as confirmed for the publication of the *First* Gospel.

The Flavian Period

The year 85 C.E. places us directly in the center of the Flavian Period of Roman history. "Flavius" was the family name of a dynasty of three emperors, Vespasian and his two very different sons, Titus and Domitian, who together ruled a total of twenty-eight years, from 68 to 96 C.E. These three decades frame the political setting for *Matthew's* Gospel.

After Nero's excesses, 54-68 C.E., and the brief, ineffective reigns of his three successors, Galba, Otho and Vitellus, all within a few months, life under Vespasian, 68-79 C.E., must have provided a welcome respite for the Antiochene Christian community. Vespasian liked Antioch and owed it a great debt of gratitude. It had supplied most of the recruits and logistics for his conquest of Israel, 66-70 C.E. Furthermore, it was the official Antiochene leadership which in 68 C.E. championed Vespasian as the next emperor, preparing the way for his triumphal return to Rome.

There was only one disquieting official act during Vespasian's ten year reign that is of special interest to us however. It involved his reallocation of Jewish Temple tax funds to the reconstruction of the Capitoline Temple to Jupiter in

Rome. This *Fiscus Judaicus,* or "Jewish Tax," was a very bitter pill for Jews to swallow, and since many Christians were of Jewish extraction it must have been extremely difficult for them as well.

Titus, 79-81 C.E., — young, capable, sympathetic — was in many ways a better emperor than his father. Even before he ascended the throne, however, it was his misfortune to become enmeshed in a dangerous civil dispute involving the Antiochene citizenry. When he returned to Antioch as the triumphant General after the destruction of Jerusalem in late 70 C.E. he was met by a large delegation of the populace demanding that all Jews be expelled from the city. Included in the mob was a young Jewish renegade named Antiochus, the son of a local Jewish council, βουλη, president.[7] Apparently to keep the opprobrium of others from being heaped on himself, Antiochus accused his fellow Jews of conspiring to burn the city and dispel prevailing municipal authority. Titus, however, though a hardened General already by age thirty, was too politically astute to fall for such opportunistic demagoguery. Rather, as Josephus[8] informs us, Titus was content simply to embarrass the Jews using spoils from Jerusalem to redecorate the southern gate of the city near the Jewish quarter and to order the re-construction of the synagogue in Daphne as a theater. To rub the disgrace still further into Jewish wounds, a tablet was emblazoned on the wall of the Daphne theater declaring EX PRAEDA JUDAEA, "From Jewish Spoils." With such a diplomatic slap on the wrist, temporarily painful as it was for the Jews of Antioch, Titus quelled the riot, satisfying the populace's desire for vengeance without substantively changing the status of the Jewish population. Life was permitted to return to normal in a relatively short time.

Titus' enlightened reign, unfortunately, was also marred at its outset by the disastrous eruption of the Mt. Vesuvius volcano in 79 C.E., burying the cities of Pompeii, Herculaneum and Stabiae in southern Italy and claiming the lives of thousands including one of the ancient world's most famous naturalists, Pliny the Elder. A walk through the deserted streets of these excavated cities today, visiting their temples, baths, villas, bakeries and even houses of prostitution, provide the visitor with as good a glimpse of life on an average day in the ancient Roman world as one might hope to experience. Except for some inevitable cultural differences this was in essence also the world of Matthean, Roman/Syrian Antioch.

As we know, Titus' official tenure as Emperor lasted only two years, until 81 C.E., when he died at age 42. His younger brother, Domitian, now ascended the throne and remained there for the next fifteen years. He was as undisciplined as Titus had been responsible. Although totally committed to Roman traditions, restoring, for example, the old national shrines in Rome and constructing a temple of Asclepius, the god of health, in Antioch, Domitian's personal vanity was so overweening, especially after his previously mentioned victories in northern Europe, that he began to fancy himself a son of Jupiter and insisted on being worshipped as such. Subsequently, he publicly declared himself *Dominus et Deus*, " Lord and God," and demanded appropriate adoration.

Kings and Emperors had long flirted with deification, especially in the East. Egyptian Pharaohs, of course, from time immemorial had been identified with one Nile River god or another. Greek Seleucid kings were only slightly more modest. Antiochus I chose Soter, "Savior," as his personal designation just as Antiochus IV declared himself, "Epiphanes," implying that he was a manifestation of the divine. Generally speaking, Roman emperors since Julius Caesar had desisted from assuming divine privileges during their lifetimes, content to permit the Roman Senate to deify them posthumously.

Caligula and Nero, of course, were unrestrained in their self-aggrandizements, but they were viewed as largely demented exceptions. Vespasian was undoubtedly more characteristic. Suetonius records his sardonic deathbed quip: "Woe is me. I think I am about to become a god."[9] With Vespasian's second son, Domitian, however, the tide toward deification overflowed. The time for the *"Augustales,"* i.e., official Roman emperor worship, had begun in earnest.

While there is no hard evidence of widespread persecution of dissenters in Antioch during the early half of Domitian's reign,[10] one can imagine the intense qualms of conscience experienced especially by such monotheistic groups as Jews and Christians when they considered the seemingly inevitable national trend toward emperor worship. Perhaps the irony of it all is that Domitian was one of only three emperors, along with the likes of Caligula and Nero, who was awarded the *"damnatio memoriae,"* by the Roman Senate following his assassination. Not only was he thereby denied deification, but his name and accomplishments were officially erased from the annals of the empire. Adding insult to injury, Domitian's end apparently came with the connivance of his own wife, Domitilla, in 96 C.E.

The Economy

As uncertain as the political situation may have been during the Flavian period, economically these must have been comparatively prosperous times for Antioch. As the capital city of the Roman Syrian Province, there were huge amounts of government funds flowing into and through the region. With its port at Seleucia Pieria, Antioch was a commercial gateway to the wealth of the East. Vestiges of the ancient Roman road system converging on the city, especially the famous Via Maris running the full length of the Mediterranean Sea's eastern shore, are still visible today and witness to the city's function as an overland transportation and communications nerve center. Busy caravansaries, we may imagine with some certainty, huddled outside its walls as motels and warehouses do most western metropolises today. Add to these assets the productivity of the adjacent Amik plain and a composite picture of a very vibrant economy appears, explaining, perhaps, at least in part, the exaggerated financial quotations in the *First* Gospel.

Unfortunately, economic prosperity does not necessarily imply individual happiness or contentment. Ostensibly, real wealth was limited to a very small upper crust of Roman elites, Senators and Equestrians, occupying opulent villas in Daphne and surrounding areas. Even smaller was an enterprising middle class of bakers, butchers, public servants, actors and educators who enjoyed a modest level of independence. Most ordinary citizen day-laborers, however, risked a hand-to-mouth subsistence while an estimated one fifth of the total populace consisted of slaves living menial, destitute lives.

In one sense, in fact, everyone was a slave. While some temples served as trusted depositories for private wealth, no centralized, public banking system was available. Patronage was the uncomfortable reality of the day with everyone borrowing from, and becoming at least temporarily indentured to, everyone else. This patronage/class system, while controlled by some respected social conventions, generally made for very sensitive and fragile community relationships. There was a predominant dog-eat-dog mentality where such values as generosity, mercy, compassion and forgiveness were viewed as signs of weakness and irresponsibility. It is highly instructive to keep this index of virtues (or vices?) in mind when considering the redactional Parables of the Talents, Mt. 18:23-36, and Laborers in the Vineyard, Mt. 20:1-16. The reference to being imprisoned for failure to repay debts in 18:30, for example, is tell-tale evidence of a Roman legal provenance for this parable since, as far as we can tell, such practice was unknown within Jewish jurisprudence.

Arts and Entertainment

As with most large Greek and Roman cities, cultural opportunities were numerous in Antioch during the Flavian period. Actors, athletes, orators and storytellers abounded. Both Antioch and Daphne boasted large outdoor theaters for the presentation of classic Greek dramas and contests of various kinds. A hippodrome for chariot races, the favorite sport of Roman audiences, loomed large on the island near the imperial residence (cf. Map 3, p.7). By this time, too, Antioch had already become the permanent home of the Greek Olympic Games produced every five years unless preempted by war or natural disaster. The city enjoyed its own central library although its primary purpose was to serve as a repository for government records. The Temple of Asclepius, the god of healing, similarly doubled as a hospital.

Among Antioch's foremost treasures, then as now, however, must have been the mosaic floors in some of its larger villas with their graphic depictions of Greek and Roman mythological figures as well as natural flora and fauna.[11] Their art, in terms of perspective, color and shading, is unsurpassed in the ancient world.

Education

Classical rhetoric was the focus and cynosure of Greco-Roman education at the time. Everything from philosophy, to oratory, to the scribal arts was taught using the Socratic method of questions and answers, but with some written exercises thrown in. Facts were not viewed as so important in themselves as in their suitability to persuade. Language was power. The orator, the literati, the professional reader and storyteller, therefore, were among the most respected professions in Antiochene society.

Marcus Fabius Quintilianus, or simply Quintilian, c. 35-95 C.E., was unquestionably the leading educator and rhetorician of the Flavian period, and a direct contemporary of the first evangelist. Having arrived in Rome from Spain around 70 C.E., he soon became the teacher of Domitian's two royal sons and, in effect, the "first teacher" of Rome and the "Secretary of Education" for the entire Roman empire. His most famous work, INSTITUTIA ORATORIA, must have been written at the same time as the *First* Gospel, or only shortly thereafter. Surely, Quintilian's influence was felt also within the literary circles of Antioch, including those of the early Christian community located there.

Although still quite young when the *First* Gospel was being written, the most popular philosopher of the day, undoubtedly, was Epictetus, c. 50-138 C.E., from Phrygia in central Asia Minor. His was a most unusual story. Born into slavery he grew up to become a celebrated Stoic philosopher, a rare type of optimistic cynic, with a strong religious bent. A profound moralist he had the ability to articulate his teachings in simplest terms and sometimes even with humor. Typical of his views and style is this quotation: "If a man could only subscribe heart and soul, as he ought, to this doctrine, that we are all primarily begotten of God, and that God is the father of men as well as of gods, I think that he will entertain no ignoble or mean thought about himself."[12] How reminiscent of our own less dignified adage: "God doesn't make junk!" While no direct connection, either linguistic or theological, between Epictetus and *Matthew* can be demonstrated, it is clear that they shared similar moral and religious inclinations.

These were the days, too, of the Roman world's greatest historians. Flavius Josephus, 37-c.95 C.E., was a young, capable, but not entirely self-sacrificing Jewish general in the early years of Jewish resistance to Rome, 66-70 C.E. His birth name was Joseph ben Matthias. After his capture by Vespasian, however, his personal charisma and diplomatic skill won him an early pardon. In return, he adopted the dynastic surname, Flavius, and became a Roman citizen. Without the detailed records in his book, THE WARS OF THE JEWS, we would know little about the Roman East during the period just prior to and contemporaneous with the *first* evangelist.

Plutarch, c. 46-120, Tacitus, c. 55-117, and Suetonius, c. 69-140 C.E. were also contemporaries and covered much of the same time and material in their histories and biographical sketches on the reigns of the first twelve emperors. Morality, or lack thereof, is a common theme. Obviously, *Matthew* was not alone. One has to be amazed at the moral preoccupation and the literary vitality of the age.

Of immediate interest to us, too, is the visit to Antioch of the famed wonder worker and Pythagorean "divine man," Apollonius of Tyana, about this same time, as recorded by his biographer and protagonist Philostratus.[13] The exact date of this visit is unknown, but since we are told that Apollonius died as a very old man during the reign of Nerva, 96-98 C.E., Domitian's successor, the chances are good that Apollonius came to Antioch some time during the Flavian period. Apparently, he was not impressed with the city or its inhabitants. He found some shrines closed and even the Temple of Apollo in Daphne lacking a house of studies. His caustic comment was probably reminiscent of the myth of Daphne's origin: "O Apollo, change these dumb dogs into trees, so that at least as cypresses they may become vocal."[14] Still, we are told, he eventually relented and left Antioch with a talisman at the eastern gate to defend against the north wind, plus a small bronze statue of a scorpion to protect the inhabitants from stings, and a solemn mantra to ward off gnats. Again there is no evidence of direct contact between the *first* evangelist and Apollonius, but the latter's possible presence in Antioch

61

around the same time as the Gospel's composition does help to personalize the comment found only in Mt. 7:15: *"Beware of false prophets, who come to you in sheep's clothing but inwardly are ravenous wolves."*

Religion

Little is definitely known about religious groups represented in the city at the time, but much can be inferred. Polytheism was certainly the norm. Cybelline worship in its various forms, undoubtedly, was widely practiced. Cybelle, the Great Mother of the Gods, began as an ancient, local Phrygian deity of nature and fertility. Over time, however, she became identified with a host of other ethnic and regional goddesses: Astarte in Syria, Demeter in Greece, Isis in Egypt and Ceres in Rome. Surely, too, Mithraism was popular especially among the Roman military stationed in Antioch. The familiar pantheon of Greek and Roman deities were also visible everywhere, especially Zeus (Lat. Jupiter) and Apollo, the patron gods of Antioch and Daphne respectively. Domitian, as previously indicated, demanded worship of himself as the Son of Jupiter. Among other popular cultural symbols, as testified to by remnants of the mosaic floors, were beatific personifications of Fortune, Τυχης, and Health, Σωτηρια.

Generally speaking, the Flavian period must have been a time of spiritual ferment with a rising tide of mystery religions and recrudescent cults contesting Domitian's efforts to reestablish a national religion along traditional mythological lines, with himself, of course, prominently displayed.

Curiously, however, the danger of encroaching polytheism does not seem to be a major concern in the *First* Gospel. We will discuss the probable reasons for this failure at another time.

Judaism was also well represented in Antioch by the previously mentioned large and beautiful synagogue, the

Kenesheth Hashmunith, "the Assembly of the Eight," so named after the seven Maccabean martyrs and their mother (2 Macc. 7:1-42, 4 Macc. 8-17). With this synagogue located prominently toward the southwestern end of the celebrated colonnaded street, within the Kerateion Jewish sector, we wonder whether the passage in 4 Macc. 17:3 may not be broadly descriptive of its grandeur:

"Nobly set like a roof on the pillars of your sons, you held firm and unswerving against the earthquake of the tortures." (NRSV)

That possibility is easy to entertain since the composition of 4 Maccabees is also often associated with Antioch sometime in the seventh decade of the first century C.E.. We wonder, too, if this famous structure may not have been the immediate object of *Matthew's* scorn when frequently referring directly to *"your"* and *"their"* synagogue in his Gospel? Mt. 4:23; 9:35; 10:17; 12:9; 13:54; 23:34.

Undoubtedly most unfortunate for us is the fact that, in terms of hard extra-biblical evidence, the least of all can be known about Antiochene Christianity during the Flavian period. Without images, statuary or even distinctive "church" buildings early Christianity left no physical artifacts to be discovered.[15] We can, therefore, only rely on late literary memories, many of them third and fourth hand, fragmentary and inconsistent.

Nevertheless, it would appear that the *First* Gospel was written at a crucial, watershed time in the history of the Antiochene church. The Christian community there had reached a critical juncture. It was entering its third generation, the stage where initial commitments wane and vision degenerates into practicalities. Like an orphaned teenager the Antiochene congregation was groping for maturity and identity. The mother church in Jerusalem was no more, its membership scattered to the four winds, the original disciples dead and gone. The formerly stabilizing traditions were now being challenged by new situations. What should be discarded, what retained, what accommodated, what resisted? There were no codified or widely accepted standards of orthodoxy, except for a few cherished formulae, rituals and conventional practices.[16] The "Bible" most accessible to the public was the Septuagint, i.e., the Old Testament in Greek translation. The Gospel of Mark was obviously available, but still had not attained stature as inviolate Scripture. Paul's Letters, too, were no doubt widely discussed, but their collation and distribution remained projects for the future. "Truth," therefore, was primarily a matter of the perceived reliability of the one who professed it. Conversely, "heresy" was whatever that person opposed. Desperately needed, therefore, were authoritative leaders, consistent patterns of belief, action and behavior, organization and a renewed vision of the kingdom. *Matthew*, apparently, set out to provide these foundational necessities.

The organizational structure of the fledgling church was undoubtedly somewhat predetermined by state and city requirements. From its inception Antioch was considered a free city, meaning that its non-slave inhabitants were automatically designated citizens of the Roman empire with the right to select their own leaders and design their own organizations. It is likewise assumed that Antioch, like other Roman cities, had its registry of voluntary associations called *collegia*. Religious associations were accordingly known as *collegia sodalicia*, each with its own leader, treasurer, secretary, legal officer, priest and steward. These groups were allowed to set their own schedules and find their own meeting places, public or private, as long as they kept the responsible authorities informed. No doubt the early "house congregations" common in the nascent church were of this type and form, some of them area based, others ethnically determined, and still others more or less tradition-bound in their theological perspectives and religious practices. In a city the size of first century Antioch there probably were as many as thirty to fifty such Christian *"collegia,"* with a total membership of several thousands. Although the title "Bishop" was undoubtedly anachronistic and premature before the final decade of the first century C.E., the previous mention of Evodius in a leadership role in the larger Antiochene Christian community does suggest a certain early level of central authority and an attempt at establishing a degree of uniformity. It was only later, with Ignatius, that this role seems to have become codified and vested with the accouterments of ecclesiastical power, privilege and official responsibility, but even then not without resistance.

All things considered, the Flavian period in the 70s, 80s and 90s of the first century C.E. rates an above average grade, especially as far as Antioch-on-the-Orontes was concerned. They were not spectacular, but it was twenty-eight years of peace and prosperity, free from major natural disasters (except for the Vesuvius eruption in southern Italy), and manifesting a palpable level of social progress. The aging Vespasian's reign can only be described as benign. Titus' promising tenure was too short to allow for comparison. Domitian became increasingly pompous and autocratic through the years, but never to the level of insanity that characterized Caligula and Nero. The most persistent irritants to Roman unity and stability during the period seem to have been in the areas of religion and its companion, popular morality, as evidenced by the works of Epictetus, Tacitus, Plutarch and, of course, *Matthew.*

Political Reflections

We will have occasion to discuss the religious and ethical perspectives of the age as viewed by the *first* evangelist in more detail in subsequent chapters. There will also be opportunity later to evaluate the impact of contemporary methods of education on *Matthew's* editing and his response to the problem of order and authority in the Antiochene church. Our focus in the remainder of this chapter, however, will be on the pervasive political pressures present in Antiochene life in the mid 80s and how they are reflected in *Matthew's* Gospel. After all, *Matthew* must have performed his scribal tasks in the shadow of the most powerful political center in the eastern half of the Roman world of his day.

An initial survey of the text might suggest, with some justification, that there isn't much to go on. For example, there is no direct confrontation over emperor worship or explicit signs of severe, current and widespread persecution evident in the Gospel. Yet, a closer review would indicate that this comparative silence on these subjects and the delicate handling of those few political matters that are explicitly dealt with in the Gospel do not reflect disinterest, but, conversely, a very cautious handling of an extremely touchy and potentially volatile political situation in the Antiochene community and church.

Consider, if you will, the unique attitude *Matthew* displays toward Pontius Pilate. Contrasted with Mark which uses "governor," ηγεμων, only once when referring to Pilate, the *First* Gospel does so on nine occasions thus exhibiting remarkable deference toward Roman authority. Pilate's official status is recognized and granted.

Then we have the account of Pilate's wife in 27:19 pleading Jesus' case because of a dream she had had. Only *Matthew* includes this dramatic interlude in his Passion narrative. But what is the point? Surely it is to demonstrate Jesus' innocence as recognized even by one whom the readers might normally think of as belonging to Jesus' opposition. Indirectly, however, it also portrays this highly placed Roman woman as honest and unbiased, if not actually committed to Jesus.

Next we come to the Pilate-Washes-His-Hands episode, again found only in Matthew, 27:24-25. While many modern preachers are quick to see this action as descriptive of Pilate's duplicity, it seems fairer to say, on the basis of context, that the evangelist's own intention was to portray Pilate positively as trying everything imaginable to ward off the unjustified determination of the Jewish mob and their leaders to have Jesus crucified.

This judgment is further confirmed by a third *Matthean* addition, the story of the guards at Jesus' tomb, 28:11-15. There, when the chief priests hear of Jesus' resurrection they offer to pay the guards to alter their testimony, promising to defend them from any possible recrimination on Pilate's part. Pilate, or we might read Rome, accordingly, had no role or responsibility in this ultimate deception — a ruse, however, which *Matthew* caustically concludes is prevalent among *"the Jews to this day,"* 28:15.

Perhaps the most explicit statement of the *Matthean* attitude toward the Roman state is found in the so-called Temple Tax account, again found only in the *First* Gospel, 17:24-27. If we correctly understand the implication of this traditional story as transparently referring to the *Fiscus Iudaicus* initiated by Vespasian to replace the old Jewish Temple Tax then it is the Roman tax-gathering authorities to whom Jesus' words refer when he says to Peter: *"However, so that we do not give offense to them, go to the sea and cast a hook; take the first fish that comes up; and when you open its mouth, you will find a coin; take that and give it to them for you and me."* Giving offense, σκανδαλιζω, as we will have further occasion to learn, is a major concern of the *first* evangelist. While he would have had every right to refuse the Roman demand for taxes, *Matthew's* Jesus, by redaction, does not wish a confrontation with the Roman authorities. If we may retain the marine metaphor, then, *Matthew* is determined not to rock the Roman boat.

This conciliatory stance does not imply that the evangelist was oblivious to all political dangers. The problem is that most other political statements in the *First* Gospel are not unique to it, but were taken over from *Matthew's* precursor texts, Mark and Q. This fact makes it hard to assess their significance specifically in the Antiochene context late in the first century C.E. For example, the well known text, "*Give...to the emperor* Καισαρος, *the things that are the emperor's, and to God the things that are God's,*" Mt. 22:21, is repeated from Mark 12:17. It sounds like a very accommodating principle on Jesus' part. It is entirely proper for his followers to pay taxes to Caesar. However, if one considers that the most popular coin during the time of Jesus' ministry was one which displayed the bust of the emperor Tiberius, 14-37 C.E., and also bore the inscription, "Son of the deified Augustus," then Jesus' seemingly level-headed comment was in fact an indirect negative inferring that Caesar is NOT God. If such was the passage's import during the reign of Tiberius as recorded in Mark how much more devastatingly appropriate would it have been during the tenure of Domitian as suggested by its inclusion in the *First* Gospel?

The same considerations apply when attempting to answer the much debated question of whether or not the *First* Gospel reflects a situation of on-going persecution in Antioch's Christian community. Eusebius, as previously noted, wrote that Domitian early in his reign determined to implement the punitive program of genocide against all "descendants of David" that his father, Vespasian, had only threatened, or may have actually pursued in some individual cases in Rome.[17] However, Eusebius also quotes Hegesippus, a late second century C.E. Christian historian, as reporting that after grilling two humble, Galilean grandchildren of Judas, Jesus' brother, Domitian decided that Jewish Christians did not pose a threat to his throne and called off the whole effort.[18]

Now, it is true that Jesus' dire predictions in Mt. 10:16-22a, based for the most part on Mark 13:9-11, sound very much like post-eventu, i.e., after-the-fact, prophecies:

> *"See, I am sending you out like sheep into the midst of wolves...Beware of them, for they will hand you over to councils and flog you in their synagogues; and you will be dragged before governors and kings because of me, as a testimony to them and the Gentiles ... Brother will betray brother to death, and a father his child, and children will rise against parents, and have them put to death; and you will be hated by all because of my name."*

But do these words imply continuing serious persecution in Antioch? Not necessarily. Surely, the wider Christian community, directly and indirectly, had experienced threatening times, especially under Nero after the burning of Rome and during the war with Israel, as undoubtedly reflected in the Gospel of Mark, but there simply is not sufficient corroborating evidence in Matthew or in secular histories of the period to conclude that a widespread condition of persecution persisted in Antioch at the time of Matthew's composition.

Again, we hear the direct warnings in the Beatitude: *"Blessed are you when people revile you and persecute you and utter all kinds of evil against you falsely on my account,"* 5:11, and in Jesus' declaration about *"those who lose their life for my sake"* in 10:20. In the concluding eschatological flashback in 25:31-46, however, we are told that final judgment will not be based on having endured persecution but on the more routine expectations of the Christian life and ethic, giving food to the hungry, drink to the thirsty, clothing to the naked, succor to the sick, and visiting those in prison.

While the *first* evangelist, then, is very aware of negative past experiences within the wider Christian community and may well still anticipate future local problems coming from Gentile sources, he does not portray them with sufficient intensity to imply a situation of current and consistent persecution within the immediate congregation. Rather, the most serious threats he envisions in the text of the *First* Gospel are those emanating from rival Jewish groups as attested in chapter 23. Much more on this subject later.

Finally, there is one other curious phenomenon in Matthew which may or may not have political roots. Why is "Savior," Σωτηρ, not used as a Christological title in the *First* Gospel? It is not found in Mark either, but Matthew has the unique quote of the angel to Joseph in 1:21: *You are to name him Jesus, for he will save,* σωσει, *his people from their sins."* The theological basis for the possible use of such a title then is certainly present. Still it is never employed. Why not? Several logical reasons have been advanced for its omission. 1) The title, "Savior," had long been used to describe the gods of Greek and Roman mythology, also those of some current mystery cults, such as Mithraism. *Matthew* wished to avoid any such denigrating comparisons with Jesus. 2) The Greek verb σωζω, "to save," often has the meaning "to heal" in the *First* Gospel.[19] Healing, as previously noted, was associated with the god Asclepius in Roman culture. Domitian had built a temple to Asclepius in Antioch. Later mosaic floors in Antioch and Daphne also portray "Health" and "Long Life" as the demigoddess Σωτηρια, "Salvation." Could it have been a desire to differentiate Jesus from Asclepius or other common "healers" that prompted the omission? 3) Vespasian, when assuming the emperorship, chose the accolade Soter, or "Savior," fashioning himself as the rescuer of the Roman state after the Neronian debacle. Was it to avoid the suggestion that Jesus was only the equivalent of a deified Vespasian that the evangelist side-stepped the title as applying to Jesus? It is impossible to tell. Perhaps it was "all of the above." At any rate, it was left to Luke/Acts, the Gospel of John, and the Deuterocanonical letters attributed to St. Paul to introduce the designation "Savior" which today has undoubtedly become one of the most commonly used titles of the Christ.

All in all, the serious reader of Matthew acquires an unavoidable sense that the evangelist is seriously, yet only marginally, concerned with matters political.

The rewarding aspect of delving more deeply into the political, economic, cultural and religious context of the *First Gospel*, as we have attempted to do in this chapter, is that it opens up new vistas of understanding and new challenges for interpretation. Like an artist's portrayal of an aesthetic concept, the resultant picture stimulates one's imagination. Yes there is some speculation involved, but there is also the enhanced experience of empathetic identification with *Matthew's* original readers. Above the melody line of *Matthew's* narrative detailing Jesus' life and ministry we are also able to hear the descant of the Antiochene church's struggle, faith and devotion. The harmony is exhilarating.

Chapter 3 Endnotes

[1] Most of the historical material underlying this chapter is taken from Glanville Downey, A HISTORY OF ANTIOCH IN SYRIA, Chap. 9, on the Flavian Dynasty, pp. 202-210.

[2] In Turkish travel guides it is known as the Gariz Tunnel of Samandag.

[3] Cf. Eusebius, ECCLESIASTICAL HISTORY III, V, 2f.

[4] Cf. Georg Strecker, DER WEG DER GERECHTIGKEIT; 3rd expanded edition, Vandenhoeck & Ruprecht, 1971, pp. 45-49, 184-188; Also Jack Dean Kingsbury, MATTHEW AS STORY; Fortress Press, Minneapolis, 1986, pp. 38-40; MATTHEW, STRUCTURE, CHRISTOLOGY; KINGDOM; Fortress Press, Philadelphia, 1975, pp. 25-37.

[5] Downey, A HISTORY OF ANTIOCH, op cit. p. 286.

[6] Ibid. Cf. also my book, PETER IN MATTHEW, Discipleship, Diplomacy and Dispraise. Liturgical Press, Collegeville, MN., 1992.

[7] Cf. Downey, HISTORY, op. cit., p. 206.

[8] Josephus, THE WARS OF THE JEWS, Bk. 7, chapters 3 & 5, pp. 752-54, 756.

[9] Suetonius, THE LIVES OF THE CAESARS, Book VIII, "The Deified Vespasian," p. 319, in the Loeb Classical Library.

[10] But see Eusebius, op. cit., III, xvii, xix, p. 101f. for another debatable view.

[11] Many of these floors are on display at the Hatay Archeological Museum in Antakya. They are also reproduced in book form in ANTIOCH ON THE ORONTES; Fatih Cimok, ed., A Turizm Yayinlari Ltd. Sifa Hamanmi Sokak 18, Sultanahmet 34400, Istanbul, 1994.

[12] EPICTETUS, Bk. 1, Ch. 3, 1 in the Loeb Classical Library. Trans. W. A. Oldfather. Harvard University Press, Cambridge, 1925, p. 25.

[13] Cf. Philostratus, THE LIFE OF APOLLONIUS OF TYANA, 2 Vols. Trans. F.C. Conybeare in the Loeb Classical Library, Harvard University Press, Cambridge, 1912.

[14] Ibid., Bk. I, Ch. xvi. p. 45.

[15] A famous, beautifully adorned silver communion cup known as the "Chalice of Antioch" was uncovered there in 1910. Some enthusiastically considered it the "Holy Grail." Its origin, however, is late, perhaps fourth or fifth century C.E. Today it is on display at the Metropolitan Museum of Art in New York City.

[16] Cf. the *Didache,* or *Teaching of the Twelve Apostles* in APOSTOLIC FATHERS, Bk. 1; Trans. Kirsopp Lake in the Loeb Classical Library, Harvard University Press, Cambridge, 1912, pp. 305-333.

[17] Eusebius' ECCLESIASTICAL HISTORY; Baker Book House, Grand Rapids, Michigan. chapters XVII, XIX and XX, pp.101-103.

[18] Ibid.

[19] Cf. e.g., 9:21-22.

Chapter 4

An Alias for the Author[1]

Public phones at the Istanbul International Airport require tokens of various values for calls of differing lengths. As instructed, I dialed the number of the local tourism office and asked for Menter Yugliri. A female voice greeted me in Turkish, then left the phone apparently to find someone who spoke English. I waited. Finally another female voice intoned: "Can I help you?" "I want to speak with Menter Yugliri," I replied. "What information do you need?" she asked. "I need to speak with Menter Yugliri," I insisted. "I am Menter Yugliri!" she responded with some firmness. Just then the allotted time expired.

I was embarrassed. I had assumed "Menter" was masculine and accordingly had insulted the first Turkish person who had tried to befriend me. Lesson learned: It is very important to be clear about the proper use of names wherever you are.

Now the question is: Who, in fact, was the *first* evangelist? Few questions are more critical in a study such as this. The editor, or author, determines the content and sets the tone of the piece. The quality of the finished product is largely dependent upon that person's commitment, abilities, education, experience, tastes, time and resources. And no matter how objective or historically accurate an author aspires to be, something of his or her own personality and subjective perspective is bound eventually to show through and influence the conclusions drawn in the literary product. Some acquaintance with the author, therefore, is sure to be beneficial, if not essential, for understanding the text. The more intimately the individual reader, or the listening audience generally, can identify with the writer emotionally and situationally the more personally vital and poignant the redacted message becomes.

The mini-prologues introducing each chapter, such as the one above, for example, are intended, similarly, to serve as clues for you, the reader, to understand what interests, amuses and motivates me, the present writer, thereby enabling you more readily to align your thinking with my purposes in this book. Empathy is the handmaid of authorship, the heart of the art of persuasion.

Unfortunately, we are haunted and handicapped in our quest to become better acquainted with the *first* evangelist not only by the fact that the *First* Gospel is anonymous but by the added baggage of an attractive though discredited traditional belief that the author was a direct disciple/companion of Jesus. There is, therefore, much inertia to overcome and only inferential possibilities and statistical probabilities on which to build an alternative consensus.

Our plight is graphically illustrated by the reproductions of artists' conceptions of the *first* evangelist populating the covers and dust jackets of numerous commentaries on the Gospel of Matthew. A cursory review of my desk-side collection reveals that, generally speaking, all portray a male in quasi-ancient garb, looking properly emaciated and clasping a sacred text. That many of these depictions are more theologically than historically motivated is clear from the further fact that often the evangelist is haloed, shown with a right hand uplifted in a Trinitarian gesture, and occasionally even bedecked with the suggestion of angelic wings.[2] Obviously the intention, consistent with traditional, pious fancy, is to portray a saintly, out-of-this-world evangelist, a hallowed disciple of Christ, even an embodied *alter ego* of the Holy Spirit. As well intended as these presentations may be they are misleading and unfortunately often serve to cloud our view of the Gospel text itself. We cannot relate to it as genuine literature addressing practical, every day, human issues. Instead, we are more inclined to simply stand in awe of it as "Sacred Scripture" — untouchably immaculate, incomprehensibly divine and unchallengeably authoritative. Such triumphalist attitudes constitute part of our present day plague of pretexts as described in Chapter One. Old sanctimonies die hard and these representations of the evangelist as someone super-saintly sadly tend only to perpetuate them.

Happily, two renditions in my collection of Matthean book covers break the mold. One projects the bust of a portly "Friar Tuck" type with full face, flashing dark eyes, balding forehead, short black hair and a long, straight Roman nose. Apparently the artist used his local Italian priest as a model.[3] But imagine, *Matthew,* a Gentile!?

The second depiction is even more amazing, and frankly more to my liking because it is more honest.[4] It portrays the evangelist as a comparatively young man, casually dressed, with cropped, curly hair, sitting at his writing pedestal out in the open air with fields and forests, and even a classical Greco-Roman building, visible in the background. Here at least, and at last, the evangelist is portrayed as a normal human being, albeit a literary artist, living and working in real time and place. That situation makes him a part of our own experience and environment, enabling us to identify more personally with him and his Gospel.

Our challenge now is to provide this translucent artist's conception with a resumé, to add as much flesh and blood, character, personality and motivation to this proposed author as we responsibly can. This means asking ourselves some very down-to-earth questions about the *first* evangelist, some of which may even seem sacrilegious, such as: What was his real name anyway? Up to now, in this book, we have continued to identify him by his traditional cognomen, *Matthew,* but in view of currently accepted answers to the Synoptic Problem are we still justified in doing so, even for convenience sake? For that matter, are we even sure the evangelist was a single individual or a male? If so, how old was he? What race? How well educated? Married...with children? How did he make a living? What were his political views and how did he get along with his neighbors?

Most of these topics will be treated in subsequent paragraphs, but a few will be left to later chapters allowing for more relevant and extended presentation there.

First, we must ask: Was the *First* Gospel the work of an individual or a group? There was an interesting suggestion a half century ago that a "school" of St. Matthew was responsible for its composition.[5] Seeing the Gospel as the residue of several minds may help to explain some of its apparent variety of conflicting traditions, its sometimes lofty form of argumentation, and its seemingly ambivalent treatment of certain subjects such as the Torah in the Sermon on the Mount. The possibility of multiple authorship, however, is no longer seriously entertained. It represented a possible, but by no means necessary solution. Individual authors are equally capable of employing an assortment of sources and approaches. As a matter of fact, some rhetorical strategies require a degree of indirection, inconsistency and irony. Over all, however, this Gospel exhibits too much integrity of style, perspective and organization to have been the product of a committee. The evangelist, we confidently conclude with the preponderance of scholars, was an individual.

Was this individual, then, male or female? The artists, referred to above, were most likely correct in portraying the evangelist as a male. Perhaps he was even somewhat of a chauvinistic one. The basis for such an audacious suggestion, in part, is the statistical fact that normally in the ancient Greek and Roman worlds boys received whatever formal education was available, especially on the secondary level, girls much more rarely so. Clearly, as the vocabulary, style, structure and content of the *First* Gospel attest, the *first* evangelist was well schooled, and therefore, no doubt, male.

Furthermore, the treatment of women in the text, with the possible exception of Pilate's wife, 27:19, tends toward the negative. In contrast to Luke's birth narrative, for example, where Mary plays the leading role, responding to the angel's announcement and giving birth to the infant Jesus, in this Gospel's Christmas story, Mt. 1:18-25, 2:13-23, it is Joseph, Mary's husband, who is the center of all action and attraction, receiving divine direction through dreams for the naming and care of the holy child. Although the evangelist presumably does so for ultimately good reasons, it is noteworthy, too, that the four female ancestors of Jesus whom he lists in his genealogy of Christ, 1:1-17 — Tamar, Rahab, Ruth and Bathsheba — were all "shady ladies," either Gentiles or prostitutes and adulteresses. Similarly, Mark's Syrophoenician woman in Mk. 7:26 is culturally down-graded in the Matthean parallel account, 15:22, to a Canaanite. The compelling Markan story of the poor widow who contributed all she possessed, Mk. 12:41-44, is entirely omitted. Perhaps most telling, is the further omission in Matthew 19:9 of Mark's suggestion of a woman's right to divorce, found originally in Mk. 10:12. Was that possibility simply inconceivable in the mind of the *first* evangelist? In general, then, the *First* Gospel portrays a man's world and reflects a correspondingly pervasive male editorial perspective with masculine values and views, nouns and pronouns, predominating.

Well then, was the evangelist a married man? Of course we are not explicitly told and the sample of relevant material is too small to be definitive. All things being normal, we would be inclined to assume that he would have been married. Clearly, he was old enough, prosperous enough, and sufficiently well educated to be respected as an outstanding family man in the community. Nevertheless, in view of some of the comments unique to this *First* Gospel, one is left to wonder. Why, for instance, is Matthew the only gospel to discuss the legitimacy of eunuchs in the kingdom of heaven in 19:10-12? There the disciples ostensibly ask Jesus if it would not be better for a man to remain unmarried if the repercussions and penalties of a possible divorce are so severe. Jesus, by redaction, answers approvingly. Yes, some men have even made themselves eunuchs for the sake of the kingdom. Jesus, again by redaction, then adds a forceful final admonition: *"Let anyone accept this who can."* If you will excuse the pun, the evangelist here, at least in principle, clearly espouses celibacy as an acceptable, if not preferable, form of Christian asceticism. But does this unparalleled perspective and level of concern reflect a personal commitment to the ideal of remaining unmarried on the author's part? It's your guess, but I must admit I am tempted to think so.

Naturally, if the evangelist's marital status is uncertain so is the question whether or not he had a family. What he has to say about children is for the most part taken over from Mark, cf. Mt. 18:1-5/Mk. 9:33-37; Mt. 19:13-15/Mk. 10:13-16. One observation, however, is in order here. The author's frequent use, especially in chapter eighteen, of οι μικροι, translated *"little ones"* in the NRSV, does not necessarily refer to children, but rather envisions anyone, regardless of age, whose faith is young and vulnerable. There is no distinctively parental attitude displayed in the *First* Gospel.

Now more materially significant: Was the evangelist a Jew or a Gentile? Was he a Christian Jew or a Jewish Christian? An older view, apparently still indebted to the traditional commitment to *Matthew*, the Galilean disciple of Jesus, as the author, practically assumed that the evangelist was a Jew both by race and original religion. One popular notion even saw him as a converted rabbi.[6] In support of this perspective, scholars observed the emphasis on Torah in the Sermon on the Mount, the author's facility with the Hebrew Bible, his rabbinical style of argumentation, and the number of unexplained Jewish customs assumed to be understood by a Jewish readership. In time, however, these arguments were individually countered by contrary observations. After all, the gospel was written in Greek, not in Hebrew or Aramaic as one would expect from a Jewish writer. There are several egregious errors (see below) in the author's knowledge of Jewish history and Judean geography; and, perhaps most importantly, it is thought by some scholars that no Jewish author would or could ever make the kind of anti-Judaism comments found in Mt. 23. Some commentators, therefore, have gone to the opposite extreme concluding that the evangelist must have been a Gentile.[7]

My own opinion is a compromise, or better, a combination of the views. Both sets of conflicting observations listed above cannot be denied. It is reasonable, therefore, to conclude that the evangelist was in fact a Diaspora Jewish Christian, reared in a first or second generation Jewish Christian home, but educated in Greco-Roman schools, and living in Roman-Syrian Antioch in the concluding decades of the first century C.E.

Very possibly his residence was located within the Kerateion, the Jewish quarter of the city, near the Daphne gate and not too far from the Kenesheth Hashmunith synagogue. There, we can easily imagine, he grew up speaking the Aramaic language at home and becoming sensitized to the cultural and religious stresses and strains occurring within that larger Jewish community. Simultaneously, however, as a citizen of this free city and of Rome, he also learned the Greek language as a youth on the streets of Antioch, was privileged to receive a formal education in one of Antioch's schools of rhetoric, and frequently, whether at work or at worship, interacted with Gentiles of varying nationalities, cultures and values.

As exhibited in his Gospel, the *first* evangelist, while primarily concerned with and influenced by his Jewish religious and cultural surroundings, was remarkably cosmopolitan. At times, we are surprised to hear common anti-Gentile epithets such as *"let such a one be to you as a Gentile and a tax collector,"* issuing from Jesus' lips, 18:17. Then again we are just as often made to marvel at the extraordinary faith credited to Gentiles, such as the Roman centurion mentioned in 8:5-13, and the humble Canaanite woman in 15:21-28. Obviously, *Matthew* was writing to two cultural worlds at once seeking to bring them together into what he views more globally as "the kingdom of heaven(s)," or less frequently, as "the church."

Now, how old was *Matthew*? Age, of course, is relative, but this much can be safely asserted: the *first* evangelist was mature, experienced and self-assured, but still mentally agile and open to change. As previously observed, he was respectful of official government authority, but not intimidated by Jewish leadership, cf. ch. 23. He appreciated venerable traditions, 5:17-18, but was not so enamored of them that he followed them mechanically, 5:31-32. His familiarity with human nature, 20:10-12, with legal and penal institutions, 5:21-22, with taxes, 17:24-27, illnesses, 15:30, with social graces and faux pas, 22:11-14, all indicate an active public life.

Nowhere was he more experienced, however, than in the field of religion, in pursuing a life oriented toward God. A keen observer of spiritual fluctuations in his own community, he had obviously thought long and deeply of God-pleasing solutions to the church's problems. *The "little-faiths"* required strengthening, 6:30f., the *"little ones"* protecting, 18:6, the "sinning brothers" forgiveness, 18:21-36. All in all, the *first* evangelist must have been a very aware, resilient and profound — but not uncomplicated — man in the prime of his professional life.

What precisely was his profession? Surely, as the *First* Gospel exemplifies, he was an experienced writer, a compiler of sources and traditions, an observer of the contemporary scene, a storyteller, a teacher, a theologian, an editor, and an author in his own right. In short, and in terms of the comparatively brief list of social categories available in ancient times, he was a *literatus*, a respected literate member of Antiochene society, or at least of its Christian community. Perhaps, speaking more generally, we can say simply that he was a scribe.

The term "scribe" when applied to all ancient societies covers a broad subset of derivative professions from a humble, somewhat despised, public letter-writer seated in the dust on a street corner, to a bookkeeper, teacher, or famous author/ orator, like Cicero in Rome or Antioch's own Libanius. As a class, scribes were usually highly regarded and much in demand as public servants, businessmen, lawyers, playwrights, professional readers, entertainers, and Sophists. The best among them attained considerable wealth, fame and influence, so much so that even the imperial households were occasionally obliged to listen to scribal tirades against their arbitrary, self-serving actions. In a world without television, radio or telephones, scribes of one type or another were at the heart of all communication.

Was the *first* evangelist, then, a professional scribe, or writer? His facility with words and rhetorical conventions, plus his dexterity in conflating disparate traditions, as demonstrated in the *First* Gospel, would certainly suggest that he was, but probably not in an exclusively religious sense. The potential readership and support base in the church was undoubtedly too small to make any literary project profitable or even fiscally possible. It was in the secular field, then, that we can imagine this scribe earning his living. I can see him, for example, working as a clerk in the imperial archives in the city's center, collating and categorizing official documents and writing brief abstracts of their contents. This kind of responsible governmental position would more possibly have supplied the experience and financial resources needed for a talented and committed author to undertake a task of Gospel proportions.

It may very well have been in the capacity of an avocation, therefore, that the *first* evangelist undertook the composition of this *First* Gospel. As described in the previous chapter, citizens of "free" Roman cities like Antioch enjoyed the prerogative to organize their own ethnic, civil or religious groups or councils called *collegia*. As a well educated, middle class, semi-independent Jewish Christian man, the *first* evangelist undoubtedly belonged to one of these *collegia sodalicia* located in the vicinity where he lived. Perhaps, this assembly, εκκλησια, even met in his comparatively comfortable home. It is entirely conceivable, too, that in the course of time he served in its various official capacities as president, αρχων, chaplain, ιερευς, or secretary, γραμματευς. These offices undoubtedly would have brought him into contact with all the other Christian *collegia* in Antioch and its environs — their leaders, experiences and problems — broadening his vision of both the fledgling church's needs and its spiritual assets. We might well imagine that it was in that last position as scribe, secretary or *amanuensis* that he felt most professionally comfortable, competent and responsible to contribute to the stabilization of the larger Christian community by composing this *First* Gospel.

We have the comparable contemporary examples of Tertius, St. Paul's *amanuensis,* in Romans 16:22, and of Clement, who apparently while serving as the secretary to the second Bishop of Rome sometime around 80 C.E., wrote his

First *Letter to the Corinthians,* today better known as *I Clement.*[8]

Now, perhaps, we can also understand why that curious concluding eighth parable in Matthew 13:52 has attracted so much scholarly attention. It reads: *"Therefore every scribe,* γραμματευς, *who has been trained for the kingdom of heaven is like the master of a household who brings out of his treasure what is new and what is old."* Could this passage referring to a scribe *"trained for the kingdom,"* rather than the Mt. 9:9 Matthew-as-tax-collector account, represent the evangelist's true tactic of self-identification in his Gospel? Although stated in plural terms as applicable to numerous scribes the description here of their using things *"new and old"* fits the evangelist's own practice perfectly. Four of the previous parables in this 13th chapter, for example, may be considered "new" insofar as they are found only in this Gospel while the other three are "old" having been taken over from Mark and Q. Certainly, in contemporary terms, this evangelist/scribe saw himself as a journalist and publicist for the kingdom of heaven.

We can now safely and finally forget the old, pious idea that Mt. 9:9 where Jesus calls a tax-collector named *Matthew* to be a disciple represents the author's desire to associate himself with this gospel. There simply is no internal evidence to suggest that the *first* evangelist was an eye-witness companion of Jesus, a tax collector, a Galilean fisherman or any other such role usually associated with being one of the "Twelve." The evangelist clearly had a different reason for changing *"Levi,"* as in the parallel passage, Mark 2:14, to *"Matthew."* No doubt, the alteration was made to bring the Mt. 9 commissioning account into compliance with the list of disciples given shortly thereafter in Mt. 10:2-4/Mark 3:16-19 where no "Levi" is included. As many commentators have observed, the Greek for *"Matthew,"* Μαθθαιος, closely parallels in

85

sound and spelling the Greek for "disciple," μαθητης, perhaps suggesting the exchange. Abandoning the comforts of the venerable tradition, then, about *Matthew, Apostle and Evangelist,* let us realize that the true writer of this *First* Gospel was not an original disciple of Jesus but an unknown scribe living in a distant land, Syrian Antioch-on-the-Orontes, and at a later date, in the ninth decade of the first century C.E.

An Alias for the Scribe,[9] *Author and Evangelist*

But if the author of the *First* Gospel was not *Matthew,* the disciple, then how do we identify him?

The established, traditional title of the work is The Gospel According to St. Matthew, or simply "Matthew." Nothing, apparently, can be done to change that designation at this late date, although an alternative suggestion will be made in Chapter Five. Continuing to refer to both the Gospel and the evangelist as Matthew, however, even for convenience sake, actually represents an unjustified and unwarranted concession to a skewed form of religiosity unworthy of even the average Christian's intelligence. Since the author's true name and identity are not recoverable, however, the ascription of some kind of alias or *nom de plume* seems advisable. Up to this point in this book, we have made the minimal adjustment, referring to the *first* evangelist as *Matthew,* in italics, to distinguish him from Matthew, in block letters, indicating the written text of the Gospel. On occasion, we shall continue to do so. In my own study, however, I prefer to think of and to refer to the author by employing a more distinctive pen-name to reflect his true identity in terms of both ethnicity and occupation. I call him "Ben Grammateus." "Ben" in Hebrew means "son" while "Grammateus," as we have learned, is Greek for "scribe." Employing this designation for the evangelist, it seems to me, introduces us more directly to a real, human author, a Diaspora son of a Jewish Christian family, but one educated in Greek and serving as a scribe within his own time, place and situation. Simultaneously, such a bold exchange of names, it seems to me, helps us rid our minds of lingering, pietistic hidden agendas involving a haloed saint composing this gospel in some beatific vacuum. As the sovereign reader of this book, of course, you are free to decide upon an alias of your own choosing.

Recent explorations into Composition Criticism, Narrative Criticism, Reader Response and Audience Criticism have greatly magnified our appreciation of the scribal arts as practiced by the evangelist and represented in the *First* Gospel.

There was a time when biblical scholarship considered the Gospels as comprised essentially of a series of unrelated anecdotes, historical vignettes, parables and miracle stories. Each pericope could be studied independently, in isolation, as representing a theological cosmos of its own. The inspired writers of the Gospels were viewed simply as compilers of these stories, traditions and sayings of Jesus. Then a half century ago along came Redaction Criticism. It elevated the role of the evangelist. He was seen as not only collecting and combining his sources, rather arbitrarily, but as consciously and purposefully rearranging them, omitting some, adding others and nuancing their theological import. Evangelists, in other words, had become editors. Today, however, even Redaction Criticism in some respects appears increasingly obsolete. While still retaining older traditions, the evangelists are seen as having reworked their sources so thoroughly in order to interweave parallel themes, appeal to the interests of their immediate readers and arrive at a consistent over-all plot that they are now viewed as having gone beyond mere editing to actual authorship. On the one hand, traditional materials retained from other sources are now seen as potentially as significant as those originated by the redactor himself, especially if repeated or augmented by reinforcing arguments. On the other hand, present day scholars also recognize the possibility that, consistent with some rhetorical strategies, evangelists may occasionally even include materials which they themselves do not intend to be accepted literally or absolutely. Rather, to be properly understood by the reader, each part has to be viewed, interpreted and perhaps even corrected from the perspective of the whole.

So, enter *Matthew,* or Ben Grammateus, scribe, evangelist and author. As a scribe, his stock in trade was rhetoric. As noted earlier, he had been trained in it from his youth in an Antiochene school where, we can well imagine, he had been introduced to Quintilian's elementary exercises,[10] implementing the art of rhetorical invention as popularized by Cicero,[11] 106-43 B.C.E., of *stasis* theory going back to Hermagoras of Temnos in the second century B.C.E., and the various strategies of persuasion associated with Isocrates, Aristotle and Homer.[12] He had learned his lessons well and in time became an accomplished journalist of the kingdom.

In the *First* Gospel we find this scribe using a wide variety of rhetorical conventions and strategies technically known as *"topoi."* His favorite topos was *"synkrisis,"* i.e., comparison or contrast. It was his chief pedagogical method. Its instances are too numerous to note here, but undoubtedly the most familiar examples of *"synkrisis"* are the introductory clauses to the six Antitheses in the Sermon on the Mount: *"You have heard that it was said to those of ancient times....But I say unto you...,"* 5:21, 27, 31, 33, 38, 43. There are also comparisons and contrasts between Jesus and John the Baptist, 11:18-19, Jesus and Peter, 14:28-33, the disciples and the prophets, 13:17, and many others.

A second important, but seldom noted, topos, as previously mentioned, is called *"stasis." Stasis* functions in a variety of ways. Cicero used the Latin word *"insinuatio,"* to define *stasis,* that is, something that insinuates itself into the reader's subconscious mind. It may also be viewed as a resolve in a debate, a proposition to be analyzed and, if necessary, modified. A *stasis* statement, therefore, is not the last word on a subject, but the first, introducing in often slightly outrageous terms a topic to be argued. A good illustration may be the controversial passage found in the Sermon on the Mount, 5:18: *"For truly I tell you, until heaven and earth pass away, not one letter, not one stroke of a letter, will pass away from the law until all is accomplished."* This is a strong statement, but it is obvious from what follows where he modifies the law almost at will that Ben Grammateus, the scribe, did not intend these words to be understood in any woodenly literal, or absolutist, sense. Rather, he was setting the parameters for discussion on the topic of appropriate moral and ethical behavior in the kingdom of heaven. We will have occasion to note other examples of *stasis* as we proceed.

Invention is a third rhetorical tactic employed by the evangelist. This is a troublesome concept for some modern day Christians, suggesting an irresponsible form of unhistorical "make believe" or fabrication. As G.W. Bowersock,[13] however, insists, invention does not involve "willful mendacity" but conforms more closely to what Frank Kermode defined as "benign deceit," shading the facts to enlighten the reader. No doubt one of the best examples of the art of invention in the *First* Gospel is the author's intentional misquoting of Micah 5:2 in Mt. 2:6, changing the Old Testament description of Bethlehem as *"one of the little clans of Judah"* to one which recognized it as *"by no means least among the rulers of Judah."* In the *first* evangelist's mind, the spiritual significance of Jesus' birthplace far outweighed its historical and geographic insignificance, justifying the literary reversal.

Biblical scholars have uncovered a host of smaller rhetorical conventions and rubrics employed in the *First* Gospel. There are *chreia,* brief anecdotes with an authoritative punch line. We might think of the account of Jesus eating with tax-collectors in 9:10-13, concluding with the saying: *"I have come not to call the righteous but sinners."* There is *paronomasia,* i.e., puns or plays-on-words — the best known, and most troublesome, example, undoubtedly, being the Peter-Rock, Πετρος–πετρα, combination in 16:18. Again, *prolepsis* refers to anticipations or flash-forwards such as when Jesus is heard to use the anachronistic metaphor of taking up one's "cross" and following him in 16:24 long before there was any explicit mention of Jesus' impending crucifixion. *Inclusios* are identical or at least very similar phrases opening and closing units of thought. Consider the early identification of Jesus as *"Emmanuel,"* i.e., *"God is with us"* in 1:23 and his own final promise *"I am with you always"* in 28:20, embracing the entire gospel. The statement in 11:11 that *"among those born of women no one has arisen greater than John the Baptist; yet the least in the kingdom of heaven is greater than he,"* is reminiscent of the rhetorical strategy Cicero called *laudandi et vituperandi,* praise and dispraise, honor and shame. One rhetorician lists more than thirty such *topoi.*[14] *Matthew,* or Ben Grammateus, seems to have been familiar with most of them.

More difficult, but undoubtedly also more fundamentally important to ascertain even than these practiced rubrics of classical rhetoric are the author's personal attitudes, perspectives and editorial practices which appear to be both culturally and theologically influenced. An illustrative case-in-point which has long titillated exegetes is the evangelist's inconsistent use of Old Testament texts.[15] There are more than one hundred such references and allusions found in the *First* Gospel, including eleven direct "fulfillment quotations," introduced by the formula: *"This was to fulfill what had been spoken by the Lord through the prophet..."* (cf. 1:22-23; 2:15, 17-18, 23; 3:3; 4:14-16; 8:17; 12:17-21; 13:35; 21:5; 27:9-

10). Some times *Matthew,* the scribe, employed the Hebrew text (cf. Mt. 27:46 vs. Mk. 15:34), at others he preferred the rendition of the Greek Septuagint. Then again, he could be either very free, daring even to misquote the Micah 5:2 passage about the significance or insignificance of Bethlehem in 2:6, or rigidly literalistic as in 21:5 where he seems completely oblivious to Hebrew poetic parallelism insisting that there were two beasts of burden, a donkey and its colt, rather than one as the original text in Zechariah 9:9 clearly attested. On the one hand, then, the *first* evangelist as we have come to know him obviously holds the Sacred Scriptures in high regard, but on the other is quite loose in their application. How can one understand or justify such ambivalence?

In response, scholars have been quick to remind us that the concept of an inspired canon had not yet matured at *Matthew's* time, neither for the Old Testament nor for the New. The texts were sacred, but not sacrosanct, highly respected but not inviolate. Approximately another century would be required for the 22 Hebrew books of the Old Testament[16] to attain the level of canonical authority, and another three centuries for the 27 Greek books of the New Testament to achieve that same degree of acceptance in the church.

Furthermore, some supportive evidence can be cited to indicate that other translations and versions of the various texts, each displaying their own theological nuances, could have existed and been in use in the first century C.E.

The discovery of the Dead Sea Scrolls, similarly, reflects an extant "pesher" perspective whereby the prevailing, current situation is accepted as the standard for understanding the Old Testament "anticipations" or "prefigurations," rather than *vice versa,* as the concept of "fulfillment" traditionally suggests.

As true and tantalizing as these observations are, a better explanation of the *first* evangelist's idiosyncratic stance and approach, it seems to me, may be found in the attitude that subsequently developed in the neighboring Constantinopolitan Church, known generally today as Eastern Orthodoxy. To appreciate the essence and genius of Eastern Orthodoxy, Steven Runciman insists, one must be able to entertain an almost intuitive appreciation of the "apophatic." In definition of this manifestly esoteric term, Runciman, speaking of the "Great Church," explains:

> "Its genius is apophatic, dwelling on the ignorance of man face to face with the Divine: all that we can know about God is that we know nothing: for His attributes must from their nature be outside the realm of worldly knowledge. Its theology and its practices are characterized by antinomies that are not easily resolved by a logical observer...The objective student before he begins his study must charge himself with sympathy and must forget the taste for dialectical precision that is apt to characterize Western theology."[17]

In other words, God's wisdom operates on an entirely different and superior level from human intelligence. The intuitive takes precedence over the cognitive. While profoundly committed to religious truth, the apophatic mindset ultimately shies away from absolutes. Logic is limited. Dogma is suspect. Facts do not necessarily add up to truth. Human language can only approximate, but never capture, divine omniscience. In contrast to western rationalistic and scientific preoccupations, then, the Eastern Orthodox Christian must be content to live with some imprecision, relativity, uncertainty and ambivalence. This attitude is simultaneously freeing and frustrating, open to experiment, and leaving a growing edge, yet often evolving into mysticism, traditionalisim and ritualism.

Was Ben Grammateus, living in first century Antioch, in a Greco-Roman-Jewish-Syrian cultural environment, fundamentally apophatic? I am disposed to think so, even though he was undoubtedly only incipiently and subconsciously so inclined. He clearly felt himself free to employ every rhetorical device available to maximize his positive theological points. In evidence, note his unique parable of the Laborers in the Vineyard, 20:1-16, as representative of a basic apophatic attitude. Surely, on the human level, there was no excuse for the householder's treatment of the laborers who had worked long hours through the heat of the day. It was callous, unfair, and we would think, even illegal on the basis of labor law, for him to pay these laborers the same wage as those who had worked only one hour. Yet, on the level of the transcendent, who could challenge the authority, wisdom, and generosity of the Divine Householder? No one. The evangelist, accordingly, could be equally inconsistent and in some cases seemingly as cavalier in his treatment of the sacred texts simply because from his perspective an appropriate description of God's nature, ways and will not only allowed but required it.

Several other characteristics of Ben, or *Matthew's,* style and literary tactics reflect an acute awareness of his readership or audience.[18] It has been responsibly estimated that on average no more than ten or fifteen percent of the population in Roman times could read and write. However, this is not the same as saying that these common people were illiterate. From long experience in pursuing their favorite pastimes, listening to speeches and plays of classical orators, storytellers and dramatists, they had become very sensitive to the literary tricks employed by these artists to hold their audiences' attention. We find many of these conventions in the *First* Gospel. First, there are the direct elicitors, such as *"Let the reader understand,"* 24:15/Mk. 13:14, *"Let anyone with ears, listen!"* in 11:15, 13:9, 43; and *"Let anyone accept this who can,"* 19:12. Frequently, the *first* evangelist personalizes Mark's reportage by changing the latter's historical tenses and third person verbs to direct speech employing second person verbs introduced *by "Truly I tell you..."* making it impossible for his readers or audience to escape the import of what is said. On a couple of occasions he even uses the Greek plural pronoun "you," υμεις, or a 2nd pers. pl. verb, when the speaker is responding to a single individual in the narrative, cf. 15:16, 26:40, indicating that a wider audience is actually envisioned. In addition, there are occasional summaries to keep the audience up to speed. There are questions, generalizations, repetitions, and transition indicators such the stereotyped closures to each of the five sermons in Matthew: *"When Jesus had finished saying these things..."* 7:28, 11:1, 13:53, 19:1 and 26:1. Some of these "breaks," no doubt, also served as convenient liturgical stopping and starting points when time did not permit the reading of the entire Gospel at one sitting.

Difficult to believe as it may be for some of us who have always thought of the Bible as the ultimate in serious profundity, there is even humor to be found in the *First* Gospel, a sure sign that the evangelist was considerate of the long work days of his hearers and the dim light of the rented halls where the early "house churches" met. I am not referring here to the usual jokes made about Jesus riding both the mare burro and its foal at the same time as part of his triumphal entry into Jerusalem, 21:1-7. Recognizing something of the evangelist's sensitivity about things new and old, 13:52, I am willing to consider the possibility that he had something quite serious in mind with such a portrayal. The real humor in this gospel is more studied. One variety is of the nature of tongue-in-cheek irony such as when Jesus is heard to respond *"You have said so"* to the High Priest's demand, *"Tell us if you are*

94

the Messiah, the Son of God." Only the *First* Gospel records this answer in this way, 26:64 (but see also 26:25 and 27:11 and par.). It was the scribe's coy tactic, not without some sarcasm, of indicating that the High Priest knew the truth about Jesus all along, but was too deceitfully corrupt to admit it.

Of a more playful type of humor is the rather irreverent series of six rhyming Greek words describing various physical handicaps in 5:30: χωλους, τυφλους, κολλους, κωφους, και ετερους πολλους. The English NRSV translation unfortunately ignores the humor, preferring to remain literal. It reads: *"...the lame, the maimed, the blind, the mute and many others."* What *Matthew,* alias Ben, actually wrote, however, was more like "...those suffering from arthritis, appendicitis, neuritis, gastritis and any other 'itis' you might cite us." That kind of farcical poetry should have been enough at least to bring a smile to many a tired face in the Antiochene Christian audience.

Sometimes, just stating the obvious can be hilarious as in the story of Jesus' temptations by Satan, Mt. 4:1-11. There Jesus is described as fasting forty days and forty nights. Then, the *first* evangelist, alone among the Synoptics, adds unnecessarily: *"...afterwards he was famished."* What a gross understatement! Obviously, Jesus had grown hungry long before that, as the first readers of the *First* Gospel knew all too well from their own experience with fasting.

However, this *"scribe trained for the kingdom"* also had a temper. He could use *invective* and *ad hominem* arguments as well as humor. Chapter 23 immediately comes to mind with its insistent indictments: *"Scribes, Pharisees, hypocrites!"* We think, too, of the caustic remarks he places on Jesus' lips in 15:14, again with reference to the Pharisees: *"Let them alone; they are blind guides of the blind,"* and finally to Peter in 16:23: *"Get behind me, Satan. You are a stumbling block, σκανδαλον, unto me."* Obviously, Ben Grammateus writes with emotion.

It should not surprise us that he also makes mistakes. His genealogical table in 1:2-17 presents a nest full of problems. There are several questionable spellings: *Aram*, v. 4, should be Ram according to Ruth 4:19; *Asaph*, v. 7, a name usually associated with the Psalms, should be Asa according to I Chronicles 3:10; and *Amos*, v. 10, the name of the early prophet to the northern kingdom of Israel, should be Amon according to I Chron. 3:14. *Rahab*, v. 5, is chronologically misplaced. According to Judges 2 she lived in Jericho in the days of Joshua's conquest of Canaan around 1250 B.C.E. For her to be the wife of Salmon and the mother of Boaz would require a date 100 to 150 years later. Then there are the two sets of missing kings between Joram and Uzziah, v. 8, and again between Jechoniah and the Babylonian deportation in v. 11. Finally, after the specific designation of three stylized sets of fourteen generations between Abraham and David, David and the Babylonian deportation, and the deportation to Jesus' birth in v. 17, we actually find only thirteen in the final subset.

Now, in fairness, the question must be asked: Was the *first* evangelist responsible for all of these miscues, or did he only transfer a corrupt earlier tradition? Or, are these errors, perhaps, the results of faulty transmission by copyists over time? We will probably never know, but in the light of the evangelist's subsequent redactional development of the narrative I would at least consider him responsible for the inclusion of the four special women, including the one who is misplaced, in Mt. 1: 3, 5, & 6.

There is a geographical problem in chapter 8:28ff. where the miracle story of the healing of two demoniacs is located in the *"country of the Gadarenes."* Mark 5:1-20 had placed these events in the *"country of the Gerasenes."* In view of the conclusion of the account where the swine leap over the precipice into the Sea of Galilee, Gadara is certainly an improvement over Mark's Gerasa which is nearly thirty miles distant from the sea. Yet, the distance factor is really inconsequential since Gadara is itself still six or more miles away.

We will mention only one other inconsistency. In Mt. 23:35, the redacting author apparently enlarges upon the Q passage in Luke 11:51 to make it say *"...from the blood of righteous Abel to the blood of Zechariah son of Barachiah, whom you murdered between the sanctuary and the altar."* Zechariah, the Old Testament prophet, was indeed the son of Berechiah according to Zech. 1:1. However, according to 2 Chronicles 24:20 it was another Zechariah, the son of Jehoiada, the priest, who was murdered in the court of the Lord's house. We can understand such a confusion of identical names, but in this case we have cause to wonder whether this obvious "error" may not have been intentional. Josephus[19] records an incident during the Roman siege of Jerusalem in 70 C.E. when zealot Jewish leaders unjustly accused a rich and prominent Jewish citizen named Zacharias the son of Baruch of treason and murdered him "in the middle of the temple." In this 23rd chapter of the gospel dealing with *"Scribes, Pharisees, hypocrites,"* then, could not Ben, or *Matthew,* have placed this patent misrepresentation on Jesus' lips as a cogent reminder to his embarrassed Jewish opposition of their recent and continuing injustices? Rhetorically, the procedure is called "indirection."

Our insight into all of this authorial variety, wit and deliberateness gives us a new appreciation of the *First* Gospel. It no longer seems austere, sacrosanct, or esoteric as we once may have thought. Nor, on the other hand, is it to be denigrated any longer as *kleinliteratur,* that is, "small literature," as distinct from classical writing, scribbled in uneducated *koine,* or common street-Greek, as scholars used to think. Rather, we now see it as a well-crafted work of art as well as of substance, eminently personal, practical, and provocative.

Similarly, we now find our anonymous *first* evangelist to have been an accomplished author, a professional — engaging, imaginative and disciplined — a devout man yet very human, serious but not sullen. It is no wonder that his Gospel became popular with his readers and has survived the tests of time.

The Antiochene Christian Community

The role of the first readers in this enterprise of gospel composition dare not be overlooked or underestimated either. Without an audience, immediate and/or envisioned, the evangelist would have been writing in a vacuum with only vapid results. Academic Narrative Critics today often seek accuracy in abstraction, preferring to speak of "implied" authors and "implied" readers, narrators and narratees.[20] In this book, however, we will forego pedantry for intelligibility, attempting to obtain some feel for this Gospel's real flesh-and-blood audience.

We can be sure, first of all, that many of the author's friends, those whom he knew best and cared about most, were Christians of Jewish extraction, some, perhaps, even relatives. We hear him recalling their common history and heritage in the many references to the Old Testament included in the Gospel. Simultaneously, we sense him struggling with their current cultural and religious dislocation as brought to flashpoint in chapter 23. Despite an occasional slip into a traditional racist slur such as *"...let such a one be to you as a Gentile and a tax collector,"* he also had a heart for the non-Jewish masses who swarmed about him in Antioch, especially those *"Hellenists," and "men of Cyprus and Cyrene,"* Acts 11:20, who had come to faith forty years earlier during the days of Barnabas and Paul. In fact, Ben, saw in the Gentile masses the principal hope for the church's future, 28:18-20. It was for the benefit of such a *corpus permixtum,* "a mixed body," then, that the evangelist took pen in hand.

98

But this congregation was not only mixed ethnically, culturally, politically and economically or in terms of age and gender, as we might naturally assume. Differences in spiritual commitment and quality had also begun to appear among them. We can, accordingly, detect from the scribe's varied responses to these prevailing circumstances that several categories of Christians existed within the Antiochene community.

Ben's most general category is that of *"disciple."* That he is thinking of his own congregation is clear from the specific way that he alters the traditional views of Jesus' twelve disciples as portrayed in Mark and Q. In Mark, for example, the disciples seldom, if ever, understand fully who Jesus is or what he is about, Mk. 8:17-18, 21. Their hearts are hardened, Mk. 6:52, 8:17. Typically, even the women who had just met the resurrected Jesus tell no one of his appearance *"for they were afraid,"* Mk. 16:8. In comparison, the author's characterization of the disciples in the *First* Gospel is marginally but more realistically positive. Normally here the disciples do understand, 13:51. They are called blessed because of all that they have been privileged to see and hear as followers of Jesus, 13:16-17. They worship Jesus frequently, cf. 14:33 vs. Mk. 6:52, 28:9, 17, and they correctly confess Jesus to be the Son of God, 14:33. Yet, occasionally, they still have trouble understanding, 15:16. They doubt, 14:31, 28:17, and they flee in time of trouble, 26:56. Ben's, or *Matthew's,* most frequently used description of the disciples, therefore, is *"little-faiths,"* ολιγοπιστοι, 6:30, 8:26, 14:31 and 16:8. No doubt this was also his opinion of the average member of his local *collegium* and of the entire Antiochene church. Most were devout but not deep in their Christian commitment.

This evaluation is supported by the characterization of another subset of disciples, the "sinning brothers" of 18:15-18 and 21-35. We cannot know from this small sample if the evangelist has anyone in particular in mind or if he is writing in general terms. The issue is certainly common enough, i.e., internal strife, when one brother offends, disappoints, or actually harms another. The solution proposed here is both practical and revolutionary. In 18:15-18 the evangelist codifies a progressive three step approach to resolve cases of internal friction: 1) private conversation between the respective individuals, then 2) repeated conversation with two or three objective witnesses, and finally, but only when absolutely necessary, 3) a verdict by the entire gathered community. So much for method.

The second phase, following soon after, in 18:21-35 deals with the spiritual atmosphere and environment necessary if true reconciliation is to occur. It is a surprisingly profound insight. Anyone who carefully compares the evangelist's redaction with what appears to have been the more original Q statement in Luke 17:3-4 cannot help but be impressed. The primary emphasis in the Q passage was on the necessary precondition of the sinner's repentance. In Ben's analysis, however, nothing at all is said of repentance. Rather, the focus is upon the necessity on the part of the Christian community to manifest a generous spirit of forgiveness. Thus the full responsibility for reconciliation does not rest on the sinning brother alone, but is shared by an open, receptive and caring congregation. As the redactional punch line of the Parable of the Unjust Steward in 18:35 forcefully puts it: *"So my heavenly Father will also do to every one of you, if you do not forgive your brother or sister from your heart."* We should all have patient, mutually supportive, forgiving congregations like that!

The evangelist insists on a similar attitude with regard to "straying sheep," 18:12-14. Again it is highly instructive to note the way he nuances this parable in comparison to its prototype in Q, Luke 15:3-7.[21] There the sheep are *lost*, απολεσας, while in the Matthean account they are portrayed as only straying, πλανηθη. Luke 15:7, again, is concerned that the sinner repents; Ben, or *Matthew,* only that the straying person be responsibly searched for and found before he or she is truly lost. As 18:14 concludes *"So it is not the will of your Father in heaven that one of these little ones (ever) be lost."* The issue in the *First* Gospel, then, is not one of evangelism, seeking the uninformed and the unrepentant, but of community responsibility, seeking to keep members in the fold and to avoid back-door losses.

As the above quote from 18:14 just indicated, the *first* evangelist has a special place in his heart for those whom he designates *"little ones,"* οι μικροι, including, perhaps, children, but more likely all novices, new converts, and inexperienced Christians regardless of age. The concept is introduced in 10:42: *"...and whoever gives even a cup of cold water to one of these little ones in the name of a disciple — truly I tell you, none of these will lose their reward."* And in another passage, 18:6, the evangelist again expresses what must have been his own personal exasperation but voiced in Jesus' threat: *"If any of you put a stumbling block before one of these little ones who believe in me, it would be better for you if a great millstone were fastened around your neck and you were drowned in the depth of the sea."* Then, in another saying found only in the *First* Gospel, 18:10, the evangelist warns: *"Take care that you do not despise one of these little ones; for, I tell you, in heaven their angels continually see the face of my Father in heaven."* Obviously, then, some kind of social and religious disconnect existed within the Antiochene Christian community between the older, established members and the *"little ones,"* with the evangelist's sympathies certainly favoring the latter over the former.

Finally, there were the *"righteous,"* οι δικαιοι, i.e., the "saints," living and dead, the morally good in word and in deed, those whose blessedness is assured. Ben, or *Matthew,* reveled in the thought, using the term seventeen times, having found only one prior occurrence in Mark 2:17. More of an ideal type than any identifiable group within the Antiochene Christian community, except, perhaps, for the blessed dead, the evangelist used the concept of the righteous as a standard for emulation by the living. This, at least, seems to be the thought behind the idiomatically difficult passage to translate in 10:41: *"...whoever welcomes a righteous person in the name of a righteous person will receive the reward of the righteous."* In more contemporary terms, we might say: "It takes one to know one," or, "If you ever see one you'll want to be one."

Although the concept of righteousness as a major theme in the *First* Gospel will be expanded at another time, we may say here that it carries a heavy moral content. The righteous are those who live and behave righteously and consistently in demonstration of their faithful association with the omnipresent Jesus Messiah/Christ.

In sum, the evangelist's initial audience and readers must have included a cross-section of the Antiochene population, although undoubtedly consisting mostly of Diaspora Jewish Christians like himself. Some belonged to the "old guard," going back two or three generations to the days of Barnabas and Saul, while others were recent converts still unsure of themselves in a new religious and cultural milieu. One group needed its faith rekindled, the other stabilized. All faced temptations, tensions and threats. There was the routinized spiritual nonchalance of the older Christian establishment, also the renewed attacks of false prophets coming in from the outside, and no doubt the most dangerous of all, the appeal of resurgent Judaism right there within the neighborhood. Ben Grammateus, the scribe, we conclude, hoped his Gospel could counter all these negatives at once while simultaneously providing his Christian community with courage, hope and a sense of security in the knowledge of the incarnate Lord's immediate presence among them.

Only slight changes of venue are required for us to see ourselves personally numbered among this scribe's friends, congregation and audience.

Chapter 4 Endnotes

[1] The question of the *first* evangelist's identification is frequently discussed. For an introduction to conflicting views, cf. Ernst von Dobschütz, *"Matthew as Rabbi and Cetechist,"* in THE INTERPRETATION OF MATTHEW; Graham N. Stanton, ed., T&T Clark, Edinburgh, 1983, pp. 27-38; K. Clark, *"The Gentile Bias in Matthew,"* in the JOURNAL OF BIBLICAL LITERATURE; 66, 1947, pp. 165-172; J.P. Meier, THE VISION OF MATTHEW; Paulist Press, New York, Ramsey, Toronto, 1978, p. 22. Ernest A. Abel, *"Who Wrote Matthew?"* in " NEW TESTAMENT STUDIES, 17, 1970-71, pp. 138-152, solves the question by suggesting that there may have been two Matthews, one Jewish and one Gentile.

[2] The frequent depiction of the *first* evangelist with wings recalls the traditional identification of the four evangelists with the "four living creatures" of Rev. 4:7. There, "the third living creature with a face like a human face" was thought to refer to *Matthew.*

[3] Cf. Peter F. Ellis, *MATTHEW, His Mind and His Message;* The Liturgical Press, Collegeville, Minnesota, 1974.

[4] Cf. Augustine Stock, O.S.B., THE METHOD AND MESSAGE OF MATTHEW; The Liturgical Press, Collegeville, Minnesota, 1994. The illustration in question is taken from the Gospel Book of Ebbo, Bibliothèque Municipale, Èpernay.

[5] Cf. Krister Stendahl, THE SCHOOL OF ST. MATTHEW, and Its Use of the Old Testament; Second edition. CWK, Gleerup, Lund; n.d.

[6] Ernst von Dobschütz, op. cit. Cf. footnote #1.

[7] Cf. J.P. Meier, THE VISION OF MATTHEW, Christ, Church and Morality in the First Gospel; Paulist Press, New York, 1978, p. 22. Also Georg Strecker, DER WEG DER GERECHTIGKEIT: Untersuchung zur Theologie des Matthäus; Vandenhoeck & Ruprecht, Göttingen, 1971, pp. 15-35.

[8] The argument for a later date, around 96 C.E., is reasonably rejected by William A. Jurgens in his collection of early writings entitled THE FAITH OF THE EARLY FATHERS, Vol.1; The Liturgical Press, Collegeville, Minnesota, 1970, p. 6.

[9] Cf. O. Lamar Cope. A SCRIBE TRAINED FOR THE KINGDOM; CBQ, Monograph Series #5, 1976; David E. Orton. THE UNDERSTANDING SCRIBE; in the Journal for the Study of the New Testament, Supplement Series 25, Sheffield Press, 1989; Duane F. Watson, ed. PERSUASIVE ARTISTRY; Journal for the Study of the New Testament, Supplement Series 50, JSOT Press, Sheffield, 1991; Thomas M. Conley. RHETORIC IN THE EUROPEAN TRADITION; Longman Press, New York & London, 1990.

[10] Cf. Quintilian's INSTITUTIO ORATORIA in the Loeb Classical Library. The work consists largely of suggested exercises for children.

[11] Cf. Markus Tullius Cicero. DE INVENTIONE; Trans. H.M. Hubbell in the Loeb Classical Library, Harvard University Press, Cambridge, 1949.

[12] Cf. George A. Kennedy, CLASSICAL RHETORIC AND ITS CHRISTIAN AND SECULAR TRADITION From Ancient to Modern Times; The University of North Carolina Press, Chapel Hill, 1980, especially Chapter 5: *Technical Rhetoric in the Roman Period,* pp. 86-107.

[13] G.W. Bowersock, FICTION AS HISTORY: NERO TO JULIAN; University of California Press, Berkeley, Los Angeles, London, 1994, especially p. 123. Also Frank Kermode, THE GENESIS OF SECRECY: On the Interpretation of Narrative; Cambridge, MA., 1979.

[14] Cf. Philip Shuler, A GENRE FOR THE GOSPELS. The Biographical Character of Matthew; Fortress Press, Philadelphia, 1982, p. 55f.

[15] Cf. Richard N. Longenecker, BIBLICAL EXEGESIS IN THE APOSTOLIC PERIOD; William B. Eerdmans Publishing Company, Grand Rapids, 1975, esp. pp. 140-152.

[16] Several biblical books, divided for convenience in Englsh translations, such as I, II Samuel, Kings, Chronicles, and the 12 Minor Prophets are counted only as one in the Hebrew Bible, resulting in 22 rather than 39 canonical books, excluding the Apocrypha.

[17] Steven Runciman, THE GREAT CHURCH IN CAPTIVITY; Cambridge University Press, Cambridge, England, 1968, reprinted 1995, p. 4.

[18] Cf. Robert M. Fowler. LET THE READER UNDERSTAND, Reader-Response Criticism and the Gospel of Mark; Fortress Press, Minneapolis, 1991.

[19] Flavius Josephus, *The Wars of the Jews* in THE WORKS OF JOSEPHUS; Complete and Unabridged. Trans. William Whiston. Hendrickson Publishers, Peabody, Massachusetts, 1987, Book 4, ch. 5, par. 4, p. 680f.

[20] Cf. David B. Howell, MATTHEW'S INCLUSIVE STORY: A Study in the Narrative Rhetoric of the First Gospel; in the Journal for the Study of the New Testament, Supplement Series 43. JSOT Press, Sheffield, 1990.

[21] Cf. the classic redactional study of Mt. 18:10-14 in Joachim Jeremias, THE PARABLES OF JESUS; Charles Scribner's Sons, New York, 1954, pp. 38-40.

Chapter 5

What's New and Old in the Kingdom of Heaven

The Bible is God's engagement ring to his people:
A diamond shimmering with new luster at every turn;
Twenty-four karat authenticity nested in a world of
    duplicity;
Cut to penetrate to the heart...
And at its center one silent word: αγαπη..."love."[1]

Would it increase our appreciation of the *First* Gospel if, in addition to its authorship by an anonymous Antiochene scribe we have chosen to call Ben Grammateus, we would also come to know more of what went into its actual production? I think it should. As an esteemed high school English teacher in a course on Literature Appreciation used to repeatedly advise us students: "Remember, the page was blank." In other words, a genuine appreciation of a finished product necessarily involves the recognition that every literary masterpiece began with nothing more than an idea. Considerable time, talent and technology had to combine to constitute a work of such value. Obviously, the *First* Gospel didn't float down from heaven fully formed either. Its publication required numerous intermediate steps — some physical and practical, others intellectual, artistic, emotional and spiritual — but all contributing to its ultimate power and continuing cogency.

The "How" of ancient book research and composition, manufacture and publication, thus, is another of those important considerations of context which unfortunately is seldom discussed by biblical scholars. It is usually taken for granted and overlooked as inconsequential to the work's theological content, or even worse, as somehow detracting from the Gospel's presumed sanctity as a slice of inspired Scripture. But intellectual honesty, authorial integrity and responsible hermeneutical method are also involved here. It matters greatly, for example, what sources the evangelist selected, how he arranged and edited them, thereby determining the tone and particular emphasis he desired in his presentation. True, one cannot tell a book by its cover. Yet a book without a cover, or a title page, leaves the reader somewhat adrift, disoriented and unable to identify, at least initially, with the proffered subject matter or authorial perspective. Let us try, then, to put ourselves in the evangelist's sandals as he began the process of readying the raw materials and physical tools of Gospel production. Professor Gamble of Yale will be our guide.[2]

As an aside, just thinking of the challenges facing this *"scribe trained for the kingdom"* is a bit embarrassing to me as the writer of this book. Here I am, sitting comfortably in an air-conditioned room in my home with good lighting, Claude Bolling rhapsodizing in the background on my tape deck, surrounded with bookcases, and before me a computer with printer and built-in spell-check, dictionary, encyclopedia, maps, and eight versions of the Bible including those in Hebrew and Greek. With such advantages I should be ashamed of myself if this book were not perfect. But it isn't...and I am... ashamed of myself, that is.

The Art and Anguish of Ancient Book Publication

As a professional scribe, *Matthew,* alias Ben Grammateus, was not intimidated by the challenge to provide his Christian community with an updated story of the life and work of Jesus of Nazareth as it related to the current situation in Antioch. He had an idea and was intent on its realization. Ancient writing was laborious, tedious and expensive. Yet, for the serious author nothing was more personally fulfilling. Similarly, for his enraptured audience, without film, radio or television, few opportunities for learning were more engaging. As previously mentioned, writing and reading were relatively rare talents and privileges, and were, therefore, highly esteemed.

Undoubtedly, as with most literary enterprises, the work of composing the *First* Gospel began with pencil and paper, or in this case, with *penicillus* (Lat. for "little tail," i.e., a small brush) and *papyrus*. The use of lead as a writing tool had been discovered and employed about a century earlier, but the intensity of that lead without graphite was faint reducing its legibility and popularity. Reeds and other porous materials were also used as pens for small tasks, but brushes were the more efficient and, in the long run, economical. Various inks were available with mixtures of pigments derived from powdered soils, berry juices, carbons and the dyes of Mediterranean cuttlefish and the murex sea-snail. The durability of some of these inks is remarkable.

As for the papyrus, it was made from the sliced stalks of the papyrus reed which grew in marshy areas all over the middle east, but especially along the Nile River in Egypt. For long centuries, in fact, Egypt had farmed it and was the most intentional in its regulation and harvesting. Many products were made of its leaves and fibrous stems. Sometimes its pith was even eaten. But none of its by-products was so prevalent as its "paper."

As numerous shops located along the Nile River even today are happy to demonstrate, the long, triangular papyrus stalks were first cut to specified lengths, then thinly sliced. The individual pieces were laid out horizontally on a smooth, flat surface, overlaid with a second vertical layer, pressed tightly and allowed to dry. Next, each piece of papyrus "paper" was smoothed with pumice and polished with shell.

Most of this "raw paper" was exported to regional distribution points around the Roman world. Byblos, in Phoenicia, located only a hundred or so miles to the south of Antioch-on-the-Orontes, was undoubtedly the most significant of all such centers. There the individual papyrus sheets, called *kollema* in Latin, were graded on the basis of quality and glued together side-to-side until a standard length of approximately eleven feet was attained. These *charta* or *volumen* were then rolled to form scrolls called *libri* in Latin, or βιβλια, "small books," in Greek, taking this latter name from that of the city. From Byblos these small books of differing qualities were redistributed in bulk throughout the Roman empire leaving it to the local merchant or scribe to price, cut or extend them as needed.

The art and mechanics of writing Greek in ancient times is also fascinating — and to us not a little disconcerting. There were few, if any, desks. Students normally sat or squatted on the floor surrounding their teachers, with their knees or the ground serving as "platforms" for writing. Tables, too, were very low since diners, at least on formal occasions, reclined, rather than sat, to eat. From the little available evidence it would appear that professional scribes similarly composed while sitting on the floor or low stools.

A type of shorthand was already in use at the time. If fact, Suetonius informs us that the Roman Emperor, Titus, was particularly proficient at it.[3] More common, however, is what Harry Gamble calls a "documentary hand" employing a *scriptio continua* method, that is, a form of cursive or speed writing where the individual Greek letters — all upper case, called *uncials* — were tied together with "ligatures" leaving the novice with the impression that he or she was dealing with one extremely long word. While a few abbreviations were used, usually only for familiar sacred names, there were no accent marks, no paragraphing and little punctuation of any kind. Yet, everything was arranged in neat, narrow columns two to two and a half inches wide and seven or eight inches high running vertically the length of the page, a custom maintained in most contemporary Bibles. As the writing progressed, the completed portions were attached one to another and rolled up to form a scroll, or a "book."

Now we can understand why professional readers, αναγνωστης, were needed and much in demand. Someone who could separate the individual words, determine their proper intonation and inflection, and establish their meaning was required. Reading was an art. Many readers, in fact, took the next step, memorizing long stories or entire books and making a living as public storytellers, a cherished tradition that continues in some Turkish coffee houses even today.

Once the author had completed a rough draft, often writing on both the *recto,* i.e., the "correct" side of the papyrus, with the grain, and the *verso,* or back side against the grain, he would edit and rewrite a "fair copy" using only the *recto* side of the page. This fair copy would be used for proof reading and perhaps some field-testing. If the work proved popular, and the scribe could afford it, the fair copy was then given to highly literate slaves or professional copyists who would produce "exemplars" in a fine "bookhand," an early type of calligraphy, with the individual uncials neatly separated on straight lines in well-defined columns. Often a wooden dowel (Gk. ομφαλος, Lat. *umbilicus*) was inserted into the scroll to facilitate tightening it, and a small leather flag, called a σιττυβον, with the author's name or the work's title written on it was attached to the dowel for quick and easy identification. These exemplars were then sold or loaned to public libraries or private collectors to be re-copied. The process of dissemination was thus understandably slow and expensive. It is fascinating to learn, however, that, possibly for economic reasons, Christian scrolls were among the very first — some already in the first century C.E. — to be reduced to *codices*, i.e., paged books, allowing for inscription on both sides of the page, easier handling and faster distribution at lower cost.

This procedure does not obviate the fact, however, that books were necessarily rare and highly prized in ancient times. With less than one-fifth or one-sixth of the public able to read there was limited demand and the cost of reproduction was prohibitive except for governments, public institutions and wealthy private collectors. Yet, we must be amazed when we hear of the huge library at Alexandria with 490,000 rolls and such large private collections as that of Atticus containing 20,000 volumes.

Perhaps what we need to realize and appreciate is that books in ancient times were not viewed simply as practical depositories of knowledge but as works of art with a semi-divine character. So appreciated were literary works that their authors were thought of as mystically touched by the gods. Many libraries, accordingly, were housed in temples while other repositories were referred to as *museions* (or museums) in honor of the muses, i.e., the nine patron goddesses of the arts. The Christian concept of inspiration, at least in part, is surely derivative of this venerable notion.

The Author at Work

Equipped with this information we are now ready to visualize our Antiochene scribe, *Matthew,* or Ben Grammateus, embarking on his task, whether self-appointed or commissioned, to enlarge and refocus the Gospel of Mark. He is a mature man, quite dignified, well dressed, a gentleman of some substance, not independently wealthy but, most likely, blessed with access to a wealthy patron, perhaps someone from his own *collegium sodalicium.*

Today we imagine him in his own home, a modest but comfortable villa befitting a moderately prosperous scribe. He is reclining in his *triclinium,* or dining room, with a low rectangular table in the center and the traditional couches on three sides. Next to him is his *capsa,* a round tote basket with a shoulder strap designed to carry scrolls. Perhaps it was this *capsa* that he was thinking of when he wrote metaphorically in 13:52 about the householder's *"treasure"* out of which he takes things new and old. From it the *first* evangelist now retrieves several texts of Septuagintal books, others from the Hebrew Bible, then the scrolls of Mark, Q, and possibly of Evodius' Φως, plus scraps of papyri with assorted traditions, sermon illustrations and popular stories which he has collected over time. He selects, sorts and arranges these items, occasionally rearranges them, and finally by dim candlelight begins to write.

Tomorrow we may well see him trudging along the streets of Antioch with his *capsa* at his side heading for a quiet spot with better light on the lower slopes of Mt. Silpius or on one of the spacious porticoes of a public bath. Long hours are spent in thought with occasional bursts of literary insight, writing and rewriting, and reading aloud what he has written to test its cadences.

The toils of a scribe seem endless. Days, even weeks pass. But gradually the scroll grows. Two, three, four or more papyrus βιβλια are expended. Inkwells are frequently replenished and *penicilloi* replaced. Eventually a fair copy is produced, proofread and corrected. A professional copyist is hired. The work is completed. Now it is turned over to an experienced reader to rehearse and finally introduce to the local *collegium sodalicium,* or congregation, εκκλησια, cf.

18:17. The *First* Gospel is an object of pride, representing a major accomplishment, a gift of the Spirit.

Here, however, our disciplined fantasizing ends. The rest is history.

Reasons for Writing

But why did Ben, the scribe, find it necessary to compose this Gospel in the first place? What was so deficient about his exemplars, the Gospel of Mark[4] and Q, that he felt they needed to be corrected, supplemented or replaced? Were there, perhaps, local circumstances which required immediate, authoritative resolution, or was it simply a desire to add to sacred tradition?

We can only deduce the author's reasons from his reactions, his purposes from his product.

Clearly, then, biographical completeness was an initial aim. Neither Mark nor Q contained stories of Jesus' birth. Yet, in both the Jewish and Greco-Roman worlds of thought, matters of parental fame, wealth and achievement, along with accompanying omen or irregular natural phenomena in connection with the birth of a child, were considered important for anticipating the prospects for eventual greatness in a newborn. Literary convention almost demanded them. Accordingly, Matthew, chapter 1, contains a genealogical table, at least partly fictive, identifying the infant Jesus' ancient and royal lineage, mentioning such venerable figures as Abraham, David and Solomon. It recalls fulfilled prophesies, dreams, visions and dialogues with the divine, especially on the part of Joseph, Jesus' presumed father.

Further, in chapter 2, the evangelist inserts reminiscences of a special star in the east leading extremely wealthy international dignitaries to a seemingly humble nursery in a house in Bethlehem of Judea. Fortunately, he had remembered reading about the journey King Tiridates of Armenia and his entourage of magi had undertaken across the length of Anatolia at the time of the youthful Nero's inauguration twenty years earlier.[5] This reminiscence, together with a current, popular story reported by both Suetonius and Tacitus about the appearance of a comet, portending a revolution in government, or the rise of a new emperor,[6] had provided our scribe with the raw materials for a magnificent birth narrative, Mt. 2:1-12, one which only he, among all the evangelists, records.

By means of this spectacular introduction, 1:1-4:25, composed by conflating an assortment of historical data, various Old Testament reminiscences, contemporary liturgical expressions and some local color, the stage was set for even greater developments and attainments in the later life of Jesus.

Q and Mark also omitted any post-resurrection appearances of Jesus at the conclusions of their presentations.[7] An angelic messenger in Mk. 16:7 does envision a meeting of Jesus with his disciples in Galilee, but the actual event is not recounted in the *Second* Gospel. Ben, or *Matthew,* in Mt. 28:16-20, therefore, not only answers the natural question: "What happened?" but uses the occasion in Galilee to complete and summarize the import of this entire Gospel in the authoritative words of Jesus' Great Commission.

Literary considerations also must have been part of the evangelist's thinking. While Mark's Gospel was dynamic and provocative with its frequent use of historic tenses in the third person and its "Messianic Secret" motif, whereby the disciples never understood, it simultaneously lacked stylistic variety, was often wordy, and failed to provide a comprehensive statement of Jesus' authoritative teaching. Our Antiochene scribe changed all that, cleaning up Mark's numbing kai, *"and,"* parataxis, increasing the personal aspect by exchanging direct speech and dialogue for Mark's third person narratives, and by grouping topical materials together in extended, clearly circumscribed sermons. By these means, the body of the *First*

115

Gospel's narrative was enhanced, the readers' understanding improved, and their faith commitment encouraged.

Stylistically speaking, Ben's Greek, despite rare lapses into Semitisms, is much more polished, poetic and aphoristic than Mark's. His vocabulary exhibits some variety, but even more consistency. We might call it utilitarian. Over all, there is a noticeable economy of language reducing Mark's novelistic narration to its essentials while becoming expansive only occasionally in areas of intense interest. Even his emphatic repetitions, of which there are several, are usually so nuanced as to add at least some new dimension of thought. The writer's scribal experience is thus evident everywhere.

His theological intentions, I must admit, lack some of the flair and heuristic dynamism of Mark's Messianic Secret approach. His concerns are more direct, contemporary, practical and pastoral than were Mark's, and certainly less technical and philosophical than those of St. Paul, yet they are no less intensely held or profoundly argued.

While Christology, the study of Jesus' true identity, so central to Mark's Gospel, continues here, the *first* evangelist is equally interested in encouraging consistent Christian behavior, chs. 5-7, in promoting a fearless and energetic witness, ch. 10, in resolving intra-congregational problems relating to *"little ones,"* straying sheep and sinning brothers, ch. 18, and in forearming his readers against false prophets and especially the emissaries of resurgent Judaism, ch. 23. Despite his expansion of Mark's eschatological emphases in Mk. 13 in Mt. 24 and 25, and the fact that he alone among the evangelists speaks of a παλιγγενεσια, i.e., a *"renewal of all things,"* in Mt. 19:28, there is nevertheless an inescapable "this-world" preference and emphasis evident throughout the *First* Gospel. While the thought of "deferred gratification" in the afterlife occasionally enters into the discussion, this *"scribe trained for the kingdom"* is no "pie-in-the-sky-when-we-die" theologian.

All of these issues, and more, will be discussed in detail in PART II.

The Search for a Title

How an author begins his narrative is indicative of what is to follow. On this basis the differences between the conflicting ways that the *first* evangelist and Mark introduce their respective Gospels presents us with a challenge. Mark's opening super-scription boldly declares: *"The beginning of the good news of Jesus Christ, the Son of God."* That is a title. *Matthew,* or Ben, on the contrary, opens with: *"An account of the genealogy of Jesus the Messiah, the son of David, the son of Abraham."* This is not a title, but an introduction to materials to be dealt with in only the first couple of chapters of his Gospel. We wonder: Why the change?

Book titles in general seem to have been problematic entities in ancient literature. The Hebrews were apparently content to permit the first word, or at least the first noun, of a work to serve as its title. So we have בְּרֵאשִׁית, "In the beginning...," as the Hebrew designation for the book of Genesis. Frequently, however, it seems the name of the authoritative writer was considered more significant than the subject addressed, and was therefore substituted for a title, similar to some classical musical works today which are identified only by the name of the composer and an opus number. This practice also accounts for the very early ascription of Gospels to one of the revered disciples, such as Matthew and John, or at least to a companion of one of the apostles, like Mark and Luke. Unfortunately, as Prof. Gamble informs us, ancient authors usually affixed their names only at the conclusion of a work, i.e., on the last page, which, in time, was naturally among the first lost. Much the same would apply to the flimsy σιττυβον identifying flags attached to the ends of the scroll

117

dowels. Keeping a current catalog or index of works must have been a frustrating enterprise for collectors.

The title, *"According to Matthew,"* or KATA MAΘ-ΘAION, is ancient. In fact, there is evidence for no other. Yet, the conclusions of modern research that the *First* Gospel could not have been written by the early first century Galilean, tax collector, eye-witness, disciple of Jesus named *Matthew* challenges its role as a trustworthy, eponymous designation for this book. The prevailing practice seems to reflect more the devout desire of the early church for authoritative authorship than a concern for either historical accuracy or for an appropriate summary statement of the book's content.

The bottom line, then, is that the *First* Gospel as a whole is officially untitled. Matthean commentators, consequently, have frequently attempted to encapsulate the genius of the book in their own titles such as John Meier's THE VISION OF MATTHEW, Augustine Stock's THE METHOD AND MESSAGE OF MATTHEW, and David Howell's MATTHEW'S INCLUSIVE STORY.[8] Several others, however, have focused in on that self-identifying parable in 13:52 and have accordingly named their monographs, MATTHEW, A SCRIBE TRAINED FOR THE KINGDOM OF HEAVEN, or THE UNDERSTANDING SCRIBE, or TREASURES NEW AND OLD.[9] I have decided to follow suit suggesting that the most appropriate title for this *First* Gospel may well be WHAT'S NEW AND OLD IN THE KINGDOM OF HEAVEN. This designation, inspired by the self-descriptive suggestion of the 13:52 parable, summarizes both the general content, the kingdom of heaven, and the unique operative principle of this work, combining new and old concepts and traditions in an effort to describe that kingdom of heaven as our Antiochene scribe, Ben Grammateus, envisioned it.

What's New and Old in the Kingdom of Heaven

The new/old, comparison/contrast, programmatic *topos, synkrisis,* is a pronounced characteristic of this Gospel. It is visible in the *"You have heard it said by them of old times...but I say unto you"* tactic of the Sermon on the Mount. It surfaces again in the *"first shall be last and the last shall be first"* series of exchanges in chapters 19 and 20. Nowhere is it better demonstrated, however, than in the analogy of the "Wine and the Wineskins," Mt. 9:16-17/Mk. 2:21-22/Lk. 5:36-39. Just a glance at the concluding defining Dominical statements is revealing. Mark's original verdict boldly insists *"...new wine is for fresh skins."* It expresses a radical commitment to the "new" in the fledgling Christian community's life and proclamation. Luke's concluding stance, on the other hand, leans in an opposite, traditionalist direction: *"And no one after drinking old wine desires new; for he says, 'The old is good.'"* The version of the *first* evangelist, as we might expect, however, assumes a more moderate, middle position: *"...but new wine is put into fresh wineskins, and so both are preserved."* His orientation favors the new while still retaining a latent appreciation of the old. This is the identical preference we find articulated in the critical 13:52 passage where the new, somewhat surprisingly, unnaturally and anachronistically, takes pride of place over the old: *"...every scribe...is like the master of a household who brings out of his treasure what is new and what is old."*

Ben Grammateus, or if you will, *Matthew,* thus sees himself primarily as a reformer, not a revolutionary, and his gospel as a balanced redefinition of the Christian faith and life in the present, not a total renunciation of the past. Consistent with this position are the more than one hundred Old Testament quotations[10] and references found in the *First* Gospel. Ben's community is not a New Israel, but, in his mind, a continuation and reformulation of the True Israel. This lingering

119

respect for the old also surfaces in some of the seeming "antiquarianisms" found in the text. For example, in 24:20 Jesus warns his disciples, and the Antiochene scribe his congregation: *"Pray that your flight may not be...on a Sabbath."* Matthew, or Ben, can in good conscience continue to observe and respect that Jewish holy day because *"The Son of Man is lord of the Sabbath,"* 12:8. Similarly, he can entertain as appropriate the rite of fasting in his community: *"The days will come when the bridegroom is taken away from them* (the wedding guests), *and then they shall fast,"* 9:15. Perhaps here, too, we find the explanation for the *first* evangelist's conservative omission of Mark's bold pronouncement in Mk. 7:19: *"Thus he declared all foods clean,"* saying only in the Mt. 15:20b parallel: *"...but to eat with unwashed hands does not defile."* He is cautious, and diplomatically sensitive, unwilling — at least initially — to advocate a complete spiritual or cultural break from his and his community's largely Jewish past. As far as he is concerned, and as demonstrated in the story of the Triumphal Entry into Jerusalem, Jesus simultaneously rides on both, the new colt and the old mare, 21:7. Both, Ben's literary and theological tendencies are apophatic.

Yet, when the chips are down and everything is considered, the new always wins with our *"scribe trained for the kingdom."* It takes priority. This is where the element of plot enters into this Gospel. One can almost see the conceptual landscape change toward innovation as the story of Jesus' life progresses.

Obviously, "new" does not always mean something different or novel in this *First* Gospel. It is a highly nuanced concept.[11] It can be understood as "original" as in the case of the discussion about divorce in 19:8 where Jesus rejects the practice despite Moses' relaxation of the prohibition. Jesus here rather reminds his hearers: *"...from the beginning it was*

120

not so." Permanent marriage had been God's original intention. Over time, however, that rule had been softened, then forgotten. Now, in the church, according to the *first* evangelist, it is new again for a second time. Some considerations take precedence even over Moses and Sacred Scripture.

The "current" also qualified as new. New conditions require new responses. Apparently, this principle again applied to the problem of divorce in 5:32 and 19:9. Here, immediately following the prohibition of divorce alluded to above, we are confronted by the notorious "exceptive clause," *"...except on the ground of unchastity..."* found coming only, not once but twice, from *Ben's* pen among the evangelists. This provision has long troubled Christian ethicists. The explanation, however, may well come from the prevailing circumstances in Antioch and vicinity. Daphne, the luxurious Antiochene suburb, doubled as a world class red-light district, off-limits to Roman soldiers, but frequented regularly by Generals, diplomats and the Roman world's rich and famous. Unchastity was commonplace. In such an exaggerated situation of sexual license, the *first* evangelist apparently viewed an adulterated marriage as a *de facto* divorce on the part of the offending parties. The wronged person was thus justified in officially recognizing the break. He was still acting consistently with God's original universal prohibition. This adjustment was new, but, under the circumstances, totally to be expected.

There are numerous other prevailing circumstances which called forth new, in the sense of "extraordinary," applications. The generally degenerate moral climate, for example, induces the judgment that *"...everyone who looks at a woman with lust has already committed adultery with her in his heart,"* 5:28. Similarly, in 5:21-22 anger is equated with murder, and even oath-taking, so common in ancient cultures, is discountenanced as verging on blasphemy in 5:33-37. While these perspectives have become traditional for us, they were radically new to first century Antiochenes. They were new also in the sense of logical extensions and redactional reinforcements of accepted principles within the *First* Gospel. Perhaps most offensive to our twentieth century tastes is the recognition that for our Antiochene scribe the new seems to include and allow for rhetorical invention, a topic previously discussed. As proposed in the previous chapter, Ben, or *Matthew,* is apophatic. He quotes and credits what are, at least from our vantage point, non-existent prophecies, as in 2:23 about the infant Jesus being a Nazorean, or changes them to fit new evaluations as in the prophecy from Micah 5:2 quoted in Mt. 2:6. Frequently the evangelist attributes motives to Jesus' actions and puts words in Jesus' mouth that were not found in his exemplars, Mark and Q. It must be remembered, however, that these innovations are not irresponsibly subjective, but accord with the rubrics of ancient rhetoric where the end often justifies the means. Here language is power. Therefore, if the chosen literary strategy achieves a desired, positive result the method employed is assumed to be justified. Truth, like wisdom, is *"vindicated by her deeds,"* Mt. 11:19c. New wine requires new wineskins.

Another of the new concepts in this Gospel is certainly that of the *"kingdom of heaven,"* or more literally in the plural, *"heavens,"* βασιλεια των ουρανων. The *first* evangelist, and he alone in the New Testament, uses this term, and then no less than 32 times. It is an important concept, a major reality, for him.

Matthean scholars, succumbing to their traditional Jewish, or Semitizing, orientation in evaluating a text, have usually understood the phrase as the evangelist's concession to his predominantly Jewish readership. In Hebrew, "heaven," הַשָּׁמַיִם, is a collective plural noun, so, it is surmised, the plural is also retained here in the Greek. Further, it is thought that the well-known Jewish aversion to the public use of the name for "God," the sacred tetragrammaton, YHWH, or יהוה, may also have influenced the *first* evangelist to substitute an alternative, parallel synonym such as "heaven." Perhaps. However, the fact that Ben also uses *"Kingdom of God"* four or five times, twice redactionally, argues against, if not refutes, these convenient rationalizations. No, our evangelist was more deliberate in his choice of *"kingdom of the heavens."* His reasons, I would suggest, were influenced more by his setting in a predominantly Greek Diaspora environment, in Antioch-on-the-Orontes. There the prevailing Greco-Roman cosmology, not altogether unlike the Jewish, also posited multi-level heavens ruled over by a long series of deities and powers. *"Heavens,"* then, did not imply some future place of ethereal bliss but the already extant realm of the spirits, including, of course, for Ben, the Christian God and his angels. As such, the kingdom of the heavens effectively displayed and dramatized the reality of all spiritual activity in heaven and on earth. This was his innovative ecclesiological cosmology, the church writ large, where his readers could objectively view what was in fact happening on the universal, spiritual level without being distracted and frustrated by more immediate local and temporal concerns.

Meanwhile, the parallel term, *"kingdom of God,"* as the name implies, referred more specifically to *the kingdom of the heavens* in its perfected state when God was in control. We will have much more to say on this novel idea when discussing the *first* evangelist's ecclesiology in a later chapter.

On a couple of occasions, 4:23 and 9:35, Ben Grammateus used the term *"the gospel of the kingdom."* The contexts there indicate that Jesus' own oral proclamation was referenced. Yet, there can be little doubt that in the author's own mind his written text was the closest approximation of that gospel yet available. His community needed to know

123

WHAT'S NEW AND OLD IN THE KINGDOM OF HEAVEN. The goal and potential benefits, in the evangelist's mind, were well worth the time, tedium, costs and risks involved in this Gospel's composition and publication.

The question confronting us today, however, is: Do we have enough physical, moral and spiritual fortitude to heed its message?

Chapter 5 Endnotes

[1] Excerpted from original poem: "God's Engagement Ring," No. 35, in PRACTICALLY POETRY, privately published, 5144 N. 6th St., Phoenix, Arizona, 1994.

[2] I am deeply indebted to Harry Y. Gamble, BOOKS AND READERS IN THE EARLY CHURCH: A History of Early Christian Texts; Yale University Press, New Haven and London, 1995, for most of the detailed information presented n this chapter.

[3] Cf. SUETONIUS, Vol. II, *"The Deified Titus,"* in the Loeb Classical Library, J.C. Rolfe, trans., Harvard University Press, Cambridge, MA. and London, 1914, p.323.

[4] Cf. Robert M. Fowler, LET THE READER UNDERSTAND, Reader Response Criticism and the Gospel of Mark; Fortress Press, Philadelphia, 1991, for an informative comparison of the literary agendas of the Gospels of Matthew and Mark found in a section entitled "Matthew as a Reading Grid," pp. 237-260.

[5] Cf. Luz, MATTHEW 1-7; Op cit., p. 131, N. 19; SUETONIUS, Vol. II, *Nero,* 13, p.107f.

[6] SUETONIUS, Vol. II, *Nero,* 36, p. 151; TACITUS, *The Annals,* 22, p. 147, in Great Books of the Western World, 15, Robert Maynard Hutchins, Ed. in Chief, Encyclopedia Britannica, Inc., 1952.

[7] Accepted here is the generally agreed judgment that the *first* evangelist's copy of the Gospel of Mark ended at 16:8.

[8] See the general bibliography for the publication facts for these works.

[9] These three works are authored or edited by O. Lamar Cope, David B. Howell, and David R. Bauer & Mark Allan Powell, respectively. Publication facts may be found in the general bibliography.

[10] R.E.O. White, THE MIND OF MATTHEW, counts 121 such quotations of, or allusions to the Old Testament in the *First* Gospel.

[11] Cf. G. W. Bowersock, FICTION AS HISTORY, Nero to Julian; Op. cit., p.137f., for a discussion of varying connotations between Greek synonyms for "new:" καινος and νεος, where the former, as used in Mt. 13:52, implies innovation, something radically new and different, even strange.

PART II

CONTENT

Prologue to Part II

Generating a Genre[1]

*One afternoon, while attempting to navigate the
Parmenius gorge between Mt. Silpius and Mt. Staurin, I
was confronted by a wildflower I had never seen before. It
stared me in the face with its delicate gray-blue spray of
blossoms flaring out like a sparkler on a tall roman candle
stem. I asked Erdal: "What's this?" He typically shrugged
and replied "Wild Onion."*

*After returning home to the U.S.A. I was surprised and
gratified to find that same flower at the local nursery - one
plant, $12.95, in a five gallon container. Only now its label
read "Society Garlic." Obviously, names make a difference!*

Genre makes a difference, too, when evaluating a piece
of literature. We approach a book with very different expectations if we know its type to be that of poetry, fiction, biog-
raphy or, perhaps, a how-to manual on plumbing repair. Accordingly, a brief discussion of genre here should form a helpful bridge between PARTS I and II of this book crossing over
from a review of the context of the *First* Gospel to the essentials of its content.

What type of literature is Matthew? How are we to approach it? And what can we expect from it? The variety of
proposed answers to these questions testify to their unexpected
difficulty.

Most frequently, we label this first book of the New Testament a "Gospel." This is a helpful designation. We have come
to know what that word means. Originally, and etymologically,

129

"gospel," ευγγελιον, referred to any announcement or proclamation of "good news" whether secular or sacred. Eventually, within the context of the Christian world, it came to refer primarily to the proclaimed "good news" account of the life, words and sacrifice of Jesus, the Christ, redounding to the temporal and eternal benefit of all who were, and are, influenced by its promises.

The tradition of identifying a specific written work as a Gospel, however, was undoubtedly initiated by *Mark* who, as previously noted, began his groundbreaking study with the superscription in 1:1: *"The beginning of the good news* (i.e., Gospel, ευαγγελιον) *of Jesus Christ, the Son of God."* This designation stuck, generating an unprecedented and unique literary form by which a host of later works, both canonical and pseudepigraphical, have become known.[2]

For some scholars, however, the "Gospel" identification is too broad and indistinct to be practical. They prefer to interpret the question of genre more narrowly focusing on selected theological or pedagogical designations. They argue, for instance, that the *First* Gospel is fundamentally a Christology discussing what it means that Jesus is the Christ, or an Ecclesiology defining the church, or a manual of Christian Ethics updating, as it were, the Old Testament's Pentateuch. Again, there are those authorities who see Matthew as Salvation History recounting the two or three epochs involved in God's saving enterprise, or, perhaps, as a kind of lectionary designed to satisfy the requirements of a liturgical year in the early church.[3]

But, again, there are those who disapprove of this perspective as well. These scholars object to viewing a literary work on the basis of its content rather than on its form. They point to the fact that "Gospel," as a specifically religious category, is unknown in ancient Greek literature outside the confines of the early church. Consequently, they have attempted

130

to locate the genre of the *First* Gospel more directly within the glossary of ancient classic literary nomenclature. Some have declared it a βιος, i.e., a "Life,"[4] similar to Plutarch's PARALLEL LIVES, or Suetonius' LIVES OF THE CAESARS. One commentator has gone a step farther attempting to characterize Matthew as an "Encomium," a work tending exclusively toward the praise of Jesus.[5] Others have entertained the thought of it as an "Aretalogy," lauding a virtuous divine man, as exemplified by Philostratus' THE LIFE OF APOLLONIUS OF TYANA.[6]

Undoubtedly, most disconcerting for us is the recognition that the *first* evangelist himself demurred when it came to designating his own written work as a Gospel, choosing to omit the reference in Mark 1:1 in his own introduction. He apparently preferred to speak only of the *"gospel of the kingdom"* in 4:23, 9:35 and 24:14, emphasizing again the content rather than the form of the message,[7] whether oral or written.

Within the past two or three decades it has become more popular to think of Matthew simply as "story," focusing on its narrative structure and its literary/rhetorical conventions.[8]

All of these suggestions enjoy varying degrees of validity, yet none is a perfect fit. Together they illustrate the originality, variety and vitality of the early Christian message, combining so intimately the practical, the existential and the transcendent. Simultaneously, however, they leave us with an uncertain, uncomfortable sense of disconnect in terms of genre. We seem confronted here with a collage, or potpourri, of independent materials, new and old, original and borrowed, which renders this *First* Gospel homeless in the world of ancient literature.

I do not have a conclusive answer to this genre conundrum either. Generally speaking, however, I am satisfied with the "Gospel" designation recognizing Matthew and other writings of this type as a uniquely Christian contribution to the corpus of ancient literary art.

A recognition of the work as "story" featuring a unified, coherent and comprehensive plot, is also important, I believe, as an antidote to the common temptations for pericope-hopping, proof-texting and verse-mining with commentators excavating the text line-by-line as if hoping to discover the one pure nugget of theological truth each word supposedly contains. But as we have already sensed from our study thus far, it doesn't work that way in the *First* Gospel. Here, despite initial appearances to the contrary, the story line constantly progresses, the plot follows a trajectory and the theology becomes increasingly robust until a denouement is reached in the work's closing verses.

Still, of all the proposed characterizations, I find myself most intrigued, attracted and ultimately satisfied by Prof. Robert M. Fowler's description of Matthew as a "Palimpsest," literally a "writing again," recalling the ancient practice of rubbing a skin parchment manuscript clean and then inscribing a new text over the old often resulting in a faint double image.[9] Prof. Fowler, of course, is thinking of Matthew primarily as a re-write of Mark, with all the attendant characteristics of such revisions.

This palimpsest analogy, however, is also applicable when speaking of the kind of historical transparency, or echo, we have found in the *First* Gospel whereby Ben Grammateus cleverly retells the story of Jesus in Palestine in the 20s C.E. in such a way as to make its import directly and existentially relevant to his own readership and audience in Syrian Antioch a half century later. In short, Matthew is a combined Gospel and Book of Acts of the Apostles all in one.

By further extension, the palimpsest idea also aptly describes our scribe's art in blending together varying themes so that while each emphasis is identifiably distinct in itself, usually in sermon form, it is simultaneously theologically interdependent with all other *foci* in the larger text. Thus, for example, the authority for the ethical pronouncements attributed to Jesus in the Sermon on the Mount is dependent on the Christological recognition that Jesus is *"Emmanuel ... 'God is with us'"* in 1:23 and that he speaks with *"all authority in heaven and on earth"* as stated in 28:18.

If I may be allowed to mix metaphors, this palimpsestic schematic in the *First* Gospel is the literary equivalent of a J.S. Bach fugue where several independent voices and even melodies are contrapuntally harmonized and superimposed one on top of another to produce a musical statement so comprehensive that it is among the most celestial ever terrestrially composed.

In the following chapters of this PART II you are invited to listen in to several of these complementary theological themes as artfully interwoven by Ben, our Antiochene scribe. I hope you will find their harmony equally scintillating.

Prologue 2 Endnotes

[1] Cf. the section on Genres, pp. 26-29, in THE NEW TESTAMENT IN LITERARY CRITICISM, compiled and edited by Leland Ryken; Frederick Ungar Publishing Company, New York, 1984. Also the discussion in Werner Georg Kümmel, Ed.: :INTRODUCTION TO THE NEW TESTAMENT; founded by Paul Feine and Johannes Behm; Trans. A.J.Mattill, Jr., Abingdon Press, Nashville and New York, 1965, especially p. 32.

[2] Cf. Edgar Hennecke, NEW TESTAMENT APOCRYPHA, Vol. I; Wilhelm Schneemelcher, ed., trans. R. McL Wilson, the Westminster Press, Philadelphia, 1963.

[3] For the variety of proposed perspectives see Jack Dean Kingsbury, MATTHEW - STRUCTURE, CHRISTOLOGY, KINGDOM, Fortress Press, Philadelphia, 1975; Eduard Schweizer, "The Matthean Church," in NEW TESTAMENT STUDIES, 29, 2, 1974; Robert A. Guelich, THE SERMON ON THE MOUNT, A Foundation for Understanding;_ Word Books, Waco, Texas, 1982; Gerhard Barth, "Matthew's Understanding of the Law" in TRADITIONAL INTERPRETATION IN MATTHEW; Eds. G. Bornkamm, G. Barth, H.J. Held; Trans. Percy Scott, SCM Press, London, 1963; Rolf Walker, DIE HEILSGESCHICHTE IM ERSTEN EVANGELIUMS; Vandenhoeck and Ruprecht, Göttingen, 1967.

[4] Cf. Ulrich Luz, MATTHEW 1-7: A COMMENTARY; Augsburg, 1989, p. 44f.

[5] Cf. Philip L. Shuler, A GENRE FOR THE GOSPELS: The Biographical Character of Matthew; Fortress Press, 1982, esp. pp. 45-57.

[6] English translation by F.C. Conybeare in the Loeb Classical Library, Harvard University Press, Cambridge and London, 1912.

[7] It is challenging, however, to consider the possible implications of *Matthew's* redactional addition of *"this, τουτω, gospel"* in 26:13 while referring to the account of the Anointing in Bethany.

[8] Cf. Richard A. Edwards, MATTHEW'S STORY OF JESUS; Fortress Press, Philadelphia, 1985; Jack Dean Kingsbury, MATTHEW AS STORY; Fortress Press, Philadelphia, 1986.

[9] Robert M. Fowler, LET THE READER UNDERSTAND; Fortress Press, Minneapolis, 1991, p. 234f. Fowler here credits Gerard Genette, PALIMPSESTES, La littérature au second degrè; CP, Paris, Seuil, 1982, for working out the theoretical bases for identifying the distinctive characteristics of the genre.

Chapter 6

Messiah or Christ?

I remember it happening just as we were driving into Antakya for the first time. It was noon, when suddenly we found ourselves ambushed by a dozen muezzins armed with multi-decibel amplifiers calling the faithful to prayer from an equal number of minarets. With that, Erdal, usually imperturbable, abruptly rolled up the side window on his Opel and exploded: "If there is one thing I hate it's ten priests trying to out-yell each other five times a day. Why can't one do it for the whole city, someone with a good singing voice?"

A brief, but pointed discussion on matters religious followed as we compared pet peeves. Finally quiet returned and Erdal, rolling down his window once again, thoughtfully concluded: "I was born and raised a Muslim, but if I were asked to choose a favorite prophet I guess it would have to be Ataturk" (Mustafa Kemal, the founder of modern, westernized Turkey who died in 1938). "He defined who I am."

Prophets do that. They define who we are.

Content in New Testament studies usually encompasses five major subject categories, all discussed in handy but exceedingly ponderous theological terms: 1) **Christology** — the study of the person and nature of Jesus Christ; 2) **Soteriology** — God's plan for the salvation of humankind; 3) **Ecclesiology** — the form and function of the church; 4) **Eschatology** — the study of "last things;" and 5) **Ethics** — outlining consistent Christian behavior. These categories also summarize the primary interests and contributions of early Christianity to world religion. The *First* Gospel, in its own way, but in different

137

order, and with varying degrees of emphasis, also treats these five subjects, even adding a distinctive sixth: **Polemics** — attacking the positions of its opponents. The alert reader will immediately notice the broad degree of correspondence between these general emphases and the five compact sermons in Matthew and the six subsequent chapters in this book, PART II.

Christology in the First Gospel

Unquestionably, the most pervasive topic on the evangelist's mind as he begins to discuss WHAT'S NEW AND OLD IN THE KINGDOM OF HEAVEN is Christology,[1] developing an appreciation for the person and nature of Jesus. This theme functions like an overture to *Matthew*'s Gospel fugue. No single, compact sermon is devoted to the topic, but its presence and effect frequently resurface and reinforce every other theological emphasis.[2]

Who, then, was, or is, this Jesus? And what is his role in the kingdom of heaven, in the kingdom of God, and in the life of the Antiochene Christian community of the evangelist's day? These questions are fundamental. They underlie all other considerations in the *First* Gospel. Their answers not only identify Jesus, but also define the essence of every true Christian and the fundamental nature of the whole Christian church and movement. In the mirror that is Jesus we see ourselves reflected, for better and for worse.

We run headlong into the author's Christology in the Gospel's very first sentence: *"An account of the genealogy of Jesus the Messiah* (Ιησου Χριστου), *the son of David, the son of Abraham."* What immediately captures our attention here is the unusual rendition by the 1973 NRSV Translation Committee of the Greek noun Χριστος with the English derivative of the Hebrew מָשִׁיחַ *"Messiah."* We would have expected the committee to translate it *"Christ"* as was the case consistently in the preceding edition of the Revised Standard Version of the

Bible, published in 1946. In fact, *"Christ"* is even employed in the NRSV translation of the parallel introductory statement in Mark 1:1 which reads: *"The beginning of the good news of Jesus **Christ**, Ιησου Χριστου, the Son of God."* As inconsistent as this translation practice may appear, however, I find myself wholeheartedly agreeing with its implications, although, perhaps, for different reasons. *Messiah,* (cf. John 1:41; 4:25) and *Christ,* of course, appear to be synonymous Christological titles in the New Testament, meaning "the anointed" or appointed one. But are they truly conceptual equivalents in the *First* Gospel if we consider their varying ethnic backgrounds and cultural connotations?

Jesus as Messiah

Messiah, as the English transliteration of the Hebrew מָשִׁיחַ, connotes a basic Jewish concept which carries with it some of the Hebrew Bible's vision of Israel's ancient hope for a deliverer sent from and commissioned by God. For many Jews that figure would be a military hero from David's royal line, or, perhaps, an authoritative prophet like Moses, or — for the sectarian Essenes at Qumran — a priest not unlike the Teacher of Righteousness. Among the apocalyptic visionaries in the centuries immediately bracketing the birth of Jesus, the Messiah would be an eschatological *"Son of Man"* coming in the clouds of heaven, Dan. 7:13 RSV. Whatever his identification, profession or title, however, his goal and envisioned accomplishment would be the full and final deliverance of Israel, politically, environmentally and religiously. If the non-Jewish world benefited at all from the Messiah's coming it would be only indirectly, as a by-product of Israel's ultimate triumph and bounty.

Early Christianity, emerging from this Jewish matrix, naturally adopted much of this traditional hope, seeing Jesus of Nazareth, of course, as its embodiment. Soon, however, the new faith's theological insights and Diaspora context necessitated substantive adaptations. In this Diaspora, Greek, Gentile environment, the envisioned deliverance became more spiritual than national. Christians believed themselves rescued from evil rather than just from Rome, and saw the entire Gentile world included among the primary beneficiaries of God's benefaction, not just Israel. A conceptual, theological metamorphosis, thus, transpired. The Greek Χριστος replaced the Hebrew מָשִׁיחַ "Messiah" and became "Christ." Particularism was transformed into universalism.[3]

Messiah and *Christ,* then, are not totally synonymous titles after all, even though they translate the same Greek word. Rather, they represent a continuum, a spectrum or trajectory of meaning with varying connotations. And here, I would suggest, is the key to understanding the *first* evangelist's redaction and to appreciating the NRSV Translation Committee's rendition of Mt. 1:1. In his Gospel, the *first* evangelist rhetorically recapitulates the historical experience, transforming Jesus the Hebrew particularist *Messiah* into Jesus the universal *Christ.*

Note, first, how *Matthew,* or Ben, substitutes his own minimizing introduction portraying Jesus only as "*the son of David, the son of Abraham*" in Mt. 1:1 for Mark 1:1's more exalted initial depiction of him as "*the Son of God.*" From our perspective, the *first* evangelist obviously does so because he wants to begin his presentation of Jesus on a somewhat reduced, traditional plane as the "*Messiah,*" ala the NRSV. Then, as the *First* Gospel's story proceeds, he will gradually develop his portrayal of Jesus as the *Christ* until, at the very end of the Gospel, the readers see their Lord standing triumphantly on the Galilean mountain of revelation proclaiming "*All authority in heaven and on earth has been given to me. Go therefore and make disciples of all nations...*"

Further evidence of this procedure is seen in the abbreviated genealogy which immediately follows the introductory sentence, 1:2-17. Here we can trace Jesus' descent, starting with Abraham, the recognized father of the Jewish nation and people, and proceeding through a long list of celebrated Jewish patriarchs, kings and prophets to Mary, the mother of our Lord. Now contrast this presentation, if you will, with Luke's version where Jesus' genealogy enjoys a more universal scope, including pre-Abrahamic "non-Jews" all the way back to Adam and God, Lk. 3:23-38. *Matthew's,* alias Ben Grammateus' clear intention, then, was to start on the more mundane level of his largely Jewish Christian readership, or audience, before expanding his Christological theme so that it crescendos with Jesus, the Christ, standing unchallenged and supreme at the Gospel's conclusion, proclaiming a universal mission.

Ben's, or *Matthew's* strategy of incrementally enlarging his Christological characterization of Jesus as the Hebrew Messiah continues with his concentration on several familiar allusions to Moses and the Exodus within the birth narratives in chapter 2.[4] The holy family is forced to flee into Egypt, Mt. 2:13, as were the original twelve sons of Jacob, Gen. 47:11-12. As a child, Jesus' life is threatened by a paranoid king Herod, Mt. 2:13c, as were all Hebrew infants, including Moses, by the Egyptian Pharaoh, Ex. 1:15-16. Mothers, like Rachel of old, are heard weeping for their children in a quotation from Jeremiah 31:15 found in 2:18. Similarly, the prophesy from Hosea 11:1, *"Out of Egypt have I called my son,"* is made to apply to Jesus in Mt. 2:15. Finally, in chapter 5, Jesus is portrayed as a lawgiver issuing his ethical dicta in the Sermon on the Mount, so reminiscent of Moses receiving and transmitting the Ten Commandments on Sinai. Throughout, Jesus is seen as a new and greater Moses, as the personification and recapitulation of Israel *en toto*, and as the hero of Israel's new exodus winning deliverance from all harm and evil.

Additional glimpses of Jesus' role as the Messiah are provided in the several Old Testament formula quotations. As we have already seen, according to Micah 5:2, as quoted in Mt. 2:6, Bethlehem, the nondescript birthplace of King David, becomes, with the help of the evangelist's redaction, the not-so-insignificant home of the child, Jesus. In the miracle chapters, 8 and 9, we witness Jesus' superiority over human afflictions, even demonic possession. Chapter 12:38-42 describes him as one greater than Jonah and Solomon. Chapter 16:14 contrasts Jesus with popular notions about him with some people thinking of him only as *"John the Baptist...Elijah...Jeremiah or one of the prophets."* Again, in the Transfiguration account, 17:1-9, Jesus stands in the pre-eminent position between the glorified Moses and Elijah, the two Old Testament figures who did not die natural deaths and apparently here represent the Law and the Prophets. The net effect of Ben's portrayal, consequently, is that no Old Testament hero, as great as he or she may have been, could rival Jesus in his role as Messiah.

Jesus as the Christ
Meanwhile, running parallel to his depiction of Jesus as the Jewish Messiah, our Antiochene scribe has subtly begun to challenge and alter that same limited view. The early appearance of Gentile (Anatolian?) Wise Men worshipping the Christchild in 2:1 comes as something of a shock in this Jewish birth narrative context. What are they doing here? Compared to Luke's shepherds coming in from Bethlehem fields next door, these foreigners are illegal aliens. But that is precisely the evangelist's point, without explicitly saying so. This infant Messiah is of far more universal significance than was formerly expected.

The same point is made in the accounts of the centurion in 8:5-13 and the Canaanite Woman in 15:21-28. In both cases, the author goes out of his way redactionally to have Jesus praise the exceptional faiths of these two Gentiles. After that, who could say that Gentiles were not to be included within the purview of Jesus' love, concern, and promises?

The time and person of John the Baptist appears to be pivotal in the *first* evangelist's transitional programmatic shifting the portrayal of Jesus from that of *Messiah* to *Christ.*[5] In the Q passage which *Matthew/Ben* adopted, Mt. 11:11/Lk. 7:28, Jesus says: *"...among those born of women no one has arisen greater than John the Baptist; yet the least in the kingdom of heaven is greater than he."* John belonged to the old order. Jesus, his disciples, and the Antiochene church belonged to the new. In answer to John's original question, then, yes, Jesus was the coming Messiah whom he, John, had awaited, but as everyone included in the kingdom of heaven now realizes Jesus had exploded the old understanding of what messiahship meant. Being "the anointed" now signified no ordinary human being but one with divine qualities, with all authority in heaven and on earth. Even the most humble Christian who recognized this truth was thus more blessed than John the Baptist.

Peter's confession of Jesus in 16:16 is especially revealing. In answer to Jesus' introductory question about popular notions of his identity, the disciples had listed the usual candidates. Accordingly, Jesus was being thought of as a revived John the Baptist, Jeremiah or any one of a number of prophets. In other words, he was still perceived as a Jewish type Messiah. In contrast, however, Peter's redacted answer to Jesus' next direct question: *"Whom do you say that I am?"* envisioned Jesus on an entirely different plane. Peter replied: *"You are* 'ο Χριστος,' *the Son of the living God."* Here the NRSV Translation Committee again renders the Greek as *"the*

Messiah," but I would beg to differ. At this late location in the *First* Gospel's narrative and following the list of popular Jewish candidates as Jesus' *alter egos,* Jesus is no longer to be seen simply in traditional garb as a Hebrew *Messiah,* but as the Greek noun, ο Χριστος, actually implies, as the *Christ* of universal import. This recognition is what makes Peter's confession exceptional and worthy of the acclamation Jesus' gives it in v. 17. This time the earlier RSV Translation Committee who employed *"Christ"* here wins the preferential nod over the NRSV's rendition.

On this basis, I would suggest that subsequent uses of "ο Χριστος" in 26:63 and 27:17 should also be translated *"Christ"* instead of *"Messiah,"* especially in the latter case where the question: *"Whom do you want me to release for you, Jesus Barabbas or Jesus who is called* "ο Χριστος" is asked by Pontius Pilate, the Gentile Roman governor.

As previously hinted, the final, climactic word in Ben's renewed depiction of Jesus as the *Christ* comes in 28: 18-19, the Great Commission, although the term itself is not used. Here Jesus exclaims: *"All authority in heaven and on earth has been given to me. Go therefore and make disciples of all nations..."* Can you imagine a Jewish *Messiah* making such a global statement? Hardly. This was the Hebrew particularist Messiah transfigured into the Greek universalist *Christ.* The person we see now at the end of the *First* Gospel has come a long way from the one we first met in chapter 1, verse 1.

Interestingly, *Christ,* or ο Χριστος, is never used as a proper name in Matthew as was so frequently the case already in Paul's letters, cf. Rom. 1:1 *et al.* Here, and apparently in Ben's Antiochene Christian community as well, *"Christ"* retains its role exclusively as a title, one of great substance, respect and faith.

Additional Christological Titles

A second set of significant Christological titles, beside *Messiah* and *Christ,* frequently found in the *First* Gospel are *"Son of Man"* and *"Son of God."* Their close terminological resemblance already suggests their inter-relatedness. Both come loaded with an abundance of traditional baggage, much of which the evangelist simply inherits from his sources, Mark and Q, and reproduces. The former title, *Son of Man,* especially, has a long and rich history of use in the Old Testament, in Ezekiel and Daniel in particular. Both titles, however, are used with about equal frequency, about two dozen times each, especially if phrases relating the Son with God the Father are added to the list of *Son of God* references.

Also, contrary to the popular assumption which is inclined to understand *Son of Man* as referring only to Jesus' humanity, both titles are, in fact, terms of transcendence with *Son of God* clearly acknowledging Jesus' deity while *Son of Man* reflects apocalyptic overtones recalling the one coming in the clouds of heaven to judge the world according to Dan. 7:13, cf. Mt. 24:30. In short, these two terms have much in common, are closely related, and, like *Messiah* and *Christ,* are practically interchangeable and synonymous. But again we must ask: Are they truly equivalent?

The key to understanding their distinctiveness in the *First* Gospel is, undoubtedly, detected by observing how carefully and consistently the *first* evangelist employs these titles in the text. He never allows the disciples to address Jesus as the *Son of Man,* only as the *Son of God,* while, conversely, he never redactionally permits Jesus to speak of himself as the *Son of God,* only as the *Son of Man.* This literary strategy has several natural effects. Despite its traditional character as a term of transcendence, *Son of Man* now often does appear to be somewhat self-effacing. As Jesus laments: *"The Son of Man has nowhere to lay his head,"* 8:30. There is thus something grand and yet tragic about the figure and the concept of the *Son of Man.*

The reverse situation characterizes the *Son of God.* Even God the Father on two occasions, at Jesus' baptism and again at the Transfiguration, 3:13-17 & 17:1-8, acknowledges Jesus as *"my son, the beloved, with whom I am well pleased."* Likewise, the second centurion, and those with him," confess beneath the cross: *"Truly this man was God's Son,"* 27:54. Son of God, then, is a title of confession and praise.

In sum, *Son of Man* in the *First* Gospel is the older, more traditional and diffused Jewish term while *Son of God* reflects a newer, bolder, more confessional Christological concept. In some respects, at least, we can detect here a parallel strategy to that which applied to *Messiah* and *Christ.* It is the new taking precedence over the old, 13:52. We note, with interest, for example, the close paralleling of the titles *Christ* and *Son of God* in Caiaphas' demand about Jesus' identity in 26:63 as more correctly translated in the RSV: *"Tell us if you are the Christ, the Son of God."*

This may be the logical place to discuss briefly several related circumstances demonstrating Ben's, or *Matthew's,* considerable rhetorical skill in matters Christological.

Note first the clever way, in counter-distinction from Mark 8:27, that our Antiochene scribe positions *the Son of Man* and *Son of God* titles in Jesus initial question in 16:13 and in Peter's response in 16:16. Jesus asks: *"Who do people say that the Son of Man is?"* to which Peter ultimately answers" *"You are the Christ* (RSV), *the Son of the living God."* The two titles thus combine to constitute a very complete Christological confession, although, as subsequent events will show, a still somewhat premature one, cf. 16:21-23.

Again, observe the whimsical alteration of Jesus' response to Caiaphas' indictment: *"Tell us if you are you the Messiah, the Son of the living God"* from a direct *"I am"* in Mark

14:62 to an indirect *"You have said so"* in Mt. 26:64. Not only is this reply consistent with the evangelist's practice refraining from having Jesus declare himself the *Son of God,* it also succeeds in putting the high priest on the defensive. Caiaphas already knows the correct answer, so why does he ask? For mere dramatic effect, if for no other reason, the *first* evangelist's redaction is to be preferred.

Finally, there is the problem of the trinitarian baptismal formula, *"in the name of the Father and of the Son and of the Holy Spirit"* in 28:19. Isn't it a bit premature? It is if taken at face value as a statement of the historical Jesus. Nowhere else in any of the Gospels is such a theologically mature, formulaic description of the Godhead credited to Jesus or any of his disciples. We recognize it, however, as another rather typical anachronism exposing the scribe's practice of transparency. By the evangelist's day, a half century after Jesus' death and resurrection, Christian thought had matured sufficiently to allow for such a profound formulation. Remember, St. Paul had written something similar in his "Apostolic Benediction" conferred on the Corinthian Christians already twenty-five years earlier, II Cor. 13:13.

Surely, we should not think that *Matthew,* alias Ben Grammateus, was here implying all the theological insights as well as jargonesque theologoumena that have accumulated around the doctrine of the Holy Trinity during ensuing centuries. This is "incipient" trinitarianism, simply recognizing the spiritual identification occurring when one is baptized *"in the name of"* the deity known variously and cumulatively as the Father, Son and Holy Spirit.[6]

Auxiliary Titles

But there is more. In addition to those already discussed, the *first* evangelist also employs a number of auxiliary

Christological titles which, perhaps in lesser ways, help to fill out his concept of the true nature and significance of Jesus.

"Lord," Κυριος, is, undoubtedly, the address or appellation most frequently used — some seventy-five times in the *First* Gospel — but not always referring to Jesus. In Greek and Roman times, it was a common expression of respect, as between client and patron, not unlike our contemporary use of "sir." In the New Testament, however, it also translates the Old Testament Hebrew אֲדוֹנָי, *"Lord,"* or יְהוָה, *"God."* (Cf. Psalm 110:1) This breadth and ambivalence in connotation probably explains the contradiction in its use by Ben Grammateus as well as other New Testament writers. On the one hand, *"Lord"* is often employed as a confessional address by supplicants such as the disciples who, while in a boat about to sink, cry out: *"Lord, save us. We are perishing,"* Mt. 8:25. On the other hand, we also hear Jesus declaring: *"Not everyone who says to me 'Lord, Lord,' will enter the kingdom of heaven, but only the one who does the will of my Father in heaven,"* 7:22. The Matthean scholar, Jack Kingsbury, is undoubtedly correct, then, in designating *"Lord,"* an "auxiliary title." To be at all acceptable in a Christological sense it must be accompanied by committed faith and commensurate action.

Curiously, the *"Son of David"* title in the body of the Gospel is most frequently employed by the sick imploring Jesus' aid, cf. 9:27, 15:22, 20:30, 31. Why the name of David, the great warrior king, should be so consistently associated with healing in Matthew is something of a mystery.[7] Its repeated use here — taken from Mark 9:27 and 12:30 — suggests only that it was traditional. The *first* evangelist did not make much more of it. However, I must admit to the temptation to speculate that he may have concurred in the use of this title as a tactic to counteract the prevalent notion which credited any recovery of health to the healing powers of the god

148

Asclepius whose temple in the heart of the city doubled as Antioch's primary hospital.

In 8:19, a Jewish scribe addresses Jesus as *"Teacher,"* διδασκαλος. The Pharisees, according to 9:11, think of him in the same way. And even Jesus refers to himself by that description in 23:8. What is so curiously surprising about this practice, therefore, is that, contrary to Mark's use (cf. Mk. 4:38/Mt. 8:25), our Antiochene *"scribe trained for the kingdom"* never permits the disciples to address Jesus as *"teacher."*

Jesus, of course, is a teacher in the *First* Gospel, and a great one, as his five sermons attest. He teaches *"as one having authority and not as their scribes,"* 7:29, but, for the *first* evangelist *"teacher,"* was simply not an appropriate Christological title for disciples to use. Why not? We are not told, but perhaps we might again speculate that it was, as the historian Everett Ferguson contends,[8] that "teacher" — especially on an elementary level — was not a very respected position in Greek and Roman society. Remember, there were no public schools. Those few teachers who saw the need for early instruction, therefore, were forced to beg poor, uneducated, resisting parents to pay for their children's education. Teachers, consequently, were about as welcome as tax-collectors in most Greco-Roman homes. Disciples addressing Jesus with this title, then, would not be doing him any favors. I will leave it to you, the reader, to decide if this circumstance may, or may not, have been part of the author's reasoning in limiting the use of this Christological title in his Gospel. Perhaps you can you think of a better explanation.

There is one title applied to Jesus that is used with some frequency but definitely not countenanced by the evangelist. The visiting Wise Men innocently ask: *"Where is the child who has been born 'king of the Jews?'"* in 2:2. Thereafter, however, we find *"King of the Jews"* used only in accusations, 27:11,

149

29, even in the formal indictment nailed to Jesus' cross, 27:37. As far as *Matthew*/Ben was concerned, then, *"King of the Jews"* was one thing Jesus was not. It was far too ethnically circumscribed to be of any benefit to his multi-racial readership.

Another potentially prominent designation for Jesus is not only auxiliary but is missing altogether from the *First* Gospel. This unexpected void challenges our curiosity. I refer to the title "Savior," Σωτηρ, as previously discussed. It is true that Mark does not use it either, but Paul did long before the *First* Gospel was written and Luke and John did so somewhat later as well. Why, then, did not Ben Grammateus employ it? It would seem that he had every reason and opportunity to do so since he alone among the evangelists includes a definition of the name, Jesus, in 1:21 as one who *"shall save (σωσει) his people from their sins."*[9]

As another part of the puzzle, but perhaps also of its solution, is the fact that the *first* evangelist does not use the corollary noun, "salvation," σωτηρια, either. Furthermore, sometimes when he employs the verb "to save" he does so in the seemingly non-theological sense of "to rescue from harm," 8:25, or "to heal," 9:21-22. These observations prompt two possible conclusions. One is that *Matthew,* or Ben, views "saving" holistically, indiscriminately, refusing to differentiate between saving from sin or from sickness with benefits in this life or in the next. We will have much more to say on this subject in succeeding chapters treating the topics of Ethics and Soteriology in the *First* Gospel.

The second possible, preliminary conclusion is that both Savior and salvation may have carried very different connotations in the Antiochene context than they do in ours today. For instance, one of the ancient local goddesses depicted on a remnant of a mosaic floor on display in Antakya's Hatay Archeological Museum is explicitly named Σωτηρια, "Salvation," or

"Health."[10] Also, history records that "Savior" was a popular subtitle frequently adopted by ancient Antiochene rulers such as Antiochus I Soter, who ca. 280 B.C.E. first made Antioch the capitol of his Seleucid Empire. More recently, and perhaps more cogently, Vespasian, the father of the currently reigning Flavian dynasty, had adopted the same attribution upon his elevation as the Roman emperor in 68 C.E. After the political, cultural and moral mess left by Nero, Vespasian, envisioned himself the Savior of Rome. Would not these have been reasons enough to explain the evangelist's desire to avoid ascribing this *"Savior"* title to Jesus? You be the judge. I am inclined to think both considerations may well have played a role in his conservative practice.

Although these several auxiliary titles — and the one that is missing — leave us with more questions than firm insights or answers, they do help us to focus on what Ben Grammateus views as appropriate, and inappropriate, for his community to understand about the nature, position, function and purpose of Jesus. Jesus is divine and yet human, transcendent but humble, Lord and servant, demanding but compassionate, all at the same time.

The Crescendo

As commented earlier in the Prologue to this PART II, all of the *first* evangelist's major theological themes except this one, his Christology, crescendo in an extended sermon. In this case, however, the grand denouement occurs in the climactic Great Commission, 28:18-20, concluding the entire gospel. Our Antiochene scribe certainly must have worked hard and long on this pronouncement to have come up with such a cohesive, coherent and comprehensive statement. Here we see Jesus in the full panoply of his powers — as the *Son of God* with all authority, as the *Son of Man* prepared to judge the world, as the *Christ* giving the command to make disciples of all people, as

151

the *Lord* of the church commissioning his disciples to baptize, as the ultimate *teacher* propounding the perfect curriculum. If his Antiochene Christian community could grasp this pregnant concept the author's literary struggles would be well worth his time and trouble.

But now comes the big surprise. Instead of concluding with a transcendent flourish portraying Jesus as seated eternally and triumphantly at his Father's right hand in heaven, Ben, the scribe, dramatically brings us back down to earth, to the mess that is history, to the worry that is time, as Jesus is heard in *pianissimo* consoling his Antiochene disciples, and us today as well: *"And remember, I am with you always, to the end of the age,"* 28:20b. What a masterful stroke! This is truly gospel, i.e., good news. All that Jesus was and is is now placed at the immediate service and for the continuing benefit of God's humble and helpless people.[11]

But why are we surprised? Now we recall that Ben has been hinting of this incarnational view of God's Son almost from the very beginning. Already in chapter 1, verse 23, Ben had injected as a kind of preview the quote from Isaiah 7:14: *"'Look, the virgin shall conceive and bear a son, and they shall name him Emmanuel' which means, 'God is with us.'"* We now recognize the evangelist's remarkably insightful literary purpose. It was to bracket his entire Gospel, from 1:23 to 28:20 — as if enclosing all his readers in its arms — by portraying Jesus from beginning to end as the world's one present hope and enduring consolation, its new Emmanuel. As Jesus had said in mid-gospel: *"Where two or three were gathered in my name, I am there among them,"* 18:20. Jesus' ultimate greatness, therefore, finally lay not in his transcendence, but in his immanence; not in his omnipotence, but in his omnipresense; not in his majesty, but equally in his humanity; not in his sympathy, but in his empathy; not in his austerity, but in his familiarity; not in detachment from humankind, but in his proximity to all people in need.

Our scribe's insight here is so unexpectedly profound that we wonder what brought him to such a conclusion. Divine inspiration is certainly one suggestion, but it is undoubtedly too facile for our kind of study. More fundamentally realistic is the probability that it was the daily plight of his Christian community in Antioch that led him to sense the urgent need for this kind of a "hands-on" Lord. Many, if not all, of his peers lived in the grip of fear — the fear of poverty, illness, famine, earthquake, war, suppression. Added to these temporal threats were the evangelist's own spiritual concerns about the devastating inroads of false prophets, rival resurgent Jewish scribes and rabbis, and the irrepressible advance of moral lethargy brought on by the delay of Christ's promised return. The immediate presence of an Emmanuel, then, was the perfect antidote to the moral and spiritual malaise of his days.

A third possibility may also be worth mentioning. Our lateral reading in the letters of Ignatius alerts us to the growing menace of Docetism that existed in Asia Minor and most likely also in Antioch about this time. "Docetism" is derived from the Greek verb δοκέω, "to seem" or "to appear." Accordingly, Docetists were overly zealous Christians who thought and taught that Jesus, as the Christ, only "appeared" to be human, but was in fact singularly divine, simply encased in a human shell. As such a disembodied spirit, the Docetic Christ could not be touched by human infirmities, tempted to sin, die or rise again. Heaven was his permanent address. As Ignatius protests: "Some unbelievers... say that his (Jesus') Passion was merely in semblance,"[12] and again: "For I know and believe that he was in the flesh even after the resurrection. And when he came to those with Peter he said to them: 'Take, handle me and see that I am not a phantom without a body.'"[13]

Could such an environment of nascent Docetism have been another contributing factor in the evangelist's emphasis on Jesus' immediate availability, if not tangibility? After all, there have been hints to that effect all along. We think, for example, of the insertion of the four scurrilous women in Jesus' genealogy. Certainly they testified to his very human ancestry. Then there was the quote about the *"Son of Man came eating and drinking"* in 11:19. In 18:21 we hear Jesus promise: *"Where two or three are gathered in my name, I am there among them."* Finally, in the Last Supper scene of 26:26 we note the desire to make Jesus' body and blood visible and tangible, if not digestible, in the bread and wine. Whether it was Docetism that Ben sought to counteract, or not, it is clear that throughout his gospel his one aim was to make Jesus as present and practical as possible.

Here, undoubtedly, we also find one of the secrets to the *First* Gospel's durability and continuing practicality. Thanks to the evangelist's insights, even we Christians today find reassurance in the knowledge that Jesus as the *Christ, Son of God* and *Son of Man, Lord* of heaven and earth, of Jew and Gentile, *teacher* and healer, remains present and actively involved in our daily lives as well.

Chapter 6 Endnotes

[1] For more detailed background information, see Jack Dean Kingsbury, MATTHEW: STRUCTURE, CHRISTOLOGY, KINGDOM._ Fortress Press, Philadelphia, 1975, pp. 40-127.

[2] Soteriology may be considered a second theme without a sermon dedicated to its consideration, but the "Mission Discourse" in Mt. 10 is certainly related to that general topic.

[3] Cf. Guido Tisera, UNIVERSALISM ACCORDING TO THE GOSPEL OF MATTHEW, Peter Lang Publishing, Frankfurt am Main, Berlin, Bern, New York, Paris, Wien, 1993.

[4] For an exhaustive, if not excessive, study of Mosaic motifs in the *First* Gospel see Dale C. Allison, Jr. THE NEW MOSES: A Matthean Typology, Fortress Press, Minneapolis, 1993.

[5] For a more detailed study of the role of John the Baptist in Matthew see John P. Meier, THE MISSION OF CHRIST AND HIS CHURCH, Michael Glazer, Inc. Wilmington, Delaware, 1990, pp. 180-208.

[6] Cf. Mt. 10:40-42 for some indication of what *"in the name"* of a prophet, a righteous person or a disciple implies. Some level of personal identification with the prophet, disciple or diety is indicated.

[7] Cf. Jack Dean Kingsbury, *The Title 'Son of David' in Matthew's Gospel,* JBL, 95, 1976, pp. 591-602.

[8] Everett Ferguson, BACKGROUNDS OF EARLY CHRISTIANITY, 2nd ed., William B. Eerdmans Publishing Company, Grand Rapids, 1993, p. 100.

[9] Mark Allan Powell, in his recent work, GOD WITH US, Fortress Press, Minneapolis, 1995, pp. 5-7, argues that "Jesus," in effect, stands for "Savior" wherever that name is found in the *First* Gospel. I find this difficult to accept since "Jesus" is never used in the vocative or anywhere appears in the role of a Christological title.

[10] Cf. Fatih Cimock, ANTIOCH ON THE ORONTES, op. cit. p. 33.

[11] Jack Dean Kingsbury in MATTHEW: STRUCTURE, CHRISTOLOGY, KINGDOM, op. cit., p. 41, lists the widely varying opinions among scholars in their efforts to determine which Christological title is preeminent in the *First* Gospel. My position comes closest to that of Rolf Walker, DIE HEILSGESCHICHTE IM ERSTEN EVANGELIUM, Vandenhoeck & Ruprecht, Göttingen, 1967, pp. 128-130, who speaks of the "earthly Messiah."

[12] Ignatius, *Trallians, X, 1,* in APOSTOLIC FATHERS I, Loeb Classical Library, Harvard University Press, Cambridge, MA., 1912, p. 221. Cf. also Smyrneans II,1, p. 255.

[13] Ibid, *Smyrneans,* III, 2, p.255.

Chapter 7

Exceeding or Excessive Righteousness?

Upon my return from Antakya, I invited an Arizona State University professor and his wife, both of Turkish/ Arab extraction, to an evening of reminiscing and debriefing at my home. When it came time to part, however, the professor's wife honored my wife and me with the gift of a beautiful wall ornament made of harmonic shades of blue and white glass arranged in concentric circles. It was a traditional Turkish gift, she explained, called an "Evil Eye," and was meant to be suspended over an entrance to protect the home from harmful influences.

The thought and the gift were very generous, but they presented me with a moral dilemma. The comments of Mt. 6:23 (KJV) about evil (πονηρος) eyes causing one to live in darkness immediately came to mind. By exhibiting this "Evil Eye" wouldn't I, as a Christian, be demonstrating a degree of misplaced trust in its superstitious symbolism? After several days I arrived at a personal comfort level relative to the problem. First, I arbitrarily changed the ornament's name to "Live Eye," (i.e., "evil" spelled backwards) and then suspended it above one of my office doors that is permanently locked.

Is this dissimulation?

The Roman historian, Tacitus, ca. 56-117 C.E., when reflecting on first century Judaism, criticized it as "...perverse...disgusting...inflexibly honest and ever ready to show compassion..."[1] This quizzical comment, which seems so self-contradictory to us, exposes the fundamental clash of cultural values in classical times. What was considered praiseworthy in one society was adjudged "perverse" and "disgusting" in another. Moderation here was excess there. Undoubtedly, it was precisely in the midst of this kind of moral morass that early Christianity, including the Antiochene Christian community, found itself enmeshed.

One wonders, in fact, since in the public view early Christianity was still considered a sect within Judaism, whether Tacitus may not actually have been thinking of Antiochene Christian ethics when he wrote these words. Such stipulations as we find in the Sermon on the Mount, Mt. 5-7, for example, would seem especially eligible for his kind of criticism. Here, if anywhere, we find moral idealism taken to an inflexible extreme. Listen to these words attributed to Jesus but recorded only in the *First* Gospel:

> *"Do not think that I have come to abolish the law or the prophets; I have come not to abolish but to fulfill. For truly I tell you, until heaven and earth pass away, not one letter, not one stroke of a letter, will pass from the law until all is accomplished. Therefore, whoever breaks one of the least of these commandments, and teaches others to do the same, will be called least in the kingdom of heaven; but whoever does them and teaches them will be called great in the kingdom of heaven. For I tell you, unless your righteousness exceeds that of the scribes and Pharisees you will never enter the kingdom of heaven."* Mt. 5:17-20.

Isn't this going too far, expecting too much, more than is humanly possible? Again, when we are advised in 5:29-30: *"If your right eye causes you to sin, tear it out and throw it away...And if your right hand causes you to sin, cut it off and throw it away,"* isn't this asceticism gone berserk? What has become of Christian freedom, moderation, tolerance, love and forgiveness? Isn't this perfectionism, work-righteousness, synergism, Pelagianism? In short, isn't this excessive rather

158

than exceeding righteousness that is being advocated? Thus the questions keep coming, inviting explication.

Unfortunately, the responses advanced are as varied as the questions asked.[2] Among the many opinions expressed we find that some commentators attempt to soften the impact of these uncompromising statements which seem to espouse a kind of work-righteousness and cold legalism by insisting that the sermon be read soteriologically. Jesus, accordingly, can make such extraordinary ethical demands because, ultimately, he is himself the one who will fulfill them compensating for human failure.[3] Significantly, though, there is only one passage which explicitly focuses on Jesus' vicarious atonement in the whole Gospel, Mt. 20:28: *"The Son of Man came not to be served but to serve and to give his life a ransom for many."* Seeing this one passage, located in an alien context, as the keystone to understanding the plethora of Matthean ethical demands in the Sermon on the Mount, it seems to me, is to place an unbearable weight upon it.

Others blithely inject as an antidote overriding thoughts of Christian love[4] as stated in I Corinthians 13 and in the Gospel of John, e.g., 15:9-17. As numerous and excessive as these moral maxims in the *First* Gospel may be, ultimately they all boil down to one: love, for *"love is the fulfilling of the law,"* Rom 13:10. As we shall see, love, as in *"love your enemies,"* Mt. 5:44, is embraced in the Sermon on the Mount, but nowhere in the *First* Gospel is it projected as the panacea or compensation for all evil.

Again, there are those who attempt to defuse the issue eschatologically. It is because the evangelist thinks of the end of the present age as breathlessly near that he insists on such an heroic effort toward moral rectitude. If he had known that another two millennia would pass without the *eschaton* occurring, it is assumed, such rigor would not have been advocated.

159

This, then, is "interim ethics," excessively serious, but designed only for the short term.[5]

Perhaps the most popular interpretation is to see Jesus here simply employing hyperbole,[6] speaking theoretically and idealistically, yet relatively. In spite of these absolute pronouncements, all he really hoped to accomplish was to encourage the disciples to do the very best they could. Those who hold this view can turn for support to the **Didache**, a manual of church orders also believed to have been compiled in Antioch only a decade or two later than the *First* Gospel. It reads:

> "See that no one make thee to err from this Way of the teaching, for he teaches thee without God. For if thou canst bear the whole yoke of the Lord, thou wilt be perfect, but if thou canst not, do what thou canst."[7]

Justification for this kind of relativism, as desirable as it may seem to some, is very difficult, if not impossible, to find in the Matthean text so generously sprinkled as it is with sweeping demands, indictments, threats and prohibitions.

Our own evaluation of the dynamics involved now awaits our analysis of the prevailing situation, the content, the rhetoric and the literary method employed in the *First* Gospel as composed by *Matthew,* alias Ben Grammateus, in the ninth decade of the first century C.E.

The Sermon on the Mount

The principle areas of the *first* evangelist's ethical concern are detectable from the content and style of the Sermon on the Mount as recorded and redacted in Mt. 5-7.

This discourse begins tactfully with eight beatitudes — positive, even congratulatory, statements of praiseworthy attitudes and behaviors befitting the Christian individual and community, 5:3-10. Some of the terms employed, such as *"kingdom of heaven,"* are typical of Ben as are themes of *"righteousness"* and *"mercy,"* but most of the other subjects dealt with are not repeated or treated elsewhere in the *First Gospel*. We are undoubtedly on safe ground, then, if we conclude that this poetic set of blessings, or best wishes, represents a piece of local liturgy, or hymnody, based on older Q material, cf. Luke 6:20-22. Ben, the *"scribe trained for the kingdom,"* we can imagine, had simply taken these lines from his *capsa* treasury, perhaps edited them slightly, and incorporated them at Mt. 5:3-10. Here they serve well as a kind of *exordium*[8] i.e., a very winsome, non-threatening introduction to the several more challenging statements to follow.

The ninth beatitude, vv. 11-12, however, functions as a bridge to one of the major points of the whole sermon, relations with neighboring Jews and Jewish influences. Although based on the Q passage found in Luke 6:22, it served the author's purposes perfectly. Note first of all the abrupt change in those addressed from a general *"they"* in the previous eight beatitudes to a direct and specific plural *"you"* here in v. 11. The evangelist is getting personal. Beginning with a blessing addressed to the disciple-Christians, this beatitude surprisingly concludes with a condemnation of those Jews, past and present, who have killed the prophets God had sent to them. This concern will become an ever-growing theme as we proceed and will be reviewed in full detail in Chapter Ten.

Verses 13-16 focus in on the problem. As Jesus admonished his disciples, so the Antiochene Christian community must know that if it is to survive it dare not lose its moral zeal, deteriorating like discarded salt. Rather, as a city set on a hill or a lamp on a lampstand it must let its light shine before others *"so that they may see your good works and give glory to your Father in heaven."* The glory of God, then, provides one fundamental motive and goal for all Christian behavior. Simultaneously we note, "good works" are an integral and commendable aspect of Christian faith and life.

Now, as if punctuating this prelude to the sermon, we find the uncompromising statement of 5:17-20 quoted at the beginning of this chapter. Our scribe is certainly serious about his subject. Exemplary Christian behavior is a priority with him, no doubt about it.

The Six Antitheses

With that brief prologue accomplished, Jesus, at the redactor's insistence, plunges directly into his instruction in the form of six "Antitheses," contrasting major new kingdom values with timeworn traditions, 5:21-48. The rhetorical *topos* is that of *synkrisis*, contrast and comparison.

Except for the **First Antithesis** treating the related topics of murder and anger, vv. 21-24, and the fourth Antithesis on swearing oaths, vv. 33-37, all of these comparison/contrasts have their antecedents in Marcan or Q sources, and perhaps even in Jesus' original *logia,* or sayings. Still, there are plenty of smaller redactional comments to enable us to sense Ben's own intense concern for the positive practice of Christian virtues in his local community as well.

Actual homicide, however, we can tell, was not the *first* evangelist's primary concern in this **First Antithesis**, v. 21, even though he has Jesus quoting Exodus 20:13 or Deut. 5:17: *"You shall not murder."* What really troubled him was the much more prevalent problem of congregational disharmony, intra-community squabbling, and anger leading to imprecations toward a "brother," ο αδελφος. Compare the fourfold reference to "brother" here with its equally frequent use in ch. 18:15-18 where its meaning, as sense-translated in the NRSV, is clearly *"another member of the church."* Anger, then, is as evil as murder. The emotion and the motive are the

162

equivalent of the action. Moses' temporal commandments must give way to God's eternal law demanding internal as well as external compliance. Repeated disobedience can and will lead to ever stiffer penalties including even the fires of hell, v. 22. Misdemeanors against one's brother within the community, in this way, are conceptually elevated to become sins against God. Anger, therefore, must graduate to reconciliation between Christian brothers before their oblations can be accepted by their Father in heaven, vv. 23-24.

Much the same applies generally to relationships outside the community of faith, i.e., with secular accusers. Angry words there can similarly lead to a series of cascading legal punishments, imprisonments and fines, vv. 25-26. In a society as litigious as that of Tacitus' ancient Rome, as well as Ben's Roman Antioch, where "mans' inhumanity to man" was accepted as a matter of course if not a virtue, this *First Antithesis* must have appeared to raise the standards to unattainable heights demanding a level of morality that was irresponsibly excessive.

The **Second Antithesis**, vv. 27-30, attacks what was probably the first cardinal social sin in Antioch and environs, sexual immorality. Reference is now made to the Sixth Commandment retrieved from Exodus 20:14, Deut. 5:18: *"You shall not commit adultery."*.

Like Paris and Las Vegas today, Antioch with its glitzy suburb, Daphne, was notorious for its immorality in the ancient classical world. For example, the contemporary Roman satirist, Juvenal, ca. 60-140 C.E., bemoaned the fact that: "...for years now Syrian Orontes has poured its sewerage into our native Tiber - Its lingo and manners, its flutes, its outlandish harps with transverse strings, its native tambourines, and the whores who hang out round the race course."[9] And three centuries later, Libanius, Antioch's own favorite son, was still lamenting: "...there was nothing the Antiochenes took seriously except love-making."[10]

But the evangelist wasn't concerned only about actual illicit sex. For him, Jesus' and the Father's prohibitions extended even to uncontrolled amorous glances, i.e., *"...everyone who looks at a woman with lust has already committed adultery with her in his heart,"* 5:28. Again, contrary to the prevailing mores, motives and emotions were as culpable as actions in the sight of God. The evangelist's literary intensity here mirrors his increasing level of concern.

Just how seriously God takes the sin of adultery is now illustrated in vv. 29-30: *"If your right eye causes you to sin, tear it out and throw it away...If your right hand causes you to sin, cut it off and throw it away..."* The point is that it is better to have a mutilated body in this lifetime than to suffer the eternal torments of hell.

We note, in fact, that the *first* evangelist/redactor seems to want to intensify his demands by twice inserting the word *"right,"* δεζιος, with both "eye" and "hand." It is often surmised, and with good reason, that the limbs on the right side of the human body, including the *"right cheek,"* 5:39, were accorded special honor and significance in the Greco-Roman index of values. Right hands and feet were considered the stronger and more skilled, while the left were called *sinister* in Latin, implying "unlucky," and giving rise to our English word of the same spelling used to describe something ominous or dangerously deceptive. Modern Turkish travel guides, interestingly enough, continue to advise tourists that offering anyone anything with the left hand in that country may be considered ill-mannered, if not insulting.

It appears likely, therefore, that the author, by adding *"right"* here, intended to ratchet up the degree of culpability. He was saying, in effect: "Even if your best side offends don't hesitate to amputate it."

We are forced to ask: "Did Ben, or *Matthew*, really mean this?" We can hardly believe it. In view of the fact, however, that several Moslem countries in the Middle East even today amputate the hands of convicted thieves we are challenged to take this verdict literally. Furthermore, we find the same basic thought repeated, as if for emphasis, in Mt. 18:8-9. Still, and on the other hand, it is equally clear that the evangelist here was writing metaphorically. Surely, in this context of sexual sins, there are other far more erotic appendages of the human body than eyes and hands which would deserve to be removed.

The **Third Antithesis**, 5:31-32, concerning divorce, is distinct from its predecessor in form only. Its content continues the theme of adultery's dangerous, if not fatal, contagion. In fact, not only is a divorced wife left in an adulterous condition, forced to suffer the ignominy of representing used and polluted goods, any man who subsequently marries a divorced woman also automatically shares her pollution, compounding the evil done.

If this ancient concept focusing upon the indelibility of the marital relationship appears surreal and even unfair to us when viewed from the perspective of individual human rights, especially those of women, here on the edge of the twenty-first century, imagine how incredible it must have seemed to the sex-crazy inhabitants of Daphne in the *first* evangelist's day. There divorce was easy and taken for granted. Statistics on the incidence of divorce in Roman society, in fact, are difficult to determine simply because the underlying question was almost irrelevant, especially among the wealthier Roman families. In many cases, the compromised, but still official, first wife after divorce was content to stay on as a kind of office manager for domestic affairs while the husband was permitted to remarry or maintain a stable of paramours and slave girls on the side. After all, the gods did it, and the emperors did it, why not the citizenry who could afford it?

As stringent as the evangelist's basic stand on marriage and divorce is in the Sermon on the Mount, it is further reinforced in subsequent treatment of the same subject in Mt. 19: 3-12. Here the author confronts us with an illustrative case study in the ethics of divorce. A Pharisee is depicted as asking Jesus: *"Is it lawful for a man to divorce his wife for any cause?"* The concluding phrase here, added by Ben to his Marcan source, is key.

The question of necessary preconditions justifying divorce represented a long-standing debate within Judaism with the noted rival Rabbis, Hillel and Shammai, championing opposite perspectives. Was anything more than a formal notification, as recommended by Moses in Deut. 24:1, required? Apparently not. Whatever position one held within Judaism, this *"certificate of dismissal,"* 19:7, was the bottom line. As long as this minimal prescription was fulfilled, prior justification for divorce was relatively unimportant.

In this dire circumstance, Jesus' immediate answer, as Ben records it, was to override even Moses' ancient orders to supply a certificate of divorce, returning instead to the pristine conditions prevailing at the time of the creation. God had originally created human beings as two sexes, male and female, but in marriage they became forever *"one flesh." "Therefore what God has joined together let no one separate,"* v. 6. Marriages, then, were indissoluble. Both sexes were permanently bound. Such was God's original, ultimate and continuing intention.

Was this position unrealistic and excessive, or not? The disciples, whether those of Jesus' or those of the *first* evangelist's own day, seemed to think so. In a redacted passage found only in the *First* Gospel, they ask: *"If such is the case of a man with his wife, is it better not to marry?"* That

166

is, if marriage is so immaculate, meant to be so permanent, and carries such severe penalties if broken, wouldn't it be safer never to risk marriage at all? This is a type of rhetorical question which begs for some kind of modification in the answer, but, perhaps to the surprise of all, none was forthcoming. Rather, Jesus, by Ben's redaction, approvingly references the existence of several kinds of voluntary and involuntary eunuchs, or celibates, and challenges his hearers: *"Let anyone accept this who can,"* v. 12. In other words, Jesus agreed: "Yes, you are correct in your misgivings. If you don't understand or appreciate God's sublime intention for marriage, or lack the commitment to stick with the union through thick and thin, then by all means remain unmarried." So passionately uncompromising is this redacted response that, as you may recall, we were inclined to wonder back in Chapter Four whether the *first* evangelist himself may not have opted for celibacy in his own private life.

Moving on, there are several factors about the **Fourth Antithesis**, Mt. 5:33-39, discussing the problem of oaths, which strike us as curious: 1) There are no New Testament parallels. Whether the material is traditional or not, then, it is at least clear that the evangelist consciously focused on this topic of oath-making and intentionally located it here. 2) The Old Testament reference is not taken from the lists of the Ten Commandments in Exodus 20 or Deuteronomy 5, as we might have expected from previous experience, but appears to be a rather cleverly constructed composite of several O. T. passages. Perhaps the reason for this change in procedure was the fact that the Old Testament had actually permitted, and even encouraged oaths under certain circumstances (cf. Psalm 50: 14). The underlying thought here, then, is not the elevated theological Second Commandment concern of taking God's name in vain. Rather, the focus is more on the derived mundane, practical prohibition of frivolous oaths, broken promises, unkept resolutions, and the babble of slanderous gossip. These were the very kinds of social and business interactions that were all too characteristic of an Antiochene commerce and society based on a patronage system. Note especially the descending series of examples of improper oaths in vv. 34, 35, and 36: heaven - earth - Jerusalem - one's own head - and finally a single strand of hair. Even the smallest oaths are forbidden. All expletives are unnecessary and destructive, an abuse of language, and a desecration of God's creation.

We can well understand the evangelist's concern. As a scribe/rhetorician trained for the kingdom of heaven, he knew something of the beauty, mystical power, and even sanctity of language, particularly the spoken word. Proper discourse was an art, not to be abused as slander or profanity. What the situation required was not more words but more truth, honesty, sincerity and consistent action. *"Let your word be 'Yes, Yes' or 'No, No'; anything more than this comes from the evil one,"* v. 37.

In the **Fifth and Sixth Antitheses**, Mt. 5:38-48, *Matthew,* alias Ben, returns to more general and traditional subjects based on materials found in Q, Luke 6:29-36, the errors of retaliation and hatred of one's enemies. Clearly, these issues are related. In both cases Christian behavior is to be superior to that normally practiced in the broader society, whether Jewish or Gentile. The Old Testament's *lex talionis,* the "rule of tooth and claw," found in Exodus 21:24: *"If any harm follows, then you shall give life for life, eye for eye, tooth for tooth, hand for hand, foot for foot, burn for burn, wound for wound, stripe for stripe,"* is not appropriate for the new kingdom of heaven. Retributive justice, to say nothing of punitive justice, is to be replaced by the much more positive, but also more difficult, restorative or redemptive justice: *"If anyone strikes you on* *the right cheek, turn to him the other also,"* v. 39, and *"Love your enemies, and pray for those who persecute you,"* v. 44.

The same principle applies to all other forms of aggressive behavior, vv. 40-42, because the basic Christian ethic for all social interaction is love, even toward one's foes, as the Old Testament also encourages in Leviticus 19:18: *"You shall not take vengeance or bear a grudge against any of your people, but you shall love your neighbor as yourself. I am the Lord."* God is the only appropriate model. He does not discriminate, but *"makes his sun to rise on the evil and on the good,"* v. 45. One's motives and actions, however, always need watching lest one stoops to the level of public pietism as practiced by the Gentiles where simple reciprocity, doing good only to those who do good to you, is the best that is expected, vv. 46-47. Seeking vengeance may be more natural and seemingly more satisfying, but forgiveness, returning good for evil, is the more demanding Christian approach and requirement.

In sum, then, according to these Six Antitheses the only Christian standard worth pursuing in the kingdom of heaven is one of moral and ethical perfection, following the heavenly Father's example. Average social etiquette will not do. Note in Mt. 5:48 how the *first* evangelist has redacted the Q passage in Luke 6:36 to conclude: *"Be perfect,* τελειος, *therefore, as your heavenly Father is perfect,"* rather than Luke's lesser *"Be merciful,* οικτιρμων, *just as your Father is merciful."* If we must decide the question: Is this exceeding or excessive righteousness, I think we must agree on the basis of the evidence uncovered so far that the *first* evangelist leans toward the latter end of the spectrum. His expectations are certainly serious, demanding and uncompromising, perhaps even too idealistic to be realistic.

Still, there are a couple of seemingly minor considerations that make us hesitate in our judgment that the righteousness our *scribe trained for the kingdom* demands in these Six Antitheses is truly excessive.

First, there is the rather abrupt about-face in Ben's, or *Matthew's,* attitude toward the Old Testament. In Mt. 5:18, we heard him say: *"For truly I tell you, until heaven and earth pass away, not one letter, not one stroke of a letter, will pass from the law until all is accomplished."* But then, already in 5:31, and again in 19:7-8, he deftly puts Moses' interpretation allowing for divorce in Deuteronomy 24:1-4 aside with the authoritative decree: *"...but from the beginning it was not so."* Clearly, our Antiochene evangelist, as previously noted, was not a literalist or a proponent of verbal inspiration.

An even more egregious paradox, if not a direct contradiction, occurs in the same context when, in the midst of his argument emphasizing the inviolability of marriage, the author surreptitiously slips in the infamous exceptive clause: *"...except on the ground of unchastity,"* 5:31. So there is at least one permissible exception after all.

Is this evidence sufficient to reduce our evaluation of the Matthean ethical stance from excessive to, perhaps, just exceeding? Obviously, further research is needed.

Internal Affairs: Matthew 6 and 7

Compared to the first half of the Sermon on the Mount, just reviewed, the second half, chapters 6 and 7, presents a rather formless potpourri of admonitions relating to internal, rather than external, community, or congregational, matters. The compass is narrower, the directives correspondingly less intense. The form, too, tends to be more epigrammatic and less proscriptive laying out comparatively general principles such as the Golden Rule, 7:12. Some comparison/contrasts remain, but the authoritative quotations, as found in the preceding antitheses, are missing.

As for the content, most directives articulated here — *re* almsgiving, prayer, fasting, giving offerings and avoiding the desecration of things holy — fall under the rubric of cult, ritual or liturgy. Concerns about worry and judging one another in 6:34-7:5, on the other hand, may belong within the broader category of Christian attitudes and compulsive behaviors.

As for sources, Ben found most of the material included here in Q. Only the brief sections on almsgiving, prayer, fasting and profaning the holy are unparalleled in the Gospel of Luke, suggesting their special status as matters of particular local concern to the *first* evangelist. Generally speaking, however, there is a noticeable decrease in the fervor with which these admonitions, or prohibitions, as the case may be, are presented. Our goal will be similarly limited, attempting to highlight only those insights suggested by our perspective, viewing the materials in their probable Antiochene context.

The dominant underlying concern of the first three sections on almsgiving, prayer and fasting, 6:1-6 and 16-18, is, in fact, sanctimony, the pietistic display of religiosity. The practices of giving alms, prayer and fasting are encouraged, but the arrogant display often accompanying these practices is rejected.

Ostentation is a temptation common in all religions, but perhaps more so in traditional Greek and Roman situations. There, it must be remembered, temples and local sanctuaries, while numerous and beautiful, were not used regularly for large, public gatherings except on special holidays. For the most part, therefore, religious allegiances and commitments were expressed in the devotees' distinctive manner of dress, ornamentation, or ceremonial gesture — all quite public.

The *first* evangelist, accordingly, objects to similar practices within the Christian community rejecting ostentatious charitable gifts, praying pompously in public, or disfiguring

171

oneself to emphasize the discomforts of fasting. Such egregious religiosity may gain a degree of respect from others within the Gentile society, but not before God. As the evangelist repeats: *"They have their rewards,"* vv. 2, 5 and 16. Christian piety, however, is to be quieter, deeper, less visible and more genuine.

The version of the **Lord's Prayer**, introduced in 6:9-13, shares many features with its Q source as expressed in Luke 11:2-4, and both reflect aspects of an original Jewish/Aramaic Qaddish prayer. Nevertheless, the evangelist's use in v. 7 of the onomatopoetic verb βατταλογησητε, translated *"...heap up empty phrases,"* adding *"as the Gentiles do,"* is suggestive of the kind of "batting of words," or trilling, that still characterizes Middle Eastern, Arab/Muslim prayer practices today. Of interest, too, is the fact that the form of the Lord's Prayer found here — with *"debts"* and *"debtors"*— is the same as that used in the *Didache*,[11] evidencing again some degree of shared relationship and proximity between the *First* Gospel and this latter work. One wonders: Did the additional admonition in the *Didache*, "Pray thus three times a day," also apply to this prayer's use in the Antiochene congregation? Somehow, after Ben's warning about the routine chattering of words, I tend to doubt it.

The subsequent two verses, 6:14 and 15, about the need to forgive the trespasses of other persons, are of particular interest. They follow naturally enough on the fifth petition in the Lord's Prayer, 6:12, about forgiving debts, but they also prepare us for the much more extended treatment of the subject in chapter 18:21-35 discussing relationships within the church. There Jesus, by redaction, teaches Peter to forgive, not only seven, but seventy-seven times and goes on to tell the Parable of the Unforgiving Servant which ends with essentially the same words as found in 6:15: *"So my heavenly Father will also do to every one of you, if you do not forgive your brother or sister from your heart."* This emphasis reminds us that in the *first* evangelist's hierarchy of virtues a spirit of forgiveness takes precedence even over repentance[12] or sentimental love.

Chapter 7, verse 6, on profaning the holy, attracts our attention, too, as the only remaining admonition in the Sermon on the Mount unique to the *First* Gospel. And we can probably guess why our Antiochene scribe decided to add it. There is here a clear warning to his community to avoid the public display of Christian symbols and artifacts in the prohibition: *"Do not give what is holy to dogs; and do not throw your pearls before swine."* "Dogs," of course, was a common Jewish pejorative for Gentiles while no self-respecting Jew would ever have anything to do with "swine." The sanctity of anything the Christians considered holy required that it be revered modestly and in private.

Matthew, or Ben, was careful to balance his cautions about temptations coming from the right or from the left, from Jews and Gentiles alike. In a sense, his community, consisting largely of Jewish Christians, was enduring two Diasporas at once, geographically from Israel and spiritually from its own local Jewish society.

The remaining segments of the Sermon are taken, almost entirely, from Q. These sayings of Jesus are aphoristic in nature, usually culminating in an axiom of some kind: *"Where your treasure is, there your heart will be also,"* 6:21; *"You cannot serve God and wealth,"* 6:24; *"The measure you give will be the measure you get,"* 7:2; and *"In everything do to others as you would have them do to you,"* 7:12. These are all valued admonitions. What is surprising in this part of the Sermon on the Mount, however, is the balanced nature and moderate tone of these sayings. In the light of the first half of the Sermon, for example, we surely would have expected the Golden Rule to have demanded: "Do better unto others than

173

you would have them do unto you." Obviously, then, the scribal writer is not being insensitive or unreasonably assertive in his ethical demands, as we may at first have feared. He knows the frailty of human nature very well. He can still require the high standard of a *"righteousness that exceeds that of the scribes and Pharisees,"* but he counts on a spirit of forgiveness to counterbalance that principle and serve as its ultimate expression.

The two generalizing and summarizing analogies of the Two Gates and the House Built Upon the Rock in 7:13-14 & 24-27, discussed earlier,[13] bring the Sermon on the Mount to a close. The path of Christian life may be hard, but well worth the trouble.

More Extra-Sermon Stipulations

As is always the case in the fugue-like composition of the *First* Gospel, however, variations on the various ethical themes surface again and again throughout the narrative, sometimes with even greater emphasis and import.

The question of the appropriateness of fasting returns in 9:14-15. There Ben retains the gist of his Marcan parallel, Mk. 2:18-20, confirming that while fasting, which suggests remorse, was inappropriate while Jesus, the *"bridegroom,"* was visibly, and happily, present on earth, the practice is acceptable now once again since his departure.

This passage stands as testimony to the fact, as previously stated, that while the first coming of Christ and the kingdom necessitated many "new" adaptations and modifications of "old" Jewish customs, mores and laws, it did not entirely abrogate all of them. As the **Didache** confirms, regular fasting continued in the early church, except that it was practiced on Wednesdays and Fridays instead of Mondays and Thursdays as the "hypocrites" did.[14] Exactly who these hypocrites were is questionable — very possibly the term referred to some Gentile, or heretical Christian groups in northern Syria at the time that the *Didache* was written since Jews normally honored only the Sabbath, i.e., Saturday.

As for the question of Sabbath observance, we seem to find the same principle applying. The one section, Mt. 12:1-14, discusses the issue at length, employing the noun, σαββατον, no less than eight times. The Old Testament restrictions *re* what constitutes forbidden or required "work" on the Sabbath needed some renovation, following Jesus' own example. After all, in this new time, *"the Son of Man is Lord of the Sabbath,"* 12:8. Still, the evangelist approvingly records Jesus' warning in 24:20/Mk. 13:18: *"Pray that your flight may not be in winter..."* and then specifically adds: *"or on a Sabbath."* Obviously, Sabbath observance as a social convention was still deemed appropriate even among the Jewish Christian population living in the Kerateion section of Antioch in the ninth decade of the first century C.E.

Dietary rules are treated similarly in chapter 15:1-20. At issue is the question of eating with unwashed hands, a possibility totally unthinkable to Jewish ceremonial law purists. What is of particular interest here, however, is what Jesus, and the redactor, do NOT say. The evangelist simply omits the bold statement: *"Thus he declared all foods clean,"* that his predecessor source, Mark, had recorded in 7:19. Rather, he contents himself with emphasizing the lateral principle regarding speech noting that it is not what goes into the mouth but what issues from it that is defiling. Apparently dietary law was not a topic the scribe-evangelist was prepared to argue while the abuse of language concerned him deeply.

Most curious, and bothersome, is another example of something Ben does not say. Surprisingly, there is no mention whatsoever in the *First* Gospel of circumcision, once considered the quintessential component of Jewish ceremonial law. Why is that subject avoided? We remember the

175

trouble it caused between the Antiochene and the Jerusalem Christian leadership in Acts 15:1-21. Does this omission suggest, as some have maintained,[15] that the Matthean community, wherever and whenever it was located, was still an intramural Jewish sect which regularly practiced circumcision so no discussion of its propriety was necessary? Or, was the reverse the true situation? That is, the question had been resolved earlier and our scribal editor was happy to let the sleeping dog lie. In view of the perspective accepted in this book regarding the where and when of Ben's community, the latter option appears preferable by far.

Finally, as evidence to be considered in evaluating the *First* Gospel's ethical stance, we confront the summarizing, concluding phrase in the Great Commission, Mt. 28:20a: *"...teaching them to obey everything that I have commanded you."* The comprehensive nature of this final command provides a resounding exclamation point to all the ethical statements previously enunciated in this Gospel. They were commandments, ενεταιλαμην, not just principles, guidelines or suggestions. They were not only to be accepted, but internalized and obeyed.

Conclusions

With all the most pertinent evidence now considered, what final conclusions relative to the general Matthean ethical scheme or mandate can we draw? Are these moral maxims excessively or only exceedingly demanding? I list five overarching observations:

1. Concern for ethical understanding and moral action as constitutive of the Christian faith is major in the *First* Gospel, second, perhaps, only to the pervasive Christological preoccupation discussed in the previous chapter of this book. Christian ethics is the focus of the first and longest authoritative sermon, the Sermon on the Mount, which is redactionally

placed in the most prominent position, at the outset of Jesus' public ministry in the Gospel narrative. Again, ethical themes are intermittently repeated in later chapters for emphasis. And finally, the Gospel closes with a resounding reaffirmation of all of Jesus' commandments in 28:18. There can be no question, Ben Grammateus was positively determined to upgrade the level of Christian behavior in his community.

2. Despite its prominence, however, it must be recognized that the issue of Christian ethics is not treated comprehensively in the *First* Gospel. Matthew is not an ethical manual. As noted, there is no mention of circumcision, no major prohibition of idolatry as we might have expected in this polytheistic context, and little discussion of extenuating circumstances which might influence the application of basic principles. Undoubtedly, most disconcerting of all is the absence of a single meta-ethic or an explicit hierarchy of values. Early on in the Sermon on the Mount the evangelist posits giving *"glory to your Father who is in heaven"* as a worthy goal, Mt. 5:16. Love is lauded as the proper attitude toward one's enemies in 5:44. Perfection is another ideal as expressed in the redacted statement in 5:48: *"Be perfect, therefore, as your Father in heaven is perfect."* On occasion our scribe emphasizes the importance of mercy, especially in the repeated quotation from Hosea 6:6 in Mt. 9:13 and 12:7: *"I desire mercy and not sacrifice."* In 18:22 he promotes a spirit of forgiveness quoting Jesus as telling Peter to forgive his sinning brother not just seven times, but seventy-seven times. Mt. 23:23 lists a triumvirate of values, *"...justice, mercy and faith,"* reminiscent of Paul's corresponding *"...faith, hope and love..."* in I Cor. 13:13. Significantly, however, in Matthew there is no *"...but the greatest of these..."* leaving us somewhat adrift without a true index of ultimate values, or absolutes.

3. The Matthean ethical corpus reflects a variety of sources, influences and circumstances. Some of the material

in the Sermon on the Mount was gleaned from Mark, but most originated with Q. The Beatitudes and the Matthean version of the Lord's Prayer appear to reflect popular, local community use. Similarly, the uniform cultic nature of the stipulations about prayer, fasting and the giving of alms also suggest current, intra-community issues. While the local cluster of Christians undoubtedly captured the evangelist's primary concern, he was not oblivious to the wider Gentile society either. The oppressive moral degeneracy of nearby Daphne can certainly be heard in the repeated demur, *"except on the ground of unchastity,"* in 5:32 and 19:9. Further, an explicit consciousness of a Gentile presence is revealed in the change from "sinners" in Q, Luke 6:33, to "Gentiles" in Mt. 5:47. Local color is probably most graphically represented by the use of the term, ρακα, translated "insult" in the NRSV, Mt. 5:22. The epithet, however, is most likely derived from the Greek word for "rag," perhaps used here as a colloquial metaphor for a destitute person dressed in tattered garments. The perpetrator of such demeaning language, in Ben's mind, deserved indictment before the official council. The net effect of these diverse influences manifests itself as a type of "situation ethics" which counterbalances some of the more rigorist pronouncements in the Matthean ethical discourse.

4. There are also rhetorical considerations which impact our understanding of Matthean ethics. As an *exordium,* the Beatitudes, Mt. 5:3-10, provide an appealing introduction to the Sermon on the Mount, but they do not serve as an outline of what is to come. Several of their themes and phrases are not repeated in the sermon which follows. Recognizing the *synkrisis topos* helps us appreciate and keep in perspective the many contrast/comparison analogies employed especially in the Six Antitheses. Here was the evangelist's method of balancing the new and the old in the kingdom of heaven. Perhaps most significantly, the evangelist's cavalier way of

disobeying his own prior principles, abrogating Moses' Old Testament statements and proposing at least one exception to his stated position on the inviolability of marriage, reminds us that he was adept at employing the Greek rhetorical *topos* called *stasis*. Accordingly, absolutist statements of principle were not intended to be accepted absolutely, but served, rather, as undeniable and unavoidable invitations to further discussion and possible modification. The procedure allows for a vital tension to exist between opposing positions without relativizing the conclusions. Ben preferred to preserve both the new and the old, the wine and wineskins, 9:17.

5. The *first* evangelist thinks holistically. His theology is not highly inflected. It is more practical, than philosophical. Ben Grammateus does not draw bright lines of distinction between Law and Gospel, faith and works. Rather, he views them symbiotically. Ethics is integral to faith, like two sides of the same coin. Faith and faithfulness go together, made of the same cloth. Jesus, the Messiah/Christ and the Son of Man, is Lord of the Sabbath, Mt. 12:8. Whoever would be Jesus' disciple must take up his own, not Jesus', cross and follow him, Mt. 16:24.

Ben Grammateus is not St. Paul, and we do both a grave disservice if we attempt to harmonize their positions or contrast them as representing either synergism or cheap grace. Neither is Ben a systematic theologian nor a western scientific scholar intent on bringing every question to closure. He is content to live with some ambiguity and ambivalence even in ethical matters. As such he often frustrates us, but that circumstance is at least as much our problem as his. To use something of an oxymoron, the *first* evangelist is consistently apophatic, speaking with a forked tongue, as it were, for the benefit of his audience and readers. In brief, he was a genuine son of his own culture, time and place.

In answer, then, to our topical question in this chapter: Does the evangelist insist on *Exceeding or Excessive Righteousness*? my answer to both poles of the proposition, as uncomfortably inconsistent as it may seem, must be a firm, albeit ambiguous, "Yes." Whatever moral relativizing the evangelist allows only denotes exceptions to the rule. The higher perfectionist, excessive ideals, meanwhile, remain unchanged and unchallenged.

As responsible Christians, we, like our Antiochene scribe's original readers, are challenged to live in and with that lofty, vital, unresolved moral tension, on the edge of the idealistically impossible. That's what gives the Christian life integrity, direction and focus. That is what keeps it exciting, substantial and very much worthwhile.

Chapter 7 Endnotes

P. Cornelius Tacitus, TACITUS, *The Histories;* Book IV, 5, p. 295, published by Encyclopedia Britannica , Inc., Chicago, for the GREAT BOOKS OF THE WESTERN WORLD series, Robert Maynard Hutchins, Editor in Chief, 1952.

[2] It is suggested that for introductory purposes the reader peruse the article entitled *Matthew and the Law* by Klyne Snodgrass in TREASURES NEW AND OLD; David R. Bauer and Mark Allan Powell, eds., Scholars Press, Atlanta, 1996, pp. 99-127. Snodrass lists many of the major problems associated with developing a proper understanding of Matthean ethics, and the solutions proposed, pp. 101-106.

[3] Cf. John P. Meier, THE VISION OF MATTHEW: Christ, Church, and Morality in the First Gospel; Paulist Press, New York, Ramsay and Toronto, 1979, p. 63f. Also Robert A. Guelich, THE SERMON ON THE MOUNT, A Foundation for Understanding; Word Books, Waco, Texas, 1982, especially chap. 5 on "Jesus and the Law, pp. 134-174

[4] Cf. Klyne Snodgrass, op. cit., pp. 106-111.

[5] This was the position of Johannes Weiss and Albert Schweitzer. Cf. Graham N. Stanton, THE GOSPEL FOR A NEW PEOPLE: Studies in Matthew; T&T Clark, Edinburgh, 1992, p.293.

[6] Cf. R. H. Stein, DIFFICULT SAYINGS IN THE GOSPELS; Jesus' Use of Overstatement and Hyperbole; Baker Publishing House, Grand Rapids, 1985.

[7] The *Didache*, VI, 1-2, p. 319 in APOSTOLIC FATHERS, Vol. 1; Trans. Kirsopp Lake, in the Loeb Classical Library, Harvard University Press, Cambridge, 1912.

[8] Cf. George A. Kennedy, CLASSICAL RHETORIC AND ITS CHRISTIAN SECULAR TRADITION IN ANCIENT AND MODERN TIMES; University of North Carolina Press, Chapel Hill, 1980, p. 92f. where the function of an exordium is described as making each listener well

disposed toward the speaker.

[9] Juvenal, *Satire* III, 60-64, quoted in Fatih Cimok, ANTIOCH ON THE ORONTES, op cit., p. 21.

[10] Ibid. On page 47 in the same volume is a picture of one of the famous mosaic floors of ancient Antioch and Daphne portraying a deformed young man with an enlarged, extended penis. The image is known as the "Lucky Hunchback."

[11] *The Didache,* VII:2-3, p. 321 in APOSTOLIC FATHERS I; Loeb Classical Library, trans. Kirsopp Lake, Harvard University Press, Cambridge, 1912.

[12] Contrast Mt. 18:21-22 with Lk. 17:4 noting the deletion, or omission, of all references to repenting in the *First* Gospel.

[13] Cf. Chap. Two, pages 38-39

[14] *The Didache,* VIII, 1, p. 321, in APOSTOLIC FATHERS I; op. cit.

[15] Cf. J. Andrew Overman, MATTHEW'S GOSPEL AND FORMATIVE JUDAISM: The Social World of the Matthean Community; Fortress Press, Minneapolis, 1990; also Anthony J. Saldarini, MATTHEW'S CHRISTIAN-JEWISH COMMUNITY; University of Chicago Press, Chicago and London, 1994.

Chapter 8

Living in the Presence

On the steep North slope of Mount Staurin is found the graceful outline of a female head, but with indistinct facial features, carved out of the sandstone facade. Nearby are vestiges of shrine niches. The sculpture is known as the Charonian and dated to prehistoric times making it already ancient when St. Paul visited Syrian Antioch in mid first century C.E.

According to local tradition, the portrait is that of a Syrian female deity commissioned at great expense by some forgotten king to assuage a plague threatening the community. However, the epidemic subsided before the work was completed so with the threat eliminated the goddess was economically left unfinished.

It makes one ask: Is faith really that ephemeral and deities that expendable?

At first glance, soteriology,[1] the study of God's plan for salvation, appears to play no major role in the First Gospel. For example, *Matthew*, the evangelist, pen-named Ben Grammateus, provides us with no equivalent to John 3:16. Neither is there anything like Ephesians 2:8: *"For by grace you have been saved through faith..."* Again, as previously observed, Jesus is never referred to as Savior, nor does the noun "salvation," σωτηρια, ever appear in the text. Also, while Jesus' pending passion and resurrection are predicted three times, 16:21, 20:17-19, 26:2, and the actual history of his crucifixion is graphically detailed, there is no explicit statement — much less a redactional one — associating the cross with any idea of salvific efficacy. Rather, it is presented only

183

as a symbol of responsible discipleship. As Jesus puts it in Mt. 16:25/Mk. 8:34: *"If any want to become my followers, let them deny themselves and take up their cross and follow me."* Significantly, too, Jesus' death as a saving event is never mentioned as an emphasis to be included in the disciples' missionary message. Rather, according to the commission given in 10:7-8, the disciples were only to *"proclaim the good news...Cure the sick, raise the dead, cleanse the lepers, cast out demons."* Contrast Paul's stance in I Cor. 2:2: *"For I decided to know nothing among you except Jesus Christ, and him crucified."* For Ben, then, Jesus' passion served more as an example of ethical commitment to be appreciated and imitated by Jesus' disciples, especially those now living in Antioch, than as a strictly and narrowly defined dimension in God's plan for the salvation of humankind.

In so saying, however, I certainly do not mean to imply that the salvific power of the cross is explicitly denied in the *First* Gospel, only that here, as we shall soon see, it does not receive the focus or emphasis characteristic of much of the rest of the New Testament.

Ben's distinctive use of terms usually considered soteriological is also revealing. *"Righteousness," δικαιοσυνη*, for example, is as much a favorite word of the evangelist as it was of Paul. It is employed seven times in this Gospel, all redactional, but, as noted in the previous chapter, it is a concept more appropriate to the discussion of ethics and sanctification in Matthew than to justification as in Paul's writings. It means "right living," or in 6:1 *"piety,"* instead of referring to a gracious forensic act of God whereby sinners are declared righteous, holy and sinless because of Jesus' substitutionary sacrifice. Cf. Romans 3:21-26.

Similarly, *"faith," πιστις*, as part of the triad, *"justice, mercy and faith"* in 23:23, tends to connote "faithfulness" in terms of obedience, trust, and consistent action rather than an intellectual or emotional belief in, or assent to, prescribed doctrine. The Greek verb "to save," σωζω, as used by our scribe, likewise often means to heal, cf. 9:21-22, or to rescue from physical danger, 8:25, rather than to free from the burden of sin or to gain the victory of eternal life. The *first* evangelist's concept of sin is correspondingly skewed. While he frequently employs the more general term for sins, αμαρτια, "missing the mark," his more characteristic, exclusive word is ανομια, "lawlessness," used in conjunction with verbs of "working" or "doing," 7:23, 13:41, 23:28, 24:12. Interestingly, he does not use αδικια, "unrighteousnesses," at all. Despite his emphasis upon the potential evils of motivation, thought and heart in the Sermon on the Mount, the author's natural inclination, thus, is to think of sin more in terms of actions and direct disobedience to divine law.

All things considered, then, it is very apparent that while the soteriological vocabularies of Mark, Luke, John, Paul or almost any other New Testament writer, when compared to that of Matthew, may appear quite similar, their connotations are, in fact, very different from each other. The *First* Gospel requires its own glossary.

But the situation must not be overstated. The *first* evangelist occasionally does allow some traditional soteriological terms and concepts of his peers to stand in the sense originally intended. In the Birth Narrative, for example, the messenger in Joseph's dream commands: *"...you are to name him Jesus, for he will save, σωσει, his people from their sins,"* 1:21.[2] In 20:28, *Matthew,* or Ben, quotes Mark 10:45 verbatim: *"The Son of Man came not to be served but to serve, and to give his life a ransom for many."* Similarly, in 26:28 he essentially copies Mark's rendition of Jesus' words instituting the Last Supper, Mk. 14:24: *"This is my blood of the covenant, which is poured out for* (peri, 'concerning' or 'on behalf of' rather than Mark's υπερ, 'in place of') *many*," but then adds purposefully, *"for the forgiveness of sins."* Obviously, as these borrowed passages indicate, the *first* evangelist at least had a knowledge of, if not a central commitment to, the Pauline concept of Jesus' sacrificial atonement of humankind.

That Ben Grammateus also envisioned a heavenly afterlife for those who *"have been trustworthy, πιστος, in a few things,"* can also be detected from Jesus' repeated verdict, found only in the Matthean version of the Parable of the Talents, Mt. 25:21 and 23/Luke 19:17,19: *"enter into the joy of your master."* In addition, there are several direct references to "eternal life," ζωην αιωνιον, e.g., in Mt. 19:16 and 29.

We may safely assume, therefore, that the evangelist was not fundamentally averse to the Pauline concepts of faith, grace, salvation, righteousness, redemption etc. These soteriological ideas had been disseminated and known already for the previous quarter century, especially around the larger, western, urbanized, Gentile environments within the Roman empire where Paul had been active, including, no doubt, also such a prominent eastern Roman center as Antioch-on-the-Orontes. The fact is, however, that our Antiochene scribe's view of God's plan for salvation simply had a different focus and orientation, as we shall outline later. In comparison with Paul's soteriological emphases, and in contrast to the author's own extensive moral interests, the *First* Gospel could conceivably be considered "salvation lite." When viewed in the sunshine of its distinctive integrity, however, we shall see that it makes its own significant contribution to a broadened understanding of all that the concept of salvation includes. We need to be very careful that we do not denigrate the *first* evangelist's ancient, Middle Eastern, Diaspora Jewish Christian perspectives because they happen not to match our own current, western and basically Protestant proclivities.

The First Evangelist's Soteriological Cosmos

Our Antiochene evangelist was a complex man, as discovered already in Chapter Four. Reared in a Jewish Christian home but educated in Greek schools, he incorporated the vital elements of two very different cultures, world views and spectra of values. To use Steven Runciman's term once again, *Matthew,* or Ben, was "apophatic" in orientation and practice when it came to defining religious truth. He was intensely serious, but not always totally consistent. What sometimes appears as ambivalence in his narrative may thus be one or the other side of his character or experience surfacing for the moment. His soteriological views illustrate the point.

Ben's traditional Jewish orientation is manifested in his preoccupation with the present world versus his comparative disinterest in the next. Cf. Ecclesiastes 9:1-10. Nothing is said of the afterlife, *Olam ha-Ba,* in the Torah. In the historical books of Kings and Chronicles, death is characterized only as sleeping with one's ancestors. Ideas of heaven, hell, angels, spirits and the possibility of resurrection apparently did not significantly enter Jewish religious thought until after contact with Zoroastrianism and other eastern religions in conjunction with the Babylonian Exile in the sixth century B.C.E.,[3] and then only minimally. Cf. Acts 23:8. Without the Christian acceptance of Jesus' resurrection there was little encouragement even within later Judaism to emphasize concepts of an afterlife. Although he clearly espoused the general Christian commitments to the existence of such eschatological dimensions as heaven and hell, the latter being repeatedly described in the *First* Gospel as a place where there shall be *"weeping and gnashing of teeth,"* 22:13, 24:51, 25:30, the *first* evangelist, nevertheless, seems to have remained true to his traditional Jewish frame of reference when speaking soteriologically. He much preferred to think of "salvation now" than "salvation later." Accordingly, on balance, references in the *First* Gospel to any eternal benefits accruing from confessions of faith in Christ are also few and far between. Cf. 19:28-29. Rather, the evangelist's basic attitude is perhaps best summarized in his own redactional comment in 6:34: *"So do not worry about tomorrow, for tomorrow will bring worries of its own. Today's trouble is enough for today."*

Hints of this orientation favoring the present were detectable already in our scribe's numerous, though minor, time conscious remarks discussed in Chapter Three. Similarly, as in Chapter Four, above, he employs rhetorical strategies which tend to involve himself and his immediate community directly in the life and message of Jesus. All time is collapsed. Then is now, and for all practical purposes, so is the future. The pervasive emphasis on moral living in the Sermon on the Mount and elsewhere is also clearly oriented toward life in the present. Similarly, the miracle stories which the redactor marshals in chapters 8 and 9 focus on the common vicissitudes of every day life — leprosy, paralysis, fever, storm, demonic possession, menstrual hemorrhaging and death. The eternal dimensions of the after-life, on the other hand, are usually portrayed only metaphorically. Hell, thus, is described as a place where there is *"weeping and gnashing of teeth,"* while heaven is envisaged simply as entering *"into the joy of your Master."*

There is a clever and very revealing — but often misunderstood — double entendre devised by the evangelist between 3:2 and 4:17, illustrating his temporal orientation. The very same words are used in both places: *"Repent, for the kingdom of heaven has come near,"* but the statements are not precise equivalents as though Jesus was content to begin precisely where John the Baptist had left off. What needs to be observed is that the speakers are different, John the Baptist in 3:2 and Jesus in 4:17. Furthermore, the Greek word translated *"has come near,"* ηγγικεν, can mean either "has drawn near" or simply "has come." In the earlier instance, where John, the "way-preparer," 3:3, is speaking, therefore, the first meaning announcing that the kingdom is approaching is appropriate. When Jesus, the long awaited Messiah, speaks in 4:17, however, the second definition, denoting that the kingdom has effectively arrived, is the more apropos.

That such is the intention can be demonstrated by noting the subsequent encounter between John the Baptist and Jesus in 11:2-6. There John, through his disciples, asks Jesus *"Are you the one who is to come, or are we to wait for another?"* Jesus' affirmative reply is in the form of a confirming list of evidences: *"the blind receive their sight, the lame walk, the lepers are cleansed,"* etc. In other words, the kingdom is definitely here, not just promised, or partially inaugurated, but proleptically present with all of its physical manifestations already visible though not yet universally experienced.

Note, too, the consistent use of present and aorist verbs, where the future tense may have been expected, when speaking of the kingdom of heaven. For example, while most of the Beatitudes promise future blessings, the first and eighth declare: *"...for theirs is* (εστιν, present tense) *the kingdom of heaven,"* 5:3 and 10. Likewise, 12:28 announces: *"But if it is by the Holy Spirit that I cast out demons, then the kingdom of God has come* (εφθασεν, aorist) *to you."*

This perspective whereby the kingdom of heaven is seen primarily as a present reality, unfortunately, is often misinterpreted because of a deeply ingrained desire on the part of most contemporary exegetes, lay and professional, to understand the term "heaven" exclusively in a transcendent, eschatological sense, that is, as referring to the perfect consummation of human hopes to be experienced like some ethereal Valhalla only in the afterlife. As just discussed, however, we have found the phrase "kingdom of heaven," or literally, "heavens," in the plural, to be descriptive of the spiritual realm generally in

189

the *First* Gospel, as a dimension existing already in the present as well as in the future. As Jesus, by Ben's redaction, concludes his discussion of the sin against the Holy Spirit in 12:32: *"Whoever speaks a word against the Son of Man will be forgiven, but whoever speaks against the Holy Spirit will not be forgiven, either in this age or in the age to come."* Clearly, the *first* evangelist's soteriological cosmos is anchored primarily, though not exclusively, in the present.

Further clarification of this favorite redactional term, "kingdom of heaven(s)," will follow in Chapter Nine of this book.

First Gospel Soteriology

Now we are better prepared to appreciate the author's climactic soteriological contribution, his final answer to the needs of his Christian community and the world. It is Jesus, the ever-present Christ, Emmanuel, God with us, the living Presence! This is the concluding, ultimate promise of the entire *First* Gospel: *"Remember, I am with you always, to the end of the age."* Here is Jesus' supreme legacy given to humankind: Himself! He is the healer, the provider, the source of all joy and hope. He is here to make his disciples' worship efficacious, to authenticate their prayers, to empower their witness, to stiffen their resistance, to enable them to cope with all of life's vicissitudes. He defines who they authentically are. These are the benefits which constituted salvation in the mind of the evangelist.

This, then, is immanent, rather than eschatological, soteriology. It is rooted in time. It is practical, existential, holistic. Ben, the scribe, doesn't quibble over Systematic theological distinctions. Sickness is as much of an evil to overcome as sin, and Jesus is present to heal, σωζω, both. Similarly, Jesus triumphs equally over danger, despair and death. Ethics is but the actualization of confession. Faith and faithfulness, belief and consistent action are only different cuts from the same piece of cloth. Christ is not just a Christological title to confess, but a living example to follow, 16:25, a friend to rely on, 11:28-30, and an incarnate Son of God to worship, 14:33.

Matthean soteriology, consistent with the history of the Antiochene church, is also inclusive, universalistic.[4] It was here in Antioch that disciples, including Gentiles, were first called Christians. Such openness especially to Gentiles is another of the *First* Gospel's continuing themes. Immediately after the list of Jesus' Jewish progenitors in chap. 1 comes the story of the adoration of the Gentile Wise Men. The quote in 4:15 focuses on *"...the Galilee of the Gentiles."* Along the way we are introduced to a Roman centurion, 8:5f., a Canaanite woman from the district of Tyre and Sidon, 15:21-28,[5] and in 27:54 not only to a second centurion but, as the *first* evangelist expands redactionally, also *"those with him"* who joined in his bold confession beneath the cross of Jesus as the Son of God.

The Mission Sermon in ch. 10, as it were, traces this transition from Jewish to Gentile audiences, beginning with Jesus' charge to his disciples to go only *"to the lost sheep of Israel"* in 10:6, but immediately thereafter acknowledging in a kind of *post eventu* prophecy that they will soon also be brought before governors and kings as *"a testimony to them and to the Gentiles,"* 10:18. By the time the *First* Gospel was composed in the ninth decade of the first century, C.E. such predicted confrontations with Gentile authorities were already old news. Witness the recorded trials of Paul and Peter in conjunction with the burning of Rome twenty years earlier.[6] The change in focus from Jew to Gentile is made explicit in another *post eventu* prediction in 21:43 where Jesus announces to the chief priests and elders: *"Therefore I tell you, the kingdom of God will be taken away from you and given to a people,*

191

τα εθνει, *that produces the fruits of the kingdom."* In 24:14, the universal mission is listed as one of the signs of the last times: *"And this good news of the kingdom will be proclaimed throughout the world, as a testimony to all nations, and then the end will come."* Finally, of course, we hear the climactic call in 28:19: *"Go therefore and make disciples of all nations..."* These few words have given the entire statement of Jesus its title, the Great Commission. The world has not been devoid of Christian missionaries since the day the evangelist first penned these lines. But note, disappeared now is our scribe's apparent early Jewish particularism, replaced by his later commitment to Greek, and now Christian, universalism. God's benefaction is available to all.

Such, then, was the nature and scope of soteriology in the *First* Gospel. It was contained and articulated in what *Matthew,* alias Ben Grammateus, appropriately, chose to characterize as *"the gospel of the kingdom,"* 4:23, 9:35, 24:14. It details the good news of what life in the present is like when lived under the rule and in the Presence of Jesus, the Christ. That Presence is reified in sacraments, baptism and the Eucharist. There the living Christ is actualized, made tangible, visible and even savory in the living water, the bread and the wine. As the evangelist makes explicit, 26:28, the Eucharist offers *"the forgiveness of sins"* while baptism brings one into personal and individual fellowship with the Father, Son and Holy Spirit, 28:19. In short, this Gospel is nothing if not practical. Here is a marriage of ethics and evangelism, faith and faithfulness, sanctification and justification, particularism and universalism, the present and the Presence.

Matthew, alias Ben Grammateus, Paul and Barnabas

Saint Paul, as the father of the dominant brand of Christian soteriology, would undoubtedly have had trouble with some aspects of the *first* evangelist's version of the gospel. We can imagine that he would have seen this *"gospel of the kingdom"* as a distraction, favoring a more direct and personal gospel of Jesus Christ; He might have adjudged Ben's temporal interests as majoring in the ephemeral to the neglect of the eternal verities; He would have preferred that Ben be more discreet in sanitizing the scandal of the cross, in distinguishing between faith and works, in promoting love rather than obedience to Jesus' commands or personal example as the motivation for proper Christian behavior. Yet, on the other hand, no doubt Paul would have proudly seconded our Antiochene scribe's commitment to a universal mission and his resistance to the ethnocentric machinations of the Scribes and Pharisees. He would have appreciated all of the evangelist's characterizations of Jesus as the Christ and would have concurred with his view of the sacraments.

Perhaps it is fair to assume that Ben while not opposed to Paul, was more likely a spiritual heir and theological disciple of Barnabas, open to traditional Jewish Christian perspectives while still committed to a universal mission. Remembering that Barnabas was the founding and more permanent father of the Christian community at Antioch according to Acts 11, and also that he was the one who sided with Peter and the representatives of James, the first bishop of Jerusalem, in the famous altercation recounted in Galatians 2:11ff., we probably should not find Ben's soteriological stance, as that of an Antiochene scribe, at all surprising.

My own evaluation of this down-to-earth "gospel," however, is perhaps even a bit more prosaic. What it may have lacked in soteriological sophistication it compensated for in practicality. While it may not have plumbed the depths of eternal truth to the degree that Paul's theology did, it certainly met people right where they lived, and hurt, and hoped.

193

Perhaps his distinctions between ethics and faith were not sharply enough drawn, but certainly no one can accuse the *first* evangelist of espousing "cheap grace." It was a social gospel, long on social justice, but simultaneously promising an honest and exciting transfiguration of every-day life with Christ present. Yes, the evangelist's supposed theological naiveté as seen in hindsight may have contributed to the furious, debilitating, conciliar debates over the person, nature and status of Jesus within the church in succeeding centuries, but no one had a more personal relationship with his Lord than did this *"scribe trained for the kingdom,* in his own time and manner.

One thing seems clear. Some where, some time, some how this anonymous evangelist, pen-named Ben Grammateus, must have personally experienced the living, ever-present Christ. Jesus may not have loomed large in his thinking as "Savior," but he certainly did as "Lord," as the "Messiah/Christ," and as the "Son of God" who gave his life integrity, strength and hope. Like a first century Lew Wallace, author of BEN HUR, this Ben, too, had found himself defined by Jesus, energized and captivated by him, his teaching and his example. No one could have written a gospel with such winsome allegiance to his Lord, such passion for his community or such profound commitment to kerygmatic articulation if this were not true.

Chapter 8 Endnotes

[1] For more background reading, see Mark Allan Powell, GOD WITH US: A Pastoral Theology of Matthew's Gospel; Fortress Press, Minneapolis, 1995, especially the first chapter on "Mission," pp. 1-27.

[2] Ibid., p. 6. Powell's attempt to make this Pauline soteriological definition operative wherever the name Jesus is employed throughout the *First* Gospel, however, undoubtedly goes too far. "Jesus" is never used confessionally as a replacement for "Savior."

[3] Some Jewish commentators speculate that the reason why concerns re the afterlife did not appear earlier in Hebrew literature lay in the Jewish reaction to the ancient Egyptian preoccupation with death and immortality as experienced during the Jewish exile in Egypt in the 13th or 12th centuries B.C.E. Cf. *Afterlife* in the ENCYCLOPEDIA JUDAICA, Vol. 2; Keter Publishing, Jerusalem, n.d., pp. 337-339. Also Rabbi Joseph Telushkin, JEWISH LITERACY; William Morrow and Company, Inc., New York, 1991, pp. 107, 132, 547- 8.

[4] Cf. Guido Tisera, UNIVERSALISM ACCORDING TO THE GOSPEL OF MATTHEW; Peter Lang, Frankfurt am Main, Berlin, Bern, New York, Paris, Wien, 1993.

[5] Cf. John P. Meier, *"The Canaanite Woman in Matthew 15:21-28 and the Problem of World Religions, "* in THE MISSION OF CHRIST AND HIS CHURCH; Micael Glazier, Inc., Wilmington, Delaware, 1990, pp. 209-216.

[6] Cf. Eusebius Pamphilus, ECCLESIASTICAL HISTORY; Baker Book House, Grand Rapids, Michigan, 1955, p. 79f.

Chapter 9

The Kingdom of Heaven(s), What the Church is Really Like[1]

Although it serves as a museum today, Istanbul's celebrated Hagia Sophia annually hosts hundreds of thousands of tourists who want to remember it as one of the world's most imposing religious shrines. They are never disappointed. From the outside its cascading domes appear to billow like the clouds of heaven. From the inside its soaring arches reach for the circle of the sky. Each transept echoes with the chants of history, mystery and tradition. And here and there an ancient fresco peers through worn paint to say: "This is still a holy place."

One of the *First* Gospel's major surprises is its threefold use of *"church,"* εκκλησια, in 16:18 and 18:17a&b. None of the other canonical Gospels employs the term. They rather speak of the coming of the *Kingdom of God*, i.e., a future, eschatological realm under the complete and benevolent control of God that will transcend the imminent destruction of the world, Mk. 1:15, Lk. 4:43, Jn 3:3 *et al.* The appearance here in Matthew of *"church,"* therefore, strikes the reader as an obvious anachronism, suggesting a concept of an advanced type of temporal religious organization that Jesus would not have entertained during his lifetime. It is another example of Matthean transparency.

197

This unexpected discovery, still purportedly within the parameters of Jesus' earthly ministry, has had another side effect. It has aroused a particular interest among scholars in Matthean ecclesiology, the study of the nature of the church in the *First* Gospel. When, why and how did the concept of such a continuing temporal, spiritual fellowship develop? Is the religious community, envisioned here, what we would call the "church militant" or the "church triumphant," the "visible" or the "invisible" church? Is it local or universal, democratically or hierarchically structured? And what is different, or unique, about its doctrines and values, its perspectives or procedures compared with other non-Christian religious expressions? All of these questions are of great interest to anyone involved in religious institutions of every kind even today. Imagine their supreme cogency to those early *"disciples"* living in Antioch, Syria, in those embryonic years of the Christian era when our Antiochene scribe, known to us as Ben Grammateus, originally penned this *First* Gospel.

The Kingdom of Heaven(s)

However, we dare not permit the novelty of this *"church"* anachronism here to blind us to the presence of another even more significant ecclesiological phrase, *"the kingdom of heaven(s),"* η βασιλεια των ουρανων, found no less than thirty-two times in Matthew, and conspicuously only here in all of the Bible. Its literary cousin, *"the kingdom of God,"* η βασιλεια του θεου, employed nearly sixty times throughout the rest of the New Testament, is also found here, but only on four or five occasions. Obviously, then, the *"kingdom of heaven,"* or more literally, *"heavens,"* was the evangelist's favorite expression of the two, prompting the very natural and legitimate questions: Why? Were not the two phrases synonymous? And what, if anything, was the significance of the curious plural form, *"heavens?"* We will need to devote considerable time and space to an attempt to answer these queries before we will be in a position to determine the role this important concept plays in Ben's overall ecclesiology. The near consensus explanation of the plural *"heavens"* given by scholars who think of the First Gospel as essentially Jewish in background and orientation is that the term translates the Hebrew plural collective, הַשָּׁמַיִם, "heavens," and is, therefore, merely a pious circumlocution for "God," reflecting the editor's Jewish aversion to the public pronouncement of the divine name.[2] While this answer seems plausible enough, it is undoubtedly too facile since the editor not only actually uses the phrase, *"the kingdom of God,"* several times but even adds it redactionally at least twice, 21:31 and 43. So much then for the aversion theory. Evidently, Ben, the evangelist, was comfortable enough with it, too.

The answer we suggested earlier, in Chapter Five, pp. 122-123, therefore, comports to the situation at least as well. Accordingly, *Matthew,* or Ben, was reflecting current Greek cosmology which, not too unlike that of the Jews, posited the existence of numerous levels of heavens above the earth governed by a series of planetary deities and demiurges. It even appears likely that some aspects of Plato's Cave analogy were included here whereby it was believed that the paradigms of all that is real and true exist only in the heavens reducing all that we see and experience on earth and in time as simply their diminished reflections. The plural phrase, *"...of the heavens,"* then, was not a circumlocution for "God," one and supreme, but implied more generally the larger realms of all deities and spirits - in other words, the spiritual dimension as a whole. Here the God of the Christians along with his angels are depicted as playing an important, but not necessarily an exclusive role.

That such was the popular perception is confirmed by a nearly contemporaneous statement that Ignatius, the Bishop of Antioch, made in his letter to the Smyrneans, 6:1:

> "Let no one be deceived: even heavenly powers and the glory of angels and the rulers, both visible and invisible, if they do not believe in the blood of Christ, are also subject to judgment."[3]

The *"heavens,"* then, for the *first* evangelist, constituted a multi-faceted dimension, including a pantheon of both good and evil powers, with serious implications for the spiritual and physical health of the world in the present as well as in the future. It is not a wholly eschatological idea, nor is it exclusively Christian, but it allows for more secular latitude than the phrase *"kingdom of God,"* with its distinctively Christian connotations, would permit. Perhaps it was for this reason, to broaden the concept, that our scribe evangelist in the vast majority of cases chose not to retain the term, *"kingdom of God,"* even when he found it in his sources, Mark and Q. Rather, as we shall see, he preferred to reserve it to describe only more specific circumstances in his text, as we shall learn later.

The Kingdom Parables Sermon, Matthew 13

It should not surprise us, therefore, to find this same breadth of meaning implied by the term *"kingdom of heaven(s)"* reflected and emphasized in the descriptive "Kingdom Parables Sermon" of Matthew 13. Here we find a series of seven analogies each beginning with the phrase: *"the kingdom of heaven(s) is like..."*

The Parable of the Sower, Mt. 13:1-9, 18-23/Mk. 4:1-9, 13-20, heads the list. Here the spiritual domain is compared to the different kinds of soils in which a farmer sows his seed,

13:1-9. Some soils are non-productive — too dry, heavily traveled, rocky or lacking in depth. Yet, there is also some good ground and its production is super-abundant. As Jesus then goes on to explain:

> *"When anyone hears the word of the kingdom and does not understand it, the evil one comes and snatches away what is sown in the heart...But as for what was sown on good soil, this is the one who hears the word and understands it, who indeed bears fruit and yields, in one case a hundredfold, in another sixty, and in another thirty,"* 13:18-23.

The kingdom of heaven(s), accordingly, is not the quintessence of perfection, as we normally think of heaven, but here the spiritual realm co-exists with the temporal, the evil with the good, the present and the future, with great potential for both benefit and harm. Ultimately, at the harvest, the good will triumph magnificently. In the meantime, however, Ben's readers and audience should heed the warnings contained in the quotation from Isaiah 6:9-10, recorded in Mt.13:14-17, about Israel's dull hearts and deaf ears, while simultaneously appreciating the advantages they enjoy in being able to hear and see all that God has already done for them.

The Parable, or allegory, of the Weeds and Wheat, which follows immediately in 13:24-30, is very similar to its predecessor, although more eschatologically oriented. Again, *the kingdom of heaven(s)* is compared to a householder who plants his field with good seed, but an enemy comes and sows weeds among the wheat. When the householder's servants see what has happened they want to clean out the weeds, but wisely the landowner counsels them to permit the unwelcome sprouts to grow unhindered lest in uprooting them some of the wheat is lost as well. Then, as with the previous parable, Jesus again identifies the cast of the allegory for the benefit of his disciples:

"The one who sows the good seed is the Son of Man; the field is the world, and the good seed are the children of the kingdom; the weeds are the children of the evil one, and the enemy who sowed them is the devil: the harvest is the end of the age, and the reapers are angels," 13:37-39.

Obviously, in *the kingdom of heaven(s)* concern for the preservation of the good takes precedence even over worry about the threatening presence of evil.

This parable, found only in the *First* Gospel, illustrates the vulnerability of life in *the kingdom of heaven(s)*. Here in time the kingdom is under attack by evil and there is nothing conclusive that anyone can do about it. But God is the great adjudicator. Ultimately he will send his angels to separate the wheat and the weeds, the righteous from the evildoers. The latter will be cast into the furnace of fire while the former *"will shine like the sun in the kingdom of their Father,"* 13:43. Here the kingdom is depicted in full dimension, both ephemeral and eternal, dysfunctional and functional, contaminated and purified.

The additional five parables comprising the sermon, three unique to Matthew and one each taken from Mark and Q, all highlight different aspects of *the kingdom of heaven(s)*.

The Parable of the Mustard Seed, Mt.13:31-32/Mk. 4:30-32, focuses on the potential for growth inherent in the kingdom. Now apparently as small and fragile as a mustard seed, it can mature into a tree so large that *"the birds of the air come and make nests in its branches."* In true scribal style, Ben doesn't mind a little exaggeration if it strengthens his point, and no doubt the encouragement the analogy provided

202

was well received by his numerically weak audience.

The Parable of the Leaven, 13:33/Lk. 13:20-21, similarly illustrates the tremendous potential for influencing the larger society. Size is not the determinant of success in *the kingdom of the heavens*, but the depth of conviction is. The kingdom's strategy entails permeation, like yeast in a loaf of dough, rather than subjugation.

The fact that participation in the kingdom is of such great value as to be worth any cost or sacrifice is the point made in the twin parables of the Hidden Treasure and the Pearl of Great Price, Mt. 13:44-46. It is upon such precious spiritual values as righteousness, forgiveness, mercy and the living presence of the Son of God that the kingdom's economy is based.

The opposite question of what becomes of the evil dimension still associated with life in the spiritual realm is portrayed in the Parable of the Net, 13:47-50. At the end of time, the angels of God will survey the catch, separating the good fish from the bad, the *"righteous"* from the *"evil,"* casting the latter into a furnace of fire where *"there shall be weeping and gnashing of teeth,"* the evangelist's favorite metaphor for Hades or hell, 8:12, 13:42 & 50, 22:13, 24:51, 25:30.

Before leaving this Kingdom Parables Sermon, one nagging question remains: Why did the editor reject and omit Mark's winsome Parable of the Seed Growing Secretly, Mk. 4:26-29? It would appear to have been ready-made for inclusion in the sermon. The answer, undoubtedly, lies in that parable's very secrecy motif itself. Accordingly, the seed is portrayed as growing unnoticed, automatically, without human involvement, until ready for God's harvest. What we have already learned, however, is that *Matthew,* or Ben, consistently resists any suggestion that disciples are ever free of responsibility. *The kingdom of heaven(s)* is replete with challenge, temptation and danger. Persistent awareness and preparedness are therefore required of every disciple.

These seven parables comprising this third sermon, then, are foundational for the readers' understanding of *the kingdom of heaven(s)* concept in this *First* Gospel. Unfortunately, they do not provide us with as neat, complete, coherent or systematic definition of *the kingdom of heaven(s)* as we may desire, but taken together they do present us with a gallery of individual snapshots which portray the major features and contours of that spiritual realm. *The kingdom of heaven(s),* as Ben employs the term, therefore, is a very plastic concept capable of encompassing the full panorama of spiritual experience, the good and the evil, the present and the future, the visible and the invisible. We are alerted to the kingdom's incredible value and potential, but also warned of its continuing vulnerability and possibility for immeasurable loss. The impression is given that while God, the Father, as well as the Son of Man, are active participants in the kingdom their power and authority are not yet dominant, absolute or exclusive, awaiting the final assize.

Post-Sermon References

This Parables Sermon in chapter 13, however, does not exhaust the concept of *the kingdom of heaven(s)* in the *First* Gospel. In addition, we find several more parables as the narrative proceeds. The "Church Sermon" in chapter 18, for example, concludes with the Parable of the Unforgiving Servant, 18:23-35, found only there in the New Testament. In its context, immediately following Peter's question about how often one should forgive a sinning brother, 18:21-22, this parable characterizes the kingdom as a place, or situation, where a spirit of unconditional forgiveness toward others is the prescribed norm. As God has forgiven us our huge debt of sin toward him, so we must be ready also to excuse the comparatively smaller offenses committed against us by our spiritual brethren. The final warning in 18:35 is unavoidably straight forward: *"So my heavenly Father will also do to every one of you (pl.), if you do not forgive your brother or sister from your heart."*

Faith, too, is a prerequisite for recognition in the kingdom, particularly a loving, trusting, childlike faith. As Jesus says of little children in 19:14: *"...it is to such as these that the kingdom of heaven belongs."* On the contrary, *"...it will be hard for a rich man to enter the kingdom of heaven,"* 19:23. Temporal distractions, so destructive of faith, are incompatible with life in the kingdom from the Christian perspective.

The Parable of the Laborers in the Vineyard, 20:1-16, again illustrates the unique form of inverted ethics which characterizes the kingdom. Here generosity triumphs over ordinary contractual fairness. No one should complain if the householder chooses to reward the late-comers into his vineyard/kingdom on the same level as those who have worked long through the heat of the day. This is probably as close to the Pauline concept of grace as our scribe/author ever gets. The result is also a predicted reversal in status that will obtain in the kingdom: *"So the last will be first, and the first will be last,"* v. 16.

The soteriological/eschatological question of who is eligible for reception into *the kingdom of heaven(s)* is the point of the Parable of the Wedding Feast in 22:1-14. This double analogy is so thoroughly edited by *Matthew,* or Ben, that its relationship with the similar Parable of the Great Supper in Q, Luke 14:15-24, is hard to determine. The comparison is nevertheless revealing. In brief, anyone sensitively reading or hearing the *first* evangelist's scenario cannot help but recognize that it reflects historical events, especially the destruction of Jerusalem, noting that *"the king was enraged. He sent his troops, destroyed those murderers, and burned their city," v. 7.* Also the Antiochene experience where Gentiles were first welcomed into the Christian community, as outlined in Acts 11, is only slightly veiled in Jesus' command to his messengers to go beyond the normal boundaries, διεξοδος,[4] of Israel to invite the good and the bad to the wedding feast. Perhaps, most important, however, is the extraordinary added account of the disrespectful and improperly clothed guest, found only in the *First* Gospel, 22:11-16. Even though invited in to the wedding feast, this unprepared gate-crasher is not allowed to remain, thus reminding the readers and audience of this *First* Gospel that membership in the kingdom is a privilege to be prized and not a reward to be taken for granted or assumed automatic. Here is the evangelist's replacement for Mark's Seed Growing Secretly parable. As important as the evangelist insists righteous living is, ultimately, everything depends upon God's sovereign decision. *"For many are called, but few are chosen,"* v. 14. As with the unwelcome guest at the king's wedding feast, therefore, a state of constant preparedness is required of all God's people in the kingdom of heaven(s) and, we would assume, in the church as well.

The final kingdom parable is that of the Wise and Foolish Virgins in 25: 1-13. It is unique to the *First* Gospel, but it plays an important role in the Eschatological Sermon, chapters 23-25. Its lesson is the need for constant vigilance in spite of the delay of the *parousia,* i.e., the coming of the Son of Man. *"Keep awake, therefore, for you know neither the day nor the hour,"* v. 13.

The progression in thought from the kingdom parables in the Parables Sermon, chapter 13, to those in succeeding chapters is quite evident. The earlier series of seven were of a more general nature, discussing the kingdom's value and potential both for growth and concurrent difficulty. The four subsequent examples, consistent with their topical locations, describe in more detail the definitive nature of the kingdom. For a Christian it is characterized by faith and an unqualified spirit of forgiveness. Eligibility for participation is ultimately based upon God's goodness, αγαθος, 20:15, and election, εκλεκτοι, 22:14, rather than on traditional prerogatives of ethnic privilege or moral superiority. Finally, *the kingdom of heaven(s)* has a future, eschatological dimension, a day of judgment, and a certain, though delayed, coming of the Son of Man.

We are now ready to conclude: When all of these kingdom clues are viewed *en masse*, a broad outline of one of the *first* evangelist's most important and all-encompassing concepts emerges. *The kingdom of heaven(s)* is the dominant dimension in the author's cosmology — inclusive, unlimited, timeless, inescapable, the one true reality. It is the arena of all spiritual activity. It is in this present world, co-existing with the visible kingdoms of this world, but having its own brand of ethics, economy, citizenship and politics. Here, from the Christian's perspective, God the Father is the prime actor, but by no means the only one. The devil and his children, 13:37-39, present a continuing threat. The Son of Man, with his disciple/seed, is here as well, but the impression is left that he has not yet claimed his rightful place with all authority at the Father's right hand. A time of harvest, a day of judgment, and the coming of the Son of Man await in the future. Only then will the good be separated from the bad. Those who have been invited, who have responded to the gospel of the kingdom, who have been faithful, forgiving, understanding, prepared and chosen will be welcomed into the final, great and eternal wedding feast with God, while the bad, the evil, the children of the devil, will be thrown into *"the furnace of fire where there will be weeping and gnashing of teeth."*

The Kingdom of God

In contrast to this full-orbed description of *the kingdom of heaven(s),* we now turn to the obviously related, but clearly dependent concept of the *kingdom of God.*

The four or five instances in Matthew of *the kingdom of God,"* η βασιλεια του θεου, 6:33(?), 12:28, 19:24, 21:31 and 43, undoubtedly constitute too small a sample to be definitive about the concept's parameters, but perhaps it is safe to say that the term as nuanced here envisions only *the kingdom of heaven(s)* in its ideal state, more eschatologically oriented, focusing on the perspective of its exclusivity, under the ultimate complete control of the Father.

Although resting on unsure text-critical grounds, the NRSV translates 6:33: *"But strive first for the kingdom of God and his righteousness, and all these things will be given to you as well."* Divine righteousness, then, is clearly thought of as an attribute of this *kingdom of God.*

In connection with the healing of a demoniac in Mt. 12:28/ Lk. 11:20, Jesus declares pointedly: *"But if it is by the Spirit of God that I cast out demons, then the kingdom of God has come to you."* In contra-distinction from *the kingdom of heaven(s)* where Satan is still active, here in *the kingdom of God* the Spirit of God conquers over the demons and casts them out.

The close relationship of both terms, *the kingdom of God* and *the kingdom of heaven(s),* is clearly demonstrated in Jesus' repetitive words in 19:23-24/Lk. 12:24-25: *"Truly I tell you, it will be hard for a rich man to enter the kingdom of heaven. Again I tell you, it is easier for a camel to go through the eye of a needle than for someone who is rich to enter the kingdom of God."* The difference between the two terms, then, must be one of scope, rather than of kind. They are synonyms, but not equivalents. The one is a comparative, the other a superlative.

Ben Grammateus's particular conviction that one's actual faithful performance of God's will, even if reluctant, qualifies him for the kingdom before good intentions or ethnic heritage is illustrated in the Parable of the Two Sons, 21:28-32. Here, one son at first refuses his father's command, but later obeys, while the second son does just the opposite. Jesus' final verdict, justifying the first son, is expressed loud and clear in his words addressed to the chief priests and elders: *"Truly I tell you, the tax collectors and the prostitutes are going into the kingdom of God ahead of you."* *The kingdom of God,* therefore, is the domain of final reward for all the truly obedient whatever their race, occupation or pedigree.

Finally, in one of the most cutting and crucial redactional passages in the *First* Gospel, 21:43, Jesus is again heard to say to those same Jewish leaders: *"Therefore I tell you, the kingdom of God will be taken away from you and given to a people, ται εθνει, that produces the fruits of the kingdom."* The Jews, then, have no preemptive claim on *the kingdom of God.* It is the preserve, rather, of all those who are faithfully productive of good deeds.

There are a couple of other kingdom references which though general in nature seem to fit into the kingdom of God category. In Mt. 26:29, for example, the evangelist replaces Mark's *"kingdom of God,"* Mk. 14:25, with *"the kingdom of my Father."* (Cf. also Mt. 13:43) Similarly, in Mt. 20:21, the mother of James and John requests: *"Declare that these two sons of mine will sit, one at your right hand and one at your left, in your kingdom."* The parallel statement in Mark 10:37 had read: *"...in your glory."* In response, Jesus obediently demurs, deferring to his Father as the final arbiter in matters pertaining to the kingdom: *"...to sit at my right hand and at my left this is not mine to grant, but it is for those for whom it has been prepared by my Father,"* Mt. 20:23.

While the concepts expressed in the terms *"kingdom of heaven(s)"* and *"kingdom of God,"* thus overlap in the *First* Gospel, the latter's scope appears to be narrower, referring only to the spiritual realm or dimension in its eschatologically perfected state where God the Father's absolute rule is recognized as the prevailing condition.

The Church

We return now to the term *"church," εκκλησια*. It appears only three times in Mt. 16:18, 18:17a and b, constituting an even smaller sample than *"kingdom of God"* on which to base a coherent and comprehensive definition. Our earlier insights detecting the redactor's transparent methods of addressing his own Antiochene congregation while simultaneously recounting the story of Jesus and the first disciples, however, suggest that the concept of church here is, in fact and in practice, much broader than it would at first appear, actually mirroring in large measure the dimensions and character of the evangelist's *kingdom of heaven(s)*. If *the kingdom of heaven(s)* is the movement, the *church* is its earthly manifestation. If the kingdom is the vibrant organism, the *church* is the visible organization. Conversely, if the *church* is the model then *the kingdom of heaven(s)* is its larger silhouette on the backdrop of history, enabling Ben's insecure Christian community to step back, as it were, and assess its situation as displayed in full panorama before it. In brief, *the kingdom of heaven(s)* is the *church* writ large.

The 18:17 passage undoubtedly presents the clearest picture of what is meant fundamentally by *"church"* in Matthew: *"If the member, αδελφος, refuses to listen to them, tell it to the church; and if the member, αδελφος, refuses to listen even to the church, let such a one be to you as a Gentile and a tax collector."* Here the *church* is obviously the local community, or congregation, consisting of responsible members

— and at least one who is less so. Church discipline on the local level is therefore required to maintain the brotherhood. Note the double use of "brother," αδελφος, in a religious sense in this one verse. The overall portrait of the *church,* then, is of a non-stratified fellowship rather than a hierarchy. There will be more on this subject later.

However, on the single other occasion where *"church"* is employed, the much discussed dictum of Jesus to Peter in 16:18: *"You are Peter, and upon this rock I will build my church,"* the closing expression, *"my church,"* suggests a much broader and elevated ecclesiolgical concept. Here the scribe/author seems to be thinking of the *church* as universal and triumphant. The appointment of Peter with singular authority to bind and loose also indicates some consciousness of "office," if not monepiscopacy. As we shall see momentarily, however, the redactional nature and function of this entire passage, vv. 17-19, is suspect and must await further explication.

For now, then, we are left with the transparent outline of the Antiochene church as detectable in the only slightly veiled references to a variety of current community constituencies and problems. Several of these categories were identified earlier in our study, especially in Chapter Four.

"The crowds," 5:1, undoubtedly, constituted the largest, but least defined group in the Antiochene religious community. They were the omnipresent fickle and curious, but uncommitted masses who only eavesdropped on the Christian message and life. Occasionally, they could be impressed by Jesus' teachings, 7:28, 22:33, and at least once they became the object of Jesus' compassion, 15:32, but in the end they comprised the mobs that condemned him, 26:47

Most prominent in the *First* Gospel, of course, are the *"disciples,"* referring on occasion both to the original twelve companions of Jesus fifty years earlier and to the evangelist's

211

Christian contemporaries. With our stereophonic earphones, we hear the latter disciples addressed, for example, in the traditional words of Jesus, Mt. 16:24/Mk. 8:34/Lk. 9:23: *"If any want to become my followers, let them deny themselves and take up their cross and follow me."* The anachronistic *"cross"* reference here would certainly have been confusing, if not unintelligible, to Jesus' original disciples this far in advance of his crucifixion, but for Ben, the scribe, and his Christian contemporaries, living long after Christ's passion, it would have conjured up a wide range of thoughts and emotions encouraging dutiful behavior in compliance with Jesus' sacrificial example. *"Disciples"* in the *First* Gospel, thus, includes the broad sweep of Antiochene Christians — the devout and the deficient, the strong and weak, young and old, Jewish and Gentile, all members of the extended *collegia sodalicia* who regularly came together to pray the Lord's Prayer, 6:9-13, recite the Beatitudes, 5:3-10, celebrate the Eucharist, 26:26-29, and listen to the reading of the Scriptures, i.e. the Septuagint, or perhaps occasionally even Mark or this *First* Gospel.

Many of these disciples undoubtedly also comprised the company of those whom the author liked to call *"the righteous,"* οι δικαιοι, the equivalent of "saints." We first hear of them in 10:41b: *"Whoever welcomes a righteous person in the name of a righteous person will receive the reward of the righteous."* These are the heroes of faith, the dependably committed, the tried and true, the living and the dead, past, present and future. They are so inherently good they do not objectively even know what good is, 25:44. Ultimately, as Jesus, by redaction, concluded in his explanation of the Parable of the Weeds and Wheat: *"Then the righteous will shine like the sun in the kingdom of their Father,"* 13:43.

A third category of those internal to *Matthew's,* or Ben's, community, though certainly not an organized group, were the "little ones," οι μικροι. We meet them especially in the redacted fourth sermon, in chapter 18, addressing church community concerns. Here, although a child is held up as a model of exemplary faith, the term "little ones," vv. 6, 10, 14, seems to imply all who are inexperienced, new to the faith, uninstructed in the depth of Christian teaching, and therefore vulnerable, whatever their age. Something of our Antiochene scribe's empathetic personality is visible in his particular concern for these μικροι.

"Little ones," however, are not to be confused with "little faiths," ολιγαπιστοι, implying, perhaps, more of a negative condition than a category of discipleship. Although found in one Q passage, Mt. 6:30/Lk. 12:28, Matthew, alias Ben, is the only evangelist who employs the term programmatically to describe divine disappointment in lapses of trust among the disciples. Jesus accuses Peter of little faith when, intimidated by the wind, he fails to continue to walk on the water in 14:31. Similarly, all the disciples are called little-faiths when they fear for their lives in the midst of a storm on the Sea of Galilee even though Jesus is right there with them, 8:26. On another occasion, the first evangelist typically replaces Mark's characterization of the disciples as being without understanding by accusing them of little faith, Mt. 16:8/Mk. 8:17. Whether this substitution suggests more or less of a condemnation of the disciples than in Mark's Gospel may be debated.

There are also those who function negatively as "stumbling blocks," σκανδαλοι, in the local community. Ben Grammateus introduces his ecclesiological sermon with a warning about causing others to stumble into sin. In the Temple Tax account, 17:27, Jesus counsels Peter: "However, so that we do not give offense, σκανδαλισωμεν, to them..." Then, in 18:6, in the Ecclesiological Sermon proper, he picks up the theme again, warning: "If any one of you put a stumbling block, σκανδαλιση, before one of these little ones who

213

believe in me, it would be better for you if a great millstone were fastened around your neck and you were drowned in the depths of the sea." Clearly, "*stumbling blocks,*" causing others to sin, constitutes one of the evangelist's pet peeves. Even Peter is redactionally so designated in 16:23: "*Get behind me, Satan! You are a stumbling block, σκανδαλον, to me.*" Altogether, the term and its cognates are used nineteen times in the *First* Gospel.

"Doubters" are mentioned only twice, but under rather conspicuous circumstances. The great Peter is so designated in 14:31 after fearing the wind more than trusting Jesus. And then there is that very late, sore-thumb comment in 28:17 that even after the resurrection "*some doubted.*" Obviously, then as now, some people — the best among them — were hard to convince even of that which was good for them. Do I detect some frustration on the author's part?

"Straying sheep," i.e., delinquent members, unfortunately, comprise another dimension in the Antiochene church, as the Parable of the Lost Sheep, 18:10-14/Lk. 15:3-7, by way of our scribe's editing, testifies. Back-door losses are a common experience in all congregations, ancient and modern. Faith becomes routinized. Spiritual enthusiasm cools, drowned out by a myriad of lesser concerns. Apparently, in this Antiochene congregation, an additional contributing factor was the disappointing delay of the Christ's promised return, the problem addressed in the Parable of the Wise and Foolish Virgins, 25:1-13. Making matters even worse, was the apparent lack of concern over the plight of the straying on the part of the remaining disciples. Something needed to be done or said to revive their level of commitment.

A readiness to forgive, along with individual admonition, 18:15-18, were also urgent needs, especially in the case of sinning brothers. In 18:21-22, the writer places on Peter's lips the question which in Q was asked by Jesus: "*Lord, if another member of the church,* ο αδελφος μου, *sins against me, how often should I forgive? As many as seven times?"* Somewhat to our surprise, nothing is said here about the possibility of the sinning brother repenting, as in the parallel in Lk. 17: 4. Jesus' response, therefore, is unconditional: *"Not seven times, but, I tell you, seventy-seven times."*

The Parable of the Unforgiving Servant, 18:23-35, is then immediately introduced in support of Jesus' gracious dictum. Under threat of severe punishment, the heavenly Father insists that each disciple be prepared to forgive his sinning brother *"from your heart."*

Here is Ben Grammateus' counter-balance to his earlier emphasis on moral and ethical perfection, 5:48. Ultimately, external fear and force cannot insure compliance. Only sincere forgiveness can engender in the offender the kind of inner strength needed to fundamentally transform lives.

So far we have looked only at average lay constituents in the Antiochene community, especially those replete with frailty, insensitivity and sin. Apparently, the evangelist preferred to think of his congregation as consisting of such average people, that is, a fellowship of humble, compatible, interdependent brothers and sisters in the faith. At least, he objected to any protestations of special merit or privilege. In Jesus' words, coming from the redactor's pen:

> *"But you are not to be called rabbi, for you have one teacher, and you are all students. And call no one your father on earth, for you have one Father - the one in heaven. Nor are you to be called instructors, for you have one instructor, the Messiah. The greatest among you will be your servant. All who exalt themselves will be humbled, and all who humble themselves will be exalted,"* 23:8-12.

215

We must assume, then, that those persons in the *First Gospel* who fill roles which we might wish to call clerical were viewed only as functionaries without the accouterments of any special professional status, authority or privilege. *Matthew,* alias Ben Grammateus, accordingly thought of himself as a scribe *"trained for the kingdom,"* 13:52, as previously detailed in Chapter Four. But he was not alone or even special. There were other scribes in his community. As Jesus says by redaction in 23:34: *"I send you* (or perhaps better: *"I am sending you...) prophets, sages and scribes."*

Then, too, of course, there were Jewish scribes, advisors to the Pharisees and Sadducees. And as we might expect, there is also evidence of a particular animosity between these peer group rivals. In 7:29, the *first* evangelist writes disdainfully about *"their scribes."* Again, somewhat uncharacteristically, scribes are always mentioned first in Ben's tirade against the *"Scribes, Pharisees, hypocrites"* in chapter 23. Clearly, despite Ben's self deprecating comments, the scribal role was an influential though conflicted one in his religious community.

"Prophets," προφηται, were present as well although the author does not have much to say about them. The cryptic statement in 10:41: *"Whoever welcomes a prophet in the name of a prophet will receive a prophet's reward,"* suggests that they were legitimate itinerant preachers who deserved to be welcomed. We are prompted to think of Agabus, the prophet who came to Antioch from Jerusalem during the reign of Claudius according to Acts 11:27-28. Others, however, especially those sporting charismatic gifts like Apollonius of Tyana, (cf. p. 58 above) needed to be watched for as Jesus decries in 7:22: *"On that day many will say to me, 'Lord, Lord, did we not prophesy in your name, and cast out demons in your name, and do many deeds of power in your name?' Then I will declare to them, 'I never knew you; go away from*

me, you evil-doers.'" Obviously, prophets constituted a rather suspect group in our scribe's Antiochene community.

The *"sages,"* σοφοι, listed along with *"prophets"* and *"scribes"* as sent by Jesus in 23:34, are never elsewhere defined. Perhaps they functioned as advisors, or counselors, in response to the aggressive actions of the local Jewish Scribes and Pharisees. Their limited role, however, apparently merited no further comment.

The preceding list of persons and functionaries comprising the evangelist's congregation, with the possible exceptions of the *"righteous,"* all seem to be identified with some attendant problem — causing others to sin, sinning oneself, straying from the flock, lacking in faith, doubting, giving false witness, demonstrating insensitivity or just inexperience. From the author's perspective, at least, his community was in serious danger of losing its way, its identity and its integrity.

Three threatening circumstances appear to have outweighed all others, 1) a vacuum in church leadership, 2) the inroads of resurgent Judaism and 3) the delay of the *Parousia,* i.e., the expected coming of the Son of Man in triumph at the end of time.

This concluding concern will be reviewed in Chapter Eleven below. The second, regarding resurgent Judaism, is so pronounced that our Antiochene scribe cannot seem to get away from it and ends up spending an entire chapter, ch. 23, on its consideration. We will do the same in Chapter Ten of this book. The first issue, re church leadership, however, may well have been the most sensitive of all, requiring subtle diplomacy and indirect argumentation. We will deal with it here.

The Question of Church Leadership[5]
Peter is the pivotal figure in the evangelist's brief on the nature of leadership in the church. His role in the *First* Gospel

is remarkable. Next to Jesus himself, Peter is the most prominent individual in the narrative, appearing fifteen times, making him more significant than John the Baptist, Judas Iscariot or Pontius Pilate. No other disciple, with the dubious exception of Judas, ever speaks or initiates any action. Even the inner circle, familiar from Mark, including James and John and on one occasion Andrew, is seen here to gradually fade from view. Simultaneously, Peter's star is on the rise. He is systematically portrayed almost as Jesus' *alter ego.* They both walk on water, 14:28f., and are closely associated in the Temple Tax vignette where Jesus magnanimously tells Peter to pay the fee *"for you and me,"* 17:27 The alert reader has to wonder: "What's so special about Peter?"

Part of the answer seems to rest in the location of Peter's prominence within the narrative. While the redactor has omitted five references to this *"first"* disciple, 10:2, from his Marcan prototype, he has added five more even stronger references, resulting in a total of eight all within the compass of just five chapters, 14 to 18. This is the section often referred to as Matthew's Book IV dealing primarily with matters pertaining to the church and climaxing with the Ecclesiological Sermon in 17:24 to 18:35. In the center of this section is the seemingly transcendent passage, 16:17-19, where Peter is lavishly commended by Jesus for his confession in 16:16: *"You are the Messiah, the son of the living God,"* and then promised: *"And I tell you, you are Peter and on this rock I will build my church, and the gates of Hades will not prevail against it,"* v. 18. The evangelist's redactional strategy is transparent. Peter is being symbolically portrayed here as a, if not the, leading church figure, with authority to bind and loose, i.e., to determine and interpret the will of God for all of God's people.

Unfortunately, this is about as far as the organized church in succeeding generations got in its understanding of the *First*

218

Gospel's ecclesiology. The prospect of having one authoritative Peter-type leader serving as Bishop, Patriarch or Pope to resolve the immense challenges facing the growing and diversifying church of its day was too tempting to deny. In subsequent centuries an entire theological house of cards has been constructed consisting of such supportive doctrines as the Apostolic Succession and Papal Infallibility making Peter in retrospect the first Pope, his chair the Holy See, his "bark" the ship of the church, and his "penny" the tribute of Christendom.

As careful readers of the *First* Gospel, attempting to see it in its original context, however, we know that 16:17-19 was not the end of Ben's portrayal of Peter. As a matter of fact, Peter's role, as recounted, was gradually, but relentlessly all downhill after his "elevation" at Caesarea Philippi. In the very next paragraph, 16:21-23, Jesus denounces Peter as *"Satan"* and a *"stumbling block,"* who, despite his earlier confession was still trapped within his human limitations. In 18:18, his formerly exclusive powers to bind and loose are redistributed to all the disciples, i.e., to Christians generally. His boasts in Gethsemane, promising that he would stand by Jesus at any cost, 26:33-35, eventually ring hollow. His threefold denials of his Lord, 26:69-75, are profane and disgraceful. Perhaps, the most devastating of all, however, is his conspicuous absence from the scene following Jesus' resurrection. Contrast Mark 16:7 where Peter is rehabilitated with Mt. 28:7 where he is not. In fact, the final glimpse we have of Peter in Matthew is that of the defeated disciple having been caught in his denials weeping bitterly outside of Pilate's judgment hall, 26:75. Unlike all the other gospel narratives and even Paul (cf. I Cor. 15:5), Peter in the *First* Gospel is never formally rehabilitated and plays no role in the post-Easter church. He has suffered rhetorical dispraise. If he is visible at all it is only as a cipher, one of the nameless and faceless *"eleven"* who gathered on the mountain to hear Jesus say *"All authority in heaven and on earth has been given to me,"* 28:18. The point is clear, Jesus abides no earthly rival, not even Peter.

The net effect, then, of the *First* Gospel's Petrine theme is the lesson that despite great promise, this potential supreme church leader ultimately failed the test. He was only a *disciple* after all, sharing the same deficiencies as a *"little faith,"* 14:31, 8:26, and a *"stumbling block,"* 16:23, 18:6-7. Compared to the living, present Christ, his role in the early church was not to be thought of as particularly noteworthy. As previously stated, in the *First* Gospel the church is an unstratified brotherhood with Christ its only head.

Now the rhetorically strategic role intended for the 16:17-19 passage becomes clear. The evangelist inserted this pro-Petrine Jewish-Christian tradition, replete with so many uncharacteristic Semitisms, such as *"Simon bar Jonah,"* to function as a *stasis* statement similar to 5:18, 10:8 and 23:2. In effect, Peter was set up to be knocked down so that the living, ever present Jesus could ultimately stand alone with *"all authority in heaven and on earth,"* 28:18-20.

We can easily imagine and understand the urgent circumstances surrounding this issue of church leadership in this *First* Gospel's historical context. The date of the Gospel's composition in the first half of the ninth decade, as previously proposed and determined to our satisfaction, suggests a critical period of transition in Antiochene church hegemony between Evodius and Ignatius. The questions of who would gain ascendancy and what style of leadership they would pursue were enormously important and controversial. Our scribe's solution, in human terms, was evasive, but in spiritual perspective, extremely far-sighted. It doesn't matter who the human functionaries are as long as Jesus is recognized as the present, living, authoritative leader and foundation of the church.

220

History, of course, has treated the *first* evangelist's elevated ideals poorly. Within a decade or two, Ignatius, however well intended, was claiming almost dictatorial, if not divine, powers for himself and other bishops over their territorial constituencies. We are inclined to excuse him, of course, because, after all, when he wrote his famous letters Ignatius was on his way to his own martyrdom in Rome. Nevertheless, with him the trend was set toward monarchical episcopacy, hierarchical stratification and sharper distinctions between clergy and laity in the church ever since. Undoubtedly, the church today would do well to re-read Matthew, in context, once again.

Intimations of the Transcendent

In sum, Ben's ecclesiology, like so much else in the *First* Gospel, must be viewed on two levels, that of *the kingdom of heaven(s)* and that of the *church*. Yet, they must not be thought of as opposites, as though one were perfect and the other still struggling. Rather, as previously suggested, there is here something reminiscent of "Plato's Cave" analogy whereby the earth was seen as a shadowbox of heaven. *The kingdom of heaven(s)* concept, thus, is designed to show what the church is really like. It functions as an ethereal model for the temporal church depicting its continuing challenges while also providing it with vision, encouragement and hope.

The *church*, conversely, is a reflection of *the kingdom of the heavens*. What happens there also transpires here. From the point of view of the evangelist's Christian convictions, God the Father is, and has always been, the principle actor in the kingdom, but his supremacy is not yet fully recognized. Satan and his hosts continue to sew weeds among the wheat. However, a day of judgment, though delayed, is definitely approaching. Then the Father's victory will be assured and made permanent. The sheep will be separated from the goats, the good fish from the bad, the chaff from the grain. *The kingdom of God* will have arrived. In the meantime — and the present is what most concerns Ben Grammateus — the church must hold on, fending off all attacks, both internal and external, enduring unto the end.

The major difference, and the basis for real hope, however, is that now God is with his people in the person of his beloved Son, Jesus Christ, 28:20. They are living not only in the present, but in the Presence of the divine. Jesus is in the same boat with them, 8:26, and therefore they need not fear. In him, *the kingdom of heaven(s)* has touched the earth. A bridge now arches the distance between the kingdom and the *church.* Jesus has all authority in heaven and on earth, 28:18. He is the champion of the Christians' cause, the captain of their spiritual quest. He renders their yoke easy and their burdens light, 11:30. He calms all fears and heals all diseases, 4:23. Wherever two or three Christians are gathered together in his name, there he is in their midst, 18:20. Whatever is asked the Father in Jesus' name will be heard by him, 18:19. And he, Jesus, will remain with his people until the end of the age, 28:20. The evangelist knows about a future perfect state, a time of renewal, 19:28, and of eternal life, when the *church* and *the kingdom of heaven(s)* will become one as *the kingdom of God*, but he is content for the most part to worry only about today, his day, and that of his community, in Antioch-on-the-Orontes.

Matthean ecclesiology, then, is essentially local, contemporary and even personal. Still every *"disciple"* should be aware of the intimations of the transcendent inherent in this portrayal of *the kingdom of heaven(s)* promising, in spite of continuing difficulties, weakness and spiritual lethargy, the solace of Jesus' divine presence, power, and ultimate victory.

Chapter 9 Endnotes

[1] For helpful background reading see Eduard Schweizer, "Matthew's Church," pp. 129-155 in Graham Stanton, ed., THE INTERPRETATION OF MATTHEW; Fortress Press, Philadelphia, SPCK, London, 1983. Also Ulrich Luz, "The Disciples in the Gospel according to Matthew," pp. 98-128 in the same volume.

[2] Cf. Alan Richardson, ed., A THEOLOGICAL WORDBOOK OF THE BIBLE; The Macmillan Company, New York, 1950, pp. 119-121. Ernst von Dobschütz in his 1928 article *Matthew as Rabbi and Catechist*, trans. from the German by Robert Morgan and reproduced in Graham Stantaon, THE INTERPRETATION OF MATTHEW; op. cit., p. 26, says the term was common among the rabbis. However, the MISHNAH, containing those quotes dates from a century after the composition of the *First Gospel.*

[3] Cf. Ignatius, "Smyreans" 6:1, p. 230, and commentary on pp. 235-237, plus "Trallians" 5.1, p.143, and commentary on p. 144, in William R. Schoedel, IGNATIUS OF ANTIOCH; Hermeneia Commentary Series, Helmut Koester, ed., Fortress Press, Philadelphia, 1985.

[4] Contra the translation of *"main streets"* in the NRSV. A GREEK-ENGLISH LEXICON OF THE NEW TESTAMENT; Bauer, Arndt, Gingrich, Danker, eds., University of Chicago Press, Chicago and London, p. 194, says: "the place where a street cuts through the city boundary and goes out into the open country."

[5] Cf. my own work and extensive bibliography: Arlo J.Nau, PETER IN MATTHEW: Discipleship, Diplomacy and Dispraise; The Liturgical Press, Collegeville, Minnesota, 1992.

Chapter 10

Ante- or Anti- Semitism?[1]

En route to Antakya, I spent a night in the Inci Hotel in Adana. One other comparatively young American couple, accompanied by a tiny toddler with sparkling dark eyes, was also in residence there. They had arrived more than a month earlier from New York City. Their purpose was to adopt this orphaned Turkish child. At first everything had gone smoothly, but then, despite official protestations of the Muslim Turkish authorities that everything was proceeding normally, the couple had become suspicious that concerns over the husband's Jewish ancestry had begun to cause delays. Reflected in their sad and desperate eyes one could see the menacing mask of ancient prejudice taking shape.

The weary threesome was still there, caught in the web between parental emotion and officious protocol, several days later when I returned from Antakya, Anti-Semitism had assumed a human face in their distress. It was not without sadness that I boarded the plane the next morning at the Adana airport located ironically in Tarsus, the ancient home of St. Paul. "What would that apostle, or the first evangelist, have had to say about these circumstances?" I wondered...and still wonder today.

One specter that has been haunting our path almost every step of the way since we began PART II of this book, investigating the content of the *First* Gospel, has been that of the rocky relationship existing between the *first* evangelist and his Christian community versus resurgent Judaism. Although depicted primarily in the narrative as a conflict between Jesus and Jewish authorities in Jerusalem in the early decades of the first century C.E., its parallel relevance for the comparable situation prevailing between Christians and Jews in Syrian Antioch in the 80s is patent and inescapable. We heard it in the Sermon on the Mount, Mt. 5-7, saw it in the miracle stories, chs. 8-9, and felt it where it was implicit in the parables, ch. 13.

Controversy Amid the Pax Romana.

To properly understand the local social situation in Antioch we need first to evaluate the broader regional, racial and religious context. History has shown that controversy with and within Palestine was, practically speaking, the only "fly in the ointment" within the Roman world at this point in time. This was, after all, the period of the *Pax Romana,* the approximately two centuries of world peace under Roman rule, from Augustus to Marcus Aurelius, 27 B.C.E. to 180 C.E.. A common language (Greek in the East), plus common legal, commercial and educational systems, and a general tolerance for religious and moral diversity, to say nothing of a very strong army, succeeded in developing an interdependent amalgam of races and cultures that was the Roman Empire. As the saying goes, the Mediterranean Sea had become a Roman lake. All was well, that is, except in the storied land of Judea! There resentment reigned, with broad effect reverberating throughout the Jewish Diaspora.

At home, the major Jewish parties, religious and/or political - Sadducees, Priests, Pharisees, Essenes, Herodians, Sicarii, etc. — all disagreed, sometimes violently, among themselves as well as with their political and religious adversaries, especially their Roman subjugators. The boiling pot was ready to explode, and finally did in 66 C.E. with the disciplinary invasion of Palestine by the Roman army under Vespasian and Titus.

The Roman vs. Jewish War, 66-73 C.E., upset all Jewish life at home and abroad. Antioch was the primary staging area for the Roman legions in preparation for their attacks on Galilee, Judea, Jerusalem, Qumran and eventually Masada where the vestiges of battle are clearly visible to this day. Many recruits undoubtedly came from Syria. Even some Jewish sons were conscripted. Anti-Jewish sentiment naturally ran high. Josephus, as we have previously heard, relates the tragic story of a Jewish renegade named Antiochus, the son of the ruler of Antioch's Jewish *politeuma,* who publicly advocated the expulsion, if not the genocide, of his own people living in the city.[2] The times were difficult, to say the least.

Not even the end of the war resolving the political situation, however, mollified the religious turmoil enveloping Judaism. In fact, it exacerbated it. Now, without Jerusalem, temple, priests or political leaders, Judaism began the desperate effort to redefine and reinterpret itself under the guidance of the rabbis — the lay, religious heirs of the Scribes and Pharisees. In essence, the Hebrew Scriptures with all of their possible nuances of interpretation replaced the temple with its formal rituals and sacrifices as the focus of Jewish society, study, cult and commitment.

In a strange sort of way, this unsettling situation was actually beneficial for continuing Jewish life in the Diaspora where temple worship and priesthood, never available anyway, had actually served as somewhat complicating factors. Now, with the fabled Rabbinical Council of Jamnia occurring around 85 C.E. — that is, about the same time that the *First* Gospel was being written — the distinctive patterns of a resurgent Judaism were becoming re-codified, giving Diaspora Jews, under the local rabbis, a new and heady legitimacy. All other religious movements, including Antiochene Christianity, accordingly, were forced to reevaluate their relationship with these "new"

227

Jews and to adjust their reactions. Friction was inevitable —
and enduring.

Jewish/Christian Conflict

St. Paul's genuine letters, written in the 50s and early 60s
C.E., already anticipate and document the growing Christian
vs. Jewish animosity. Christianity was in the throes of establishing its own identity, separating itself from its Jewish cultural and religious matrix. Even such internal church struggles
as the altercation between Peter and Paul at Antioch, Gal.
2:11-14, expose something of the intensity and pervasiveness
of the underlying Christianity vs. Judaism conflict.

The inherent antipathy took years to dissipate without ever
being truly resolved. For example, we still hear Ignatius of
Antioch, writing twenty years after the publication of the *First*
Gospel, exhorting his readers: "But if anyone expounds Judaism to you, do not listen to him."[3]

It should not surprise us, then, if, in this antagonistic environment, some element of polemic finds its way into the
First Gospel as well. And indeed it does. In chapter after
chapter we hear accounts of confrontations between Jesus
and the crowds, 11:7, 12:24, Jesus and the cities of Chorazin
and Bethsaida, 11:20-21, with the scribes and Pharisees, 12:24,
28, 15:1, 19:3 and 22:15, 34, with King Herod, 14:1, the chief
priests and scribes, 21:15, and the Sadducees, 22:23.

The issues were equally diverse: working and healing on
the Sabbath Day, 12:1-14, demanding signs as proof, 12:28ff.,
ritually washing one's hands before eating, 15:2, divorce, 19:3,
and the possibility of resurrection, 22:23ff.

Several of these confrontations include redactional suggestions and prophecies which demonstrate their relevance
for *Matthew's,* or Ben's, own readers in Antioch. In 11:23,
for instance, Jesus observes that *"if the deeds of power done
in you* (Chorazin and Bethsaida) *had been done in Sodom, it*

would have remained until this day." We have come to recognize such repeated insertions referring to *"this day,"* μεχρι, or εως της σημερον, 27:8, 28:15, as rhetorical red flags warning the evangelist's immediate audience of the issue's continuing relevance. The admonitions that Jesus addressed to Chorazin and Bethsaida apply just as much to Antioch and Daphne.

In view of the prevailing tensions, even the absence of any reference to circumcision in this *First* Gospel undoubtedly argues more for a condition of local volatility over the question of that Jewish rite's continuing practice among the Christians in Antioch than for any lack of interest on the author's part. It was a subject better left dormant.

What is truly surprising, however, is the very personal nature of much of the *first* evangelist's redaction and the ever increasing intensity of his anti-Judaistic criticisms. As Krister Stendahl, the Harvard Divinity School Dean, mused many years ago, the *First* Gospel seems to reflect a lively argument with a "synagogue across the street."[4] A vehement, pervasive, local controversy, perhaps taking place right there in the Kerateion, the Jewish quarter of Antioch, does appear to be at issue in this composition, making the Christian relationship with Judaism a constant, albeit penultimate, theme throughout the gospel.

Ante-Semitic Diplomacy

We note first, however, that the gospel narrative ostensibly begins on a positive note. In the genealogy of chapter 1, Jesus, the Messiah, is portrayed as a direct descendent of Jewish royalty dating back to the heroic King David and to Abraham, the mythopoeic progenitor of the Jewish people. Hebrew prophets are frequently quoted. Jesus becomes a kind of Moses redivivus, fulfilling the parallel: *"Out of Egypt have I called my son,"* 2:15. In 4:23 we are told that *"Jesus went throughout Galilee, teaching in their synagogues and pro-claiming the good news of the kingdom and curing every disease and every sickness among the people."* This initial strategy of going to Jews first and only is confirmed in Mt. 10:5-6 where Jesus commands his disciples: *"Go nowhere among the Gentiles, and enter no town of the Samaritans, but go rather to the lost sheep of the house of Israel."*

Here and there as the narrative proceeds we also detect occasional concessions to traditional Jewish mores and practices accompanied by *pro forma* slaps at corresponding Gentile deficiencies, classifying these Gentiles, for example, with tax collectors and sinners, 18:17. *Matthew,* alias Ben, the scribe, counsels his predominantly Jewish Christian readers to pray that their flight on that expected apocalyptic day will not occur in the winter or *"on a Sabbath,"* 24:20. It is hinted, too, that fasting may again be appropriate now that the *"bridegroom"* is no longer visible among them, 9:15. The evangelist even softens Mark's strong abrogation of all dietary laws: *"Thus he* (Jesus) *declared all foods clean,"* in Mk. 7:19 by simply substituting the thought that *"it is not what goes into the mouth, but what comes out of the mouth that defiles a person,"* Mt. 15:10. Meanwhile, our Antiochene scribe also cautions his Christian compatriots that when they pray they are not *"to heap up empty phrases as the Gentiles do; for they think they will be heard because of their many words,"* 6:7. A kind of temporary, left-handed compliment is even accorded Jewish leaders when, by redaction in 23:2, they are displayed as sitting on Moses' seat, apparently with all the ability and authority to interpret the Scriptures correctly.

When these kinds of indicators are viewed at face value, one could conclude, as some have,[5] that the *First* Gospel projects the image of a Christian sectarian group still existing within the walls of the parent Judaism, although, undoubtedly, struggling to define its own identity. The perspective assumed in this book, however, in the light of later developments, is that these occasional, positive comments in the gospel function only as diplomatic *ante*-Semitic demurs — somewhat condescending compliments and temporary mini concessions — designed to show balance, rationality and flexibility on the author's part, temporizing his parallel comments to the contrary. Indeed, there are some Jewish sentiments that the evangelist still condones and even celebrates. In the long run, however, these quasi pro-Judaism comments and indicators seem to be only preliminary to the evangelist's main purpose, functioning again as a type of *stasis* tactic, for the barrage of *anti*-Semitic invective to follow. One often gets the impression that the evangelist, as Ben Grammateus — Jewish by birth, but Greek by education — is struggling with himself to control his own feelings.

Anti-Semitism in the First Gospel

A second look now, reveals that *Matthew's*, or Ben's, redactional attack against his Jewish peers also starts early, although subtly. Already in 2:2, the Wise Men ask ominously: *"Where is the child who has been born king of the Jews?"* That inappropriate political title, *king of the Jews,* will not be used again until Jesus' trial in ch. 27:11, 29 and 37 where it constitutes the essence of the accusations against Jesus, nailed even to his cross. The first hint of trouble follows immediately in 2:3 as the real King of the Jews, Herod the Great, is portrayed as *"frightened, and all Jerusalem with him."* Resistance to Jesus from the start is thus seen as official and popular. As a result, the story of the Slaughter of the Innocents, as a foretaste of opposition to come, soon ensues in 2:16. The *first* evangelist's editorial skill in building his case against Judaism is clearly evident.

This anti-Jewish confrontational stance surfaces again, and frequently, in Jesus' Sermon on the Mount, chs. 5-7.

There, by redaction, Jesus upholds Christian morality in contrast to the deficient *"righteousness of the scribes and Pharisees,* 5:20. He decries the hypocrisy of those who trumpet their piety *"in the synagogues and at the street corners so that they may be seen by others,"* 6:2, 5. Finally, the sermon concludes with Jesus teaching as one having authority and not as *"their"* scribes, suggesting a we-against-them conflict. Although Mark employs this same terminology on at least one occasion, cf. Mk. 1:39, the evangelist made such indictments, using the personal possessives *"your"* and *"their"* scribes or synagogues, a routine convention of his style, cf. Mt. 4:23, 7:29, 9:35, 10:17, 12:9, 13:54, 23:34. One is left with the definite impression that a deep and permanent cleavage had occurred between Jesus and the Jews, between Christianity and Judaism, and between Ben, the *"scribe trained for the kingdom,"* and his rival Jewish counterparts in the Kerateion.

Another curious literary convention confronts us in chapter 16. Here, on four separate occasions, vv. 1, 6,11 & 12, the evangelist conjoins the two dominant but counterpoised Jewish groups, the *"Pharisees and Sadducees,"* treating them as one dimension in opposition to Jesus. No other canonical evangelist ever thought, or dared, to do so. As unhistorical and anachronistic as this tactic may be, it is effective here in the post destruction of Jerusalem situation to characterize the concerted Jewish opposition to the evangelist's Antiochene Christian community and theology.

The tempo picks up in chapter 21. The account of the Withered Fig Tree, vv. 18-22, with the tree serving as a symbol of Israel, portends the decline of Judaism as well as illustrating the power of prayer. Then follows two parables, those of the Two Sons, vv. 28-32, and the Wicked Tenants, vv. 33-44, both concluding with similar damning pronouncements toward the chief priests and Pharisees, found only in the *First*

Gospel: *"Truly I tell you, the tax collectors and the prostitutes are going into the kingdom of God ahead of you,"* v. 31, and *"Therefore, I tell you, the kingdom of God will be taken away from you and given to a people that produces the fruits of the kingdom,"* v. 43. The noose is tightening on Israel and Judaism.

The crescendo in the *first* evangelist's anti resurgent Judaism theme, of course, resounds in the sermonic Chapter 23. Although most of the basic material is gleaned from the sayings source, Q, the thunderous six-fold repetition: *"Woe to you, scribes, Pharisees, hypocrites,"* with a few occasional *"blind guides"* thrown in, vv. 16 & 25, is typical of our Antiochene scribe. The acerbic, personal nature of this attack is obvious. Despite the initial demur about the scribes and Pharisees *"sitting on Moses' seat,"* v.2, it is clear that in the writer's view these Jewish leaders can do nothing right. They are proud, insensitive, pietistic, bent on perverting the faith of their people, irrational in their ritualistic interpretations and practices. They are *"blind fools,"* v. 17, *"white-washed tombs,"* v. 27, *"snakes,"* and a *"brood of vipers,"* v. 33, 3:7, 12:34 — all invectives added here by the evangelist.

Although in v. 2 Jesus is recorded as saying *"do whatever they* (i.e., the Scribes and Pharisees) *teach..."* he, at the redactor's direction, personally countermands the very words of the Scribes and Pharaisees in v. 30 in which they try to divert from themselves culpability for the murders of the Old Testament prophets by their Jewish forefathers. Rather, he finds in their protestations and actions in decorating the tombs of the deceased heroes a confession of their own complicity. Guilt is inherited. They are the murderous sons of their murderous fathers. Jesus', and Ben's, determined refusal here to put the best construction on these Jewish disclaimers, contra the Sermon on the Mount's own Golden Rule, 7:12, testifies to the *ad hominem* nature of the altercation. This is not objective recording of history. In his editing it can be sensed that our Antiochene evangelist is so personally and directly embroiled in this *anti*-Judaistic controversy currently raging right there in Antioch-on-the-Orontes that he practically loses control of his own emotions.[6]

And the end is not yet. Undoubtedly the most self-condemnatory statement of all comes in the story of Jesus' trial before Pilate, Mt. 27:15-23. Here, in a strange and obviously contrived coincidence in names recorded only in the *First* Gospel, the Roman governor gives the crowds a clear choice between two "Jesuses," *"Jesus Barabbas or Jesus who is called the Messiah,"* 27:17. Not only do the Jewish masses select the former, but add regarding the latter: *"His blood be on us and on our children,"* v. 25. Those "children," it must be remembered, now included many among *Matthew's,* or Ben's, contemporary opposition in the Kerateion. In the evangelist's view, the damage was appallingly self-inflicted.

The apparent *coup de grace* comes in 28:15 when Ben asserts: *"And this story is still told among the Jews,* Ιουδαιοις, *to this day,"* referring to the guards' alibi that Jesus' disciples had stolen his body from the empty tomb. Not only does the time reference, *"to this day,"* imply our scribe's own day in the ninth decade of the first century C.E., but his unrestricted comment about *"the Jews,"* generally, seems of awesome consequence. Not only, then, did the *first* evangelist's opposition here in Antioch include the Jewish leaders, i.e., the rabbis, scribes and rulers of the local synagogues, i.e., the proverbial Pharisees and Sadducees, but their hapless followers as well. Our evangelist/scribe's ire thus stretched beyond matters religious to the cultural and racial, to children and adults, leaders and followers alike. If this much weight can be placed on this one word, Ιουδαιοι, or even if we view it only as a "Freudian slip," this all-inclusive statement still represents the closest that *Matthew* comes to abject anti-Semitism, in the modern sense. True, he is not advocating expulsion from Antioch, or genocide of all Jews, as the renegade Antiochus did, but the spiritual implication for Israel is, in fact, infinitely more serious, exile from the kingdom of God.

The evangelist was himself of Jewish extraction, and clearly there were aspects of his heritage which he celebrated, but simultaneously, as a Christian, there were others which he simply could not abide.

The Resolution[7]

Is there any reprieve from this loveless, anti-Semitic stance in the *First* Gospel? Fortunately, I believe we can say there is — some!

First, in partial defense of the editor, it needs to be remembered that he was writing, as he saw it, primarily for the internal benefit of his community, comprised of both Jewish and Gentile Christians, not for a Jewish audience generally or his Jewish scribal opponents exclusively. His arguments and anecdotes, accordingly, were intended to be received as tools of Christian apologetics, designed to equip his audiences to defend themselves against the attempted incursions of resurgent Judaism. Admittedly, however, the vitriolic and personal nature of the writer's approach here renders the defining line between apologetics and polemics faint indeed.

Second, our interpretive perspective aiming to see the *First* Gospel in its original context — historically, geographically, culturally, rhetorically, and theologically — emphasizes the ephemeral and local circumstances obtaining when this Gospel was originally composed. Our inclination, and commitment, therefore, is to view this conflict with resurgent Judaism as temporary, localized, and intended primarily for immediate consumption. The evangelist's objective was not to propose attitudes, values and procedures to be imitated elsewhere in all future generations. In other words, his anti-Semitism then, is no excuse for our's today. Rote, unexamined, globalized acceptance of biblical dicta, such as the invectives found here, is a recipe for ethnic and social disaster as numerous religious wars, crusades and pogroms throughout history have regrettably demonstrated.

The most compelling argument in defense of our scribe's apparent anti-Semitism, however, undoubtedly comes from his own pen. Turning once again to the Great Commission, 28:19, we hear Jesus saying by redaction: *"Go and make disciples of παντα τα εθνη."* But the Greek here can mean either "all Gentiles" or "all nations." Which is it? Are we talking about race or citizenship?

To be consistent with the anti-Jewish trajectory that the evangelist seems to have been pursuing, "Gentiles," excluding all members of the Jewish race, would no doubt appear to be the more appropriate. The missionary command, then, would have been aimed at Gentiles only. Indeed, εθνος is, in fact, used in this restrictive sense earlier in this gospel, cf. 10:5. But, that kind of rigorous, ultimate consistency, as we have seen, is not really our Antiochene scribe's style, especially not in this climactic Great Commission. Here he prefers surprise in the form of unexpected understatement — the clear, clean "ting" of the glockenspiel rather than the discordant crash of the cymbals. For example, just when we were prepared to meet the exultant, eschatological Messiah/Christ, Son of Man and Son of God, in our earlier review of Matthean Christology in Chapter Six, we were instead abruptly introduced to an immanent Lord: *"Remember, I am with you always to the end of the age,* 28:20. So here, where we might expect a restrictive μονα τα εθνη, "only Gentiles," we find, rather, an inclusive παντα, "all" peoples. The door is thus left ajar. Just as in 25:31 *"all nations,"* including Jews, are envisioned as subject to judgment, so here in 28:19, *"all nations,"* including Jews, remain eligible for discipleship.

The NRSV translators are correct, then, in rendering the Greek as *"all nations,"* just as the prototype of this passage in 24:14 anticipated. There the universality of God's gracious intentions is doubly emphasized: *"And this good news of the kingdom will be proclaimed throughout the world,* εν ολη τη οικουμενη, *as a testimony to all the nations,* πασιν τοις εθνεσιν, *and then the end will come."*

This concluding stance represents the evangelist's way of qualifying Jesus' earlier redactional *stasis* pronouncement in 10:5: *"Go nowhere among the Gentiles, and enter no town of the Samaritans, but go rather to the lost sheep of the house of Israel."* The door leading to discipleship is still open for Jews as well as Gentiles.

If such a fine line can be drawn, then, *Matthew's,* or Ben's, apophatic position was fundamentally or categorically neither *ante-* nor *anti-* Semitic, but was limited to being only anti-resurgent Judaism in Roman Syrian Antioch in the 80s of the first century, C.E.. Unlike Antioch, the host city, however, the *first* evangelist is happy to report, neither *the kingdom of heaven(s)* nor *the kingdom of God* has any solid, ethnically exclusive walls with locked gates, after all.

Chapter 10 Endnotes

[1] Background reading for this chapter is omnipresent. Almost every major commentary today accedes to the perspective that Matthew is fundamentally a Jewish work, reflecting a Jewish orientation. The 1928 article by Ernst von Dobschütz, *"Matthew as Rabbi and Catechist,"* trans. Robert Morgan, in Graham Stanton, ed., THE INTERPRETA-TION OF MATTHEW; Fortress Press, Philadelphia, 1983, has undoubtedly done the most to popularize the idea. But see also Dale C. Allison, Jr., THE NEW MOSES: A MattheanTypology; Fortress, Minneapolis, 1993, and the three volume INTERNATIONAL CRITICAL COMMENTARY on MATTHEW, by W.D. Davies and Dale C. Allison, Jr., T & T Clark, Edinburgh, 1991. The works of Andrew Overman and Saldarini also build on this premise. In opposition, cf. John P. Meier, THE VISION OF MATTHEW; The Liturgical Press, Collegeville, Minnesota, who argues cogently, if not convincingly, that the original Matthew was a Greek Gentile Christian.

[2] Cf. Chapter Three, p. 55 above.

[3] Ignatius, *"letter to the Philadelphians" 6.1*, p. 200 in William R. Schoedel, IGNATIUS OF ANTIOCH; Hermeneia Commentary Series, Fortress Press, Philadelphia, 1985.

[4] Krister Stendahl, THE SCHOOL OF ST. MATTHEW, And Its Use of the Old Testament; CWK Gleerup, Lund, n.d., p. xi.

[5] Cf. Andrew J. Overman, MATTHEW'S GOSPEL AND FORMATIVE JUDAISM: The Social World of the Matthean Community; Fortress Press, Minneapolis 1990. Also Anthony J. Saldarini, MATTHEW'S CHRISTIAN-JEWISH COMMUNITY; University of Chicago Press, Chicago and London,1994, and his chapter, The Gospel of Matthew and Jewish-Christian Conflict," *in SOCIAL HISTORY OF THE MATTHEAN COMMUNITY;* David L. Balch, ed., Fortress Press, Minneapolis, 1991, pp.38-61.

[6] Cf. Margaret Davies, MATTHEW, JSOT Press, 1993, pp. 159-165.

[7] For background reading, see John P. Meier, "Nations or Gentiles in Matthew 28:19?" pp. 141-152 in THE MISSION OF CHRIST AND HIS CHURCH; Michael Glazier, Inc., Wilmington, Delaware, 1990. Also Guido Tisera, UNIVERSALISM ACCORDING TO THE GOSPEL OF MATTHEW; Peter Lang Publishing, Frankfurt, New York, et al., 1993, esp. pp. 317-333.

Chapter 11

Immanent Eschatology[1]

*While walking the terraced paths on Mt. Silpius'
sheer incline one afternoon, Erdal and I were suddenly confronted by a shepherd with his flock. What
surprised me most was the fact that this scruffy herd
was comprised of both sheep and goats. It was actually against Turkish law, Erdal explained, to mix the
species — something about communicable diseases -
but here the government didn't interfere because the
shepherds' very subsistence depended on the combination providing, as it did, milk and mutton, wool and
valuable goat skins.*

*The experience gave new meaning to the parable
in Mt. 25:31-46. Separating the sheep from the goats
is not as easy as it may at first appear. Truly, whether
speaking pastorally or eschatologically, it's a job better left to God.*

The *first* evangelist, or Ben Grammateus as we've come
to know him, somewhat incongruously connects his anti-Jewish apologetic in ch. 23, as just discribed, with his eschatology
in chapters 24 and 25, forming one long sermon, the so-called
Eschatological Discourse, discussing "last things." It appears
the Antiochene Christian community's conflict with resurgent Judaism was considered the most obvious of the many
signs forecasting the imminence of the *parousia,* i.e., the final, visible coming of the *Son of Man.*

The literary transitional link between the two disparate
halves of this sermon is smooth enough. Jesus is portrayed

in 23:37-39 as weeping over Jerusalem and concluding: *"See, your home is left to you desolate. For I tell you, you will not see me again until you say, 'Blessed is the one who comes in the name of the Lord."* With this prediction of Jesus' climactic advent the stage is set for the *First* Gospel's last great sermon focusing on the signs preceding the anticipated arrival of the *Son of Man*, the inescapability of its approach, and the final judgment of all flesh that it portends.

Commonplace Eschatology

Despite its length and climactic position, so near to the end of Jesus' public ministry and of the *First* Gospel, however, this discourse somewhat surprisingly lacks much of the originality and vibrancy of the four earlier addresses — the Sermon on the Mount (chapters 5-7), the Mission Sermon (ch. 10), the Kingdom Parables Sermon (ch. 13) and the Discourse on the Church in chapter 18. This phenomenon is nevertheless easily explained. The evangelist here, does little more than reprint Mark's "Little Apocalypse" in Mk. 13, supplementing it only with a few thoughts from Q and attaching a parable about five wise and five foolish maidens, 25:1-13, and a judgment scene with the Son of Man separating the sheep from the goats in 25:31-46. The author's basic eschatology, thus, is traditional, even commonplace. In a sense, it is old news, but still worthy of serious consideration.

According to Mt. 24:36f., the prevailing situation is similar to the days of Noah just before the flood. Convinced that so great a deluge would not, or even could not happen, the people then lived irresponsibly. So now, Ben's Antiochene contemporaries are oblivious to the geologic, social and moral dislocations, i.e., the horrible *"birthpangs,"* ωδινων, 24:8, presaging the return of *"your Lord,"* 24:42. But, make no mistake, the end will surely come, and sooner than one may think, even though at times it appears that the *"Master is delayed,"* 24:48.

Constant preparedness is, therefore, the order of the day. *"The one who endures unto the end will be saved,"* 24:13.

A Few Distinctive Perspectives
Despite the traditional nature of the evangelist's basic eschatology here, several small but significant and very fascinating redactional nuances nevertheless emerge when this sermon is viewed from the perspective of the Antiochene Christian community in the ninth decade of the first century C.E.

The consistent use of *parousia, παρουσια,* as a theological technical term in 24:3, 27, 37 and 39, implying the *"coming of the Son of Man,"* immediately attracts our attention. The word is not found in any other Gospel, although St. Paul twenty-plus years earlier did employ it in a similar theological sense in I Corinthians 15:23. Its fourfold appearance here, therefore, testifies to the advanced state of eschatological discourse in the Antiochene congregation. The "Coming" was a concept involving considerable emotional and speculative investment.

Even more telling is the realization that most, if not all, of the prophesied signs of the last times, listed here as coming from the lips of Jesus, had already come to pass and were indelibly imprinted on the collective memories of community members by the mid-80s when *Matthew,* or Ben, composed this Gospel. *"Famines,"* and especially *"earthquakes,"* 24:7, were common experiences in Antioch. The visit of Apollonius of Tyana to Antioch about this same time immediately comes to mind when we are forewarned of false messiahs and prophets in 24:5, 11, to say nothing of the various Roman emperors, every one of whom, since Augustus first beatified Julius Caesar, claimed some connection with the divine. As for the *"desolating sacrilege,"* 24:15, which the evangelist points out is so reminiscent of the *"abomination*

243

that desolates" in Daniel 9:27, who could forget the recent frustrated attempt of a crazed Nero in 68 C.E. to have his own image erected in the temple at Jerusalem? The fact that by a stroke of divine justice, the emperor himself died before his order could be obeyed was the stuff of rye humor and lifted eyebrows within the Kerateion sector.[2] Furthermore, the destruction of Jerusalem by the Romans under Titus in 70 C.E. certainly fulfilled the prediction of *"nation shall rise against nation,"* 24:7, and Paul's missionary journeys in the 50s and 60s, begun at Antioch, similarly satisfied the prophecy that *"this good news of the kingdom will be proclaimed throughout the world, as a testimony to all nations; and then the end will come,"* 24:14. For this Gospel's readership and audience, then, these preliminary signs of the times were already part of history and could not be used as an excuse to relax anyone's guard as though they were still pending.. Any perceived delay in the coming of the Son of Man, therefore, was only imaginary, without real substance.

In two instances, our *"scribe trained for the kingdom"* reworks ideas gleaned from his chief sources, Mark and Q, and reconstructs out of these raw materials new and expanded parables — the Wise and Foolish Maidens in 25:1-13 and the Parable of the Talents in 25:14-30. Such extensive editing suggests special concern. Each parable, in its own way, accordingly, reemphasizes the evangelist's primary purpose, to remind his readers of the need for constant preparedness in view of the unknown time of the *parousia's* arrival.

The apparent delay in that day's approach, a topic accented already in 24:48, forms the backdrop for the first anecdote. Foresight, rather than procrastination, is the only wise response if one is to be ready when the bridegroom arrives at midnight, 25:6. The Christian community dare not take comfort in the apparent delay of the *parousia.*

244

The startling aspect in Ben's reconstruction of Luke's, or Q's, Parable of the Pounds, Lk. 19:11-27, in his own Parable of the Talents in Mt. 25:14-30, is its thousand-fold increase in the burden of responsibility assumed by the rich man's slaves, i.e., by inference, Ben's local "*disciples*." Ten pounds, μνας, Lk. 19:13, is perhaps the equivalent of $200.00 compared to the $200,000.00 of the *First* Gospel's five talents, ταλαντα. Using one's present opportunities responsibly, therefore, is of utmost importance and moment.

Precisely what is at stake in acting "responsibly" is illustrated in the climactic Parable of the Sheep and the Goats in 25:31-46. It is found only here in the New Testament and has all the earmarks of Matthean style, vocabulary and originality. It adds the concept of judgment as a characteristic dimension of the Son of Man's Coming. The *parousia* will be uniquely neither a day of triumph nor of wrath (cf. Joel 2:2), but of divine election when the Son of Man will judge all nations separating the sheep from the goats, 25:32, the weeds from the wheat, 13:41, the good fish from the bad, 13:49. And what will be the determining standard? Whether or not individuals in time have seen the present, living Son of Man reflected in the lives, needs, and hurts of their fellow human beings, especially their fellow Christians, and have accordingly acted with compassion. *" Truly I tell you, just as you did it to one of the least of these who are members of my family, you did it to me,"* 25:40. Here is our scribe's definitive description of the *"righteous,"* 25:46, who will enter eternal life.

Here again, we see that faith and faithfulness are of one piece from the *first* evangelist's perspective. Knowing Jesus is a transforming power, transfiguring the needs of others into saving opportunities for service to God.

A Non-Apocalyptic Apocalypse

Although this eschatological sermon in Mt. 23-25 is often referred to as the "Great Apocalypse" to differentiate it from the "Little Apocalypse" in Mark 13, it is, in fact, curiously lacking in much that can be considered characteristically apocalyptic, either conceptually or linguistically. Missing is anything like the garish symbolism found in the Johannine Book of Revelation with its sapphire throne, golden streets, crystal sea, multi-horned creatures and mysterious veils, bowls and scrolls.

Perhaps the closest we come to that kind of imagery in the *First* Gospel is the mysterious vignette in 27:52-53: *"The tombs also were opened, and many bodies of the saints who had fallen asleep were raised. After his resurrection they came out of the tombs and entered the holy city and appeared to many."* We can only guess at the writer's reasons for adding this strange account. It appears misplaced and chronologically confused with the resurrection of these saints occurring at the time of Jesus' death on Good Friday but their appearance in Jerusalem delayed until Easter Sunday. Was it Ben's intention to depict Jesus' death and resurrection as one eschatological "Christ-event" as many modern Systematics theologians opine? Or, was it a desire to add some positive relevance to Jesus' resurrection by portraying it as the precursor to the resurrection of all people on the last day? It is certainly true that without this brief interlude nothing is explicitly said in the *First* Gospel about the salvific benefits of Jesus' resurrection. Or, did this insertion simply serve to satisfy a rhetorical demand for the report of some accompanying omen to indicate the revolutionary significance of Jesus' death? We cannot be sure, but the singular awkwardness of the portrayal here suggests to me the latter reason as the primary one.

Imminent Immanent Eschatology

In all other respects, the Matthean eschatology, as we have already come to expect from related references in previous chapters, is consistently and programmatically oriented toward this world. As we learned in our review of the *First* Gospel's ecclesiology in Chapter Nine, *the kingdom of heaven(s)* is present now just as the Son of Man is already with us to the end of the age. The eternal and the ephemeral, the spiritual and the physical are thus conjoined. In 24:3 Ben, the redactor, changes the disciples' question as rendered by Mark in 13:4 from *"...what will be the sign that all these things are about to be accomplished"* to the more restrictive query: *"...what will be the sign of your coming and of the end of the age.* Note how he always views the future only from this side of the great assize. Such preoccupation with the present age, or eon, is typical of the *first* evangelist. We hear it again in the Great Commission: *"Remember, I am with you always to the end of the age."* The effect is to leave us peering over the edge of time but not yet entering the new age whatever and whenever it may be.

Ben, of course, is aware of an after-life. As previously observed, he speaks broadly of entering *"the joy of your master,"* 25:21, 23, and of *"eternal life,"* 25:46, but he doesn't dwell on these concepts. In like manner, he knows about the proverbial *"Gates of Hades,"* 16:18, and of *"eternal punishment,"* 25:46, but prefers the repeated cliché: *"There shall be weeping and gnashing of teeth,"* 8:12, 13: 42, 50, 22:13, 24:51, 26:30 to describe the essence of hell. Also, Ben's infrequent use of *"the kingdom of God,"* although seeming to envision *the kingdom of heaven(s)* in its perfected state, is not limited to becoming a reality only in the distant future. No, it arrived with Jesus, 12:28. And even the *First* Gospel's singular reference to a future *"renewal,"* i.e., a παλιγγενεσια, in 19:28, as a time when rewards will be realized (contra Mark

10:29), nevertheless suggests a concept of a new earth as the locus of the after-life rather than that of an ethereal heaven somewhere beyond space and time. Finally, the absence of any hint of an ascension of Jesus in this Gospel can only be viewed as a further confirmation of the author's intense interest in the here and now. The usual, classic list of eschatological orientations — realized, inaugurated and futuristic — then, do not comport well with the presentation here. The evangelist's eschatology partakes of them all, but rests somewhere in between. It is not strictly realized in that it does not pretend that Jesus' "presence" is already totally visible or experienced by everyone. Still, it is not simply inaugurated either, in the sense that it is only partially or incrementally manifested. Rather, its full realization is represented in the person of Jesus, the Messiah/ Christ and Son of God/Son of Man. And it certainly is not futuristic meaning that it will be realized only in the next life. There may be an element of deferred gratification when it comes to rewards, but as far as real benefits are concerned, *Matthew,* alias Ben Grammateus, wants his readers to know they can enjoy them now. The term "proleptic," then, undoubtedly comes closest to his over-all perspective. It implies an apophatic already-but-not-yet paradox. It is both present and coming. Speaking metaphorically, the victory has been won, though some battles remain to be fought. The treasure has been found and is in the bank leaving only its tabulation for tomorrow. All the blessings of the present Christ are already available if only the Antiochene disciples will entrust themselves to him, enduring unto the end.

In other words, in sum, and as previously stated, this is a very practical eschatology of imminent immanence rather than of apocalyptic transcendence. Jesus is *Emmanuel, "God is with us, "* 1:23, 28:20.

Chapter 11 Endnotes

[1] Cf. the "Kingdom" section in Jack Dean Kingsbury, MATTHEW: STRUCTURE, CHRISTOLOGY, KINGDOM; Fortress Press, Philadelphia, 1975, pp. 128-160. Also: Günther Bornkamm, "End-Expectation and Church in Matthew," in Bornkamm, Barth, Held, TRADITION AND INTERPRETATION IN MATTHEW; Trans. Percy Scott, SCM Press, London, 1963, pp. 15-24.

[2] To be fair and historically accurate, Nero did officially rescind the suicide order, but neither the suicide letter nor the repeal dispatch reached Petronius as quickly as did the news of the emperor's death. For details, see Fergus Millar, THE ROMAN NEAR EAST, 31 BC - AD 337, Harvard University Press, Cambridge, MA., 1993, p. 59.

Reprise

A Beneficial Disturbance

Finally, how does one capture, and encapsulate, the genius — not just the content — of a work like the Gospel according to St. Matthew? Wherein does its greatness lie? What is unique or distinctive about it? What constitutes its appeal? Why has it been so influential? Does it deserve its prominence? How does one explain its durability and longevity? If I have asked myself these questions once I have asked them a thousand times over the last several years of intense preparation and especially over the past two years of the actual writing of this volume.

The fact is, as any objective reader will have to admit, that there is in this *First* Gospel little that is fundamentally devotional, comforting or inspirational in any transcendent sense. It has, rather, a disturbing, argumentative edge to it. Except for the Beatitudes, the Lord's Prayer and the "comfortable words" of 11:28-30: *"Come to me, all you that are weary and are carrying heavy burdens..."* this Gospel is replete with challenges, warnings, demands, threats and indictments. Compare and contrast the Birth Narratives in Luke and Matthew. One pictures a tranquil, bucolic scene of shepherds adoring a Christ-child asleep in a manger; the other, a jealous king outraged at the thought of a baby impostor, slaughtering all the infants of Bethlehem. The Gospel of John assures its readers: *"God so loved the world that he gave his only Son, so that everyone who believes in him may...have eternal life."* Matthew, on the other hand, demands: *"He that endures unto the end shall be saved."* John, again, promises in 14:2: *"In my Father's house there are many dwelling places...I go to prepare a place for you,"* while

251

the *First* Gospel, as we have seen, leaves us teetering on the horizon of this eon peering over the edge into a ill-defined void and forcing us to pay closer attention to the here and now. Where is the expected timeless winsomeness in this portrayal?

As if on cue, however, history seems to have conspired to make this Gospel, along with others, more theologically palatable. First Papias popularized the tradition that it was written by the disciple *Matthew* in a little known Hebrew dialect. Soon it was included among those sacred books judged verbally inspired by God. It was added to the canon, and even listed first among the New Testament books. As time went on and new questions and situations demanded, Matthew became frosted with the harmonizing insights of the other canonical Gospels and Paul's Letters until all its rough edges had been worn smooth and made compatible. You will recall that we referred to this stage as "Context I" in our first chapter.

Fortunately, or unfortunately, modern scholarship did not permit these artificial props, however well intended, to stand. A plurality of Source Critics, for example, agree that Matthew was not the first Gospel written, but is in large measure a reprise, or a palimpsest of Mark. Linguists, furthermore, have noted the fluent Greek with which this Gospel is composed and deny that it could be a direct translation reflecting a Hebrew original as Papias had proposed early in the second century. C.E. The evangelist, then, was undoubtedly not a Galilean disciple of Jesus, nor, as any close comparison of the Synoptic accounts will show, are many of the words credited to Jesus in the text the *ipsisimma verba,* i.e., "the very words themselves," of our Lord, but redactional attributions of the author.

With this erosion of the pious notions underpinning the traditional view of this *First* Gospel we have come full-cycle and are again confronted with our original questions: What is the true genius of Matthew? Wherein does its greatness lie? More specifically, what makes this gospel worth all the time and effort put into a study like this one, especially after all the other studies that have preceded it? And, in particular, what new dimension has the perspective, methodology and thesis of our present examination contributed to the understanding and appreciation of this ancient composition?

My basic answer, while undoubtedly still somewhat subjective, is that this Gospel's greatness lies in its very realism as described, that is, in its direct approach to issues, blunt and unyielding as it may often appear. There is, despite its frequent apophatic imprecision, a patent authenticity and integrity about this Gospel especially when viewed from the perspective of its established context. As we have come to know it on the basis of its redactional transparency, this *First* Gospel presents a very down-to-earth, true-to-life reflection of the situation prevailing in the Antiochene church during the Flavian period of Roman history. As such it is entirely believable and almost visible, clearly suggestive of our own situation and experience today.

Setting

It is true that we cannot assume to know everything about Ben's time, its *Zeitgeist* or culture, nor can we accurately read the details of the evangelist's innermost thoughts, but some things do not radically change — the topography, the climate, the flora and fauna, and perhaps most significantly, human nature. With those basics in hand, plus a few memories from recorded history, several more tell-tale archeological scars, and the careful analysis of the conventions of Greek rhetoric, we can, at least to some extent, identify with ancient Antioch's social milieu, glimpse its life-style, experience its commerce, and eavesdrop on its conversations.

Thus, within the pages, and sometimes between the lines, of this *First* Gospel we are enabled to join the assemblies of Antioch's early Christian *collegia sodalicia, 18:17,* hear snippets of ancient sermons, chs. 5, 10, 13, 18 & 23-25, participate in congregational liturgies, 5:3-10, 6:9-13, and listen in on some of the members' dialog, 16:14, Greek humor, 15:31, gossip, 28:15, and, yes, even anger and frustration, 23:33.

Theology

However, doesn't this kind of desacralizing of the text tend to profane this Gospel's message? I don't think so. Just the opposite. It helps us appreciate all the more naturally the depth of feeling in the community, the level of commitment demanded by the evangelist, and the practicality of the advice rendered. Profundity, it must be remembered, is not determined by the number of philosophical Latinisms used to unpack the text's meaning any more than is the Gospel's sanctity dependent upon an officiant's kiss of the Lectionary. Our approach, seeing this Gospel in its original historical, geographical, redactional and rhetorical context, rather enables us to appreciate the empathy, originality, practicality and depth of its narrative and theology.

For example, I am most impressed by its immanent, incarnational, God-with-us, Christology, 1:23, 28:20b. Accordingly, ours is not a distant, detached God of the spheres, but one who is near, bearing our yoke and sharing our burdens, 11:28-30. It helps us resonate with the kind of sensitivity which recognizes that a spirit of forgiveness is equally, if not more important than an attitude of repentance as a distinctively Christian prerequisite for community harmony and peace, 18:21-35.

Contrary to some popular notions, then, the *First* Gospel is not meant to be read devotionally, sanctimoniously, for our comfort only. It doesn't sugar-coat reality, mute the opposition or minimize danger. Instead, it is a stalwart call to arms, to a higher righteousness, more genuine faithfulness, and greater endurance amid dangers of all kinds, internal or external, and at different levels. Even its repeated references to *the kingdom of the heaven(s),* as we have seen, do not present a picture of some future glory, but serve rather as a mirror where the existing church can see itself objectively reflected, only in more global, diachronic, and profound perspective.

Authorship

In this connection, some acknowledgment is due the contributions and personality of the evangelist whom we have come to know traditionally as *Matthew,* but more personally by the *nom de plume* Ben Grammateus. Some readers of this book may still feel it unnecessarily sacrilegious to credit an unknown, occasionally petulant scribe, 13:52, 23:33, with the composition of this Gospel rather than the haloed disciple of sacred memory, St. Matthew. But ask yourself, what do we really know about St. Matthew? At best, we know that he was a Galilean tax collector, Mt. 9:9, who joined Jesus' band of followers, heard his Lord's teachings, witnessed his miracles and was present among the "eleven" after Jesus' resurrection and at his ascension, Acts 1:1-9. However, he is never recorded as having said or written one word. As one of Jesus' disciples in Mt. 6:26, he is numbered among the nameless "little-faiths," with those who were *"still without understanding"* in 15:16, and those who *"deserted him and fled"* according to 26:56. Consequently, he was not present at Jesus' crucifixion or resurrection. And never, as far as we know, did he subsequently undertake anything independently. Even early Christian tradition,[1] except for Papias, seems to treat him rather unkindly, crediting him only with possibly preaching among the Hebrews in Persia and Ethiopia. Clement of Alexandria inconsequentially theorizes that Matthew was a vegetarian. There is even disagreement over whether he died a martyr's death or suffered the comparative ignominy of dying of natural causes.

Some artists, without theological foundation, like to identify and portray the *first* evangelist as a human being, but with angelic wings, in concert with the Book of Revelation's *"third living creature with a face like a human face"* described in Rev. 4:7c.[2] But Ben Grammateus, as we have come to know him quite intimately through his writing, was no angel. He had a very human temper, perhaps a bit of an ornery streak and a sharp tongue, especially when it came to his Jewish scribe peers. Yet, who can question his faith, his commitment, his industry, his meticulous artistry, the depths of his theological insights, compassion, and love for his community? Imagine, for a moment, if you can, the many sleepless nights he spent by candlelight pains-takingly piecing together the fragments of traditions found in his *capsa,* fitting them into his scenario, nuancing them redactionally to comply with his own original theological convictions and still coming up with a coherent narrative. Appreciate the ingenuity of incorporating and superimposing his "Acts," describing his analysis of the early church in Antioch, directly over and into his foundation story of Jesus' life and ministry, confirming their inescapable inter-relatedness.

True, Ben Grammateus was no angel, but he was a herald of the *"good news of the kingdom"* 24:14, and a scribe *"trained for the kingdom of heaven,"* 13:52. He was not one of Jesus' original twelve disciples, but he certainly was numbered among the *"disciples"* of his own community as he transparently describes them in his Gospel. No disrespect is intended, but pardon me if I confess that I now feel more indebted to, and better personally acquainted with, Ben Grammateus than I ever did to or with St. Matthew. Familiarity takes precedence over pious nostalgia.

Contemporary Import

Now you can undoubtedly sense where I am headed in these closing paragraphs. I wish to make an appeal that we read this Gospel again as if for the first time, identifying ourselves with its context, involving ourselves with its argument, permeating our hearts with its vision. To do so we will first need to cleanse ourselves of our many comfortable pretexts and pious self-deceptions. Forget this Gospel's pleasing King Jamesian resonances. Stop insisting on logical consistency in all aspects of its presentation. Develop a tolerance for the apophatic. Put on your historical bifocals and theological earphones so you can appreciate the full stereophonic melody of Ben's message. We need not only to reread this Gospel, but to listen to it on its own terms devoid of harmonizing decorations borrowed from Saints Paul, Mark, Luke or John. Recognize that the accumulated glitter of century-old devotion has now rusted and like tired incense has grown stale.

Here is a Gospel to which we can authentically relate. It asks the right questions, if not always providing complete and final answers. Its challenges remain urgent. In a time when we know all about improprieties and even illegalities and crimes, but have lost sight of the concept of sin, despoiling our relationship with God, we need to hear and heed the call to "exceeding righteousness." In a day when most of the Christian community is fragmented more on the bases of pet organizational structures and competing polities, formalities and financial investments, than on substantive theology, we need to be reminded that the church is a non-stratified fellowship under Christ where no one should be called or considered *"rabbi...father...or instructor,"* 23:8, to say nothing of their modern equivalents listed in an incredibly long taxonomy of ecclesiastical offices, ranks, powers and privileges.

This Gospel, discussing **What's New and Old in the Kingdom of Heaven**, when considered in context, remains

257

almost alarmingly fresh and cogent. It has its share of problems, challenges, surprises and mysteries, but as one sensitive commentator aptly concluded some years ago, this Gospel is a "beneficial disturbance,"[3] waking us up and forcing us to face the dour realities of our human condition, yet offering hope in an ever-present Christ.

Earlier I compared this Gospel's genre to a J.S. Bach fugue with several melodies and themes ingeniously interwoven. Now, in closing, I would add only that this fugue is put into the rhythm and cadence of a symphonic march. It is a call-to-arms. Hear the throbbing ebb and flow of its thematic crescendos; its shifts in key from major to minor; its impassioned surges of urgency and hope; and finally, its sustained soft note of reassurance: *"Remember, I am with you always unto the end of the age."*

With that, Ben rests his *penicillus* baton.

Bravo!

Reprise Endnotes

[1] Cf. Philip H. Phatticher, FESTIVALS AND COMMEMORATIONS; Augsburg Publishing House, Minneapolis, 1980, p. 362f.

[2] Cf., e.g., the covers of Richard A. Edwards, MATTHEW'S STORY OF JESUS; Fortress Press, Philadelphia, 1985; and Jack Dean Kingsbury, MATTHEW AS STORY; Fortress Press, Philadelphia, 1896.

[3] Cf. G. Kretschmar, *"Ein Beitrag zur Frage nach dem Ursprunfrühchristlicher Askese."* ZThK, 61, 1964, p. 67.

INDEX OF BIBLICAL TEXTS

268

INDEX OF SELECTED TOPICS

BIBLIOGRAPHY

General Reference Works

The Didache. pp. 305-333 *in Apostolic Fathers.* Trans. Kirsopp Lake. Loeb Classical Library, Harvard University Press, Cambridge, 1912.

Encyclopia Judaica. Keter Publishing, Jerusalem, n.d.

Aland, Kurt, ed. *Synopsis Quattuor Evangeliorum.* Editio septima. Württembergishe bibelanstalt, Stuttgart,1971.

Bauer, Walter. *A Greek-English Lexicon of the New Testament.* 2nd edition. Wm. F.Arndt, F. Wilbur Gingrich and Frederick W. Danker, revisers and editors. The University of Chicago Press, Chicago and London, 1979.

Danby, Herbert ed. *The Mishnah.* Oxford University Press, Oxford, 1933.

Eusebius Pamphilius. *Ecclesiastical History.* Trans. Christian Frederick Cruse. Baker Book House, Grand Rapids, 1955.

Feine, Paul; Johannes Behm, Werner Georg Kümmel. *Introduction to the New Testament.* Trans. A.J. Mattill, Jr. Abingdon Press, Nashville and New York, 1961.

Hennecke, Edgar. *New Testament Apocrypha, Vol 1.* Wilhelm Schneemelcher, ed. R. McL.Wilson, trans. The Westminster Press, Philadelphia, 1963.

Josephus, Flavius. *Josephus: Complete Works.* Trans. William Whiston. Kregel Publications, Grand Rapids, 1978.

Moulton, W.F. and A.S. Geden, eds. *A Concordance to the Greek Testament According to the Texts of Westcott and Hort, Tischendorf and the English Revisers.* Fourth edition. T & T Clark, Edinburgh, 1970.

Schaff, Philip, ed. *Nicene and Post-Nicene Fathers.* First series.

Selected Journal Articles and Books

Abel, Ernest L. *"Who Wrote Matthew?"* New Testament Studies, 17 (1970-71) 138-152.

Allison, Dale C. Jr. *The New Moses, A Matthean Typology.* Fortress Press, Minneapolis, 1993.

Anderson, Janice Capel. *Matthew's Narrative Web: Over and Over and Over Again.* Journal for the Study of the New Testament, Supplement Series 91; JSOT Press, Sheffield, 1994.

Balch, David L. ed. *Social History of the Matthean Community; Cross-Disciplinary Approaches.* Fortress Press, Minneapolis, 1991.

Bauer, David R. and Mark Allan Powell, eds. *Treasures New and Old: Recent Contributions to Matthean Studies.* Scholars Press, Atlanta, Georgia, 1996.

Blake, Everett C. and Anna G. Edmonds. *Biblical Sites in Turkey.* Redhouse Press, Istanbul,1977.

Bornkamm, G. Barth, G. and H.J. Held. *Tradition and Interpretation in Matthew.* Trans. Percy Scott; SCM Press, London, 1963.

Bowersock, G.W. *Fiction as History; Nero to Julian.* University of California Press, Berkeley, Los Angeles, London, 1994.

Breedwood, Robert F. and Linda S. *Excavations in the Plain of Antioch, The Earlier Assemblages, Phase A-J, Vol. 1* The University of Chicago Oriental Institute Publications, Vol. LXI, Chicago, 1960.

Brooks, Stephenson H. *Matthew's Community: The Evidence of the Special Sayings Material.* Journal for the Study of the New Testament Supplement Series 16; JSOT Press, Sheffield, 1987.

Brown, Raymond E. *"Not Jewish Christianity and Gentile Christianity but Types of Jewish/Gentile Christianity."* Catholic Biblical Quarterly, 45 (1983) 74-79.

Brown, R.E., Karl P. Donfried and John Reumann, eds. *Peter in the New Testament; A Collaborative Assessment by Protestant and Roman Catholic Scholars.* Augsburg Publishing House, Minneapolis and Paulist Press, New York, Paramus, Toronto, 1973.

Brown, Raymond E. and John P. Meier. *Antioch & Rome: New Testament Cradles of Catholic Christianity.* Paulist Press, New York/Ramsay; 1983.

Brown, Schuyler. *"The Two-Fold Representation of the Mission in Matthew's Gospel."* Studies in Theology, 31, (1977) 21-32.

Brown, Schuyler. *"The Matthean Apocalypse."* Journal for the Study of the New Testament, 4 (1979) 2-27.

Brown, Schuyler. *"The Matthean Community and the Gentile Mission."* Novum Testamentum, 22 (1980) 193- 221.

Cameron, Averil. *Christianity and the Rhetoric of Empire: The Development of Christian Discourse.* University of California Press, Berkeley, Los Angeles, London,1991.

Carter, Warren. *"The Crowds in Matthew's Gospel."* Catholic Biblical Quarterly, 55 (1993) 54-67.

Carter, Warren. *Matthew: Storyteller, Interpreter, Evangelist.* Hendrickson Publishers, Peabody, MA., 1996.

Cassidy, Richard J. *"Matthew 17:24-27 — A Word on Civil Taxes."* Catholic Biblical Quarterly, 41, 4 (1979) 571-580.

Childs, Brevard S. *The New Testament as Canon: An Introduction.* SCM. Press Ltd., London,1984. pp. 57-78.

Cicero, Makus Tullius. *De Inventione.* Trans. H. M. Hubbell. Loeb Classical Library, Harvard University Press, Cambridge, 1949.

Cimok, Fatih. *Antioch on the Orontes.* A Turizm Yayinlari Ltd. Sti., Sifa Hamami Sokak 18, Sultanahmet 34400, Istanbul, 1980. 1994.

Clark, Donald Lemen. *Rhetoric in Greco-Roman Education.* Columbia University Press, New York, 1957.

Combrink, H.J.B. *The Structure of the Gospel of Matthew as Narrative.* TB, 34 (1983) 61-90.

Conley, Thomas M. *Rhetoric in the European Tradition.* Longman, New York and London,1990.

Cope, O. Lamar. *Matthew, A Scribe Trained for the Kingdom of Heaven.* The Catholic Biblical Association of America, Washington, 1976.

Corbett, Edward P.J. *Classical Rhetoric for the Modern Student.* Oxford University Press, New York and Oxford, 1990.

Corwin, V. *St. Ignatius and Christianity in Antioch.* Yale University Press, New Haven, 1960.

Crowe, Jerome. *From Jerusalem to Antioch; The Gospel across Cultures.* The Liturgical Press, Collegeville, Minnesota, 1997.

Cullmann, Oscar. *Peter: Disciple-Apostle-Martyr.* Trans. Floyd V. Filson. SCM Press, London,1962.

Davies, Margaret. *Matthew.* Journal for the Study of the Old Testament Press; Sheffield;1993.

Davies, W.D. and Dale C. Allison, Jr. *International Critical Commentary on Matthew.* 3 vols. T & T Clark, Edinburgh, 1991.

Davison, J.E. *"Anomia and the Question of Antinomian Polemic in Matthew."* Journal of Biblical Literature, 104 (1985) 617-635.

Downey, Glanville, *A History of Antioch in Syria from Seleucus to the Arab Conquest.* Princeton, N.J., Princeton University Press, 1961.

Downey, Glanville. *Ancient Antioch.* Princeton, Princeton University Press, 1963.

Dumbrell, W. *"The Logic of the Role of Law in Matthew V. 1-20."* Novum Testamentum, 23 (1981) 1-21.

Edwards, Richard A. *Matthew's Story of Jesus.* Fortress Press, Philadelphia, 1985.

Ehrman, Bart D. *The Orthodox Corruption of Scripture; The effect of Early Christological Controversies on the Text of the New Testament,* Oxford University Press, New York, Oxford, 1993.

Ellis, Peter F. *Matthew - His Mind and His Message.* The Liturgical Press, Collegeville, 1974.

Epictetus. *Epictetus, Discourse, 2 vols.* Loeb Classical Library. Trans. W.A. Oldfather, Harvard University Press, Cambridge, 1925.

Farmer, Wm. F. *"The Post-Sectarian Character of Matthew and Its Post-War Setting in Antioch in Syria."* Perspectives in Religious Studies, 3 (1976) 235- 247.

Ferguson, Everett. *Backgrounds of Early Christianity,* 2nd ed., William B. Eerdmans Publishing Company, Grand Rapids, 1993.

Finegan, Jack. *Light from the Ancient Past,* Princeton University Press, Princeton, N.J., 1946.

Fowler, Robert M. *Let the Reader Understand: Reader-Response Criticism.* Fortress Press, Mineapolis, 1991.

Gamble, Harry Y. *Books and Readers in the Early Church: A History of Early Christian Texts.* Yale University Press, New Haven and London, 1995.

Garland, David E. *Reading Matthew, A Literary and Theological Commentary on the First Gospel.* Crossroad Publishing Company, New York, 1993.

Gill, David W.J. and Conrad Gempf, eds. *The Book of ACTS in its Graeco-Roman Setting.* William B. Eerdmans Publishing Company, Grand Rapids, and The Paternoster Press, Carlisle, Cumbria, U.K., 1994.

Grant, Robert M. *Augustus to Constantine.* Harper and Row, San Francisco, 1970.

Greenlee, J. Harold. *Scribes, Scrolls and Scripture: A Students' Guide to New Testament Textual Criticism.* William B. Eerdmanns Publishing Company, Grand Rapids, 1985.

Guelich, Robert A. *The Sermon on the Mount: A Foundation for Understanding.* Word Books, Waco, Texas, 1982.

Gundry, Robert H. *Matthew: A Commentary on His Literary and Theological Art.* Wm. B. Eerdmans Publishing Company, Grand Rapids, 1982.

Haines, Richard C. *Excavations in the Plain of Antioch, II, The Structural Remains of the Later Phases,* University of Chicago Press, Chicago, 1971.

Hare, Douglas R. *The Theme of Jewish Persecution of Christians in the Gospel according to St. Matthew.* Cambridge University Press, Cambridge, 1967.

Hare, D. and D. Harrington. *"Make Disciples of All the Gentiles - Matt. 28:19."* Catholic Biblical Quarterly, 37 (1975) 359-369.

Howell, David B. *Matthew's Inclusive Story.* JSOT Press, Sheffield; 1990.

Ignatius, St. *"Ignatius to Polycarp,"* in *Apostolic Fathers.* Kirsopp Lake, trans. Loeb Classical Library, Harvard University Press, Cambridge, 1912.

Jeremias, Joachim. *The Parables of Jesus.* Charles Scribner's Sons, New York, 1954.

Jurgens, William A., ed. *The Faith of the Early Fathers.* The Liturgical Press, Collegeville, Minnesota, 1970.

Kennedy, George A. *The Art of Persuasion in Greece.* Princeton University Press, Princeton,1963.

Kennedy, George A. *Classical Rhetoric and its Christian & Secular Tradition From Ancient to Modern Times,* University of North Carolina Press, Chapel Hill, 1980.

Kermode, Frank. *The Genesis of Secrecy, On the Interpretation of Narrative.* Cambridge.1979.

Kingsbury, Jack Dean. *"The Composition and Christology of Matt 28:19."* Journal of Biblical Literature, 93 (1974) 573-584.

Kingsbury, Jack Dean. *Matthew—Structure, Christology, Kingdom.* Fortress Press, Philadelphia,1975.

Kingsbury, Jack Dean. *"The Title 'Son of David' in Matthew's Gospel."* Journal of Biblical Literature, 95 (1976) 591-602.

Kingsbury, Jack Dean. *Matthew as Story.* Fortress Press, Philadelphia, 1986.

Kloppenborg, John S. ed. *Conflict and Invention: Literary, Rhetorical and Social Studies on the Sayings Gospel Q.* Trinity Press International, Valley Forge, Pennsylvania, 1995.

Koester, Helmut. *History, Culture, and Religion of the Hellenistic Age, 2nd ed.* Walter DeGruyter, New York, 1995.

Kraeling, C. *The Jewish Community at Antioch.* Journal of Biblical Literature, 51 (1932)130-160.

Kretschmar, G. *"Ein Beitrag zur Frage nach dem ursprungfrühchristlicher Askese."* ZThK, 61 (1964).

Libanius. *Autobiography and Selected Letters, Vol I.* Trans. A.F. Norman. Loeb Classical Library, Harvard University Press, Cambridge, Mass., 1992.

Libanius. *"In Praise of Antioch"* (Oration XI). Trans. Glanville Downey, Dumbarton Oaks Research Library.

Liver, J. *"The Half-Shekel Offering in Biblical and Post-Biblical Literature."* Harvard Theological Review, 56,3 ((July 1963) 173-198.

Luz, Ulrich *Matthew 1-7: A Commentary.* Trans. Wilhelm C. Linss. Augsburg Press, Minneapolis, 1985.

Malalas, John. *Chronicle of John Malalas, Books VIII-XVIII,* Matthew Spinka and Glanville,Downey, eds., University of Chicago Press, Chicago, 1940.

Malina, Bruce J. *The New Testament World: Insights from Cultural Anthropology.* John Knox Press, 1981.

Martin, James P. *"The Church in Matthew"* in Interpreting the Gospels, James Luther Mays, ed., Fortress Press, Philadelphia, 1981

Meeks, Wayne A. and Robert L. Wilken. *Jews and Christians in* Antioch In the First Four Centuries of the Common Era. SBL Sources for Biblical Study 13, Scholars Press, Missoula, Montana, 1978.

Meier, John P. *"Salvation History in Matthew: In Search of a Starting Point."* Catholic Biblical Quarterly, 37,2 (April 1975) 203-215.

Meier, John P. *"Two Disputed Questions in Matt 28:16-20."* Journal of Biblical Literature, 96 (1977) 407- 424.

Meier, John P. *"Nations or Gentiles in Matthew 28:16-20?"* Catholic Biblical Quarterly, 39 (1977) 94-102.

Meier, John P. *The Vision of Matthew. Christ, Church and Morality in the First Gospel.* Paulist Press, New York, Ramsay, Toronto, 1978.

Meier, John P. *The Mission of Christ and His Church. Studies in Christology and Ecclesiology.* Michael Glazier, Inc., Wilmington, 1990.

Millar, Fergus. *The Roman Near East, 31 BC - AD 337.* Harvard University Press, Cambridge,1993.

Nau, Arlo J. *Peter in Matthew: Discipleship, Diplomacy and Dispraise.* The Liturgical Press, Collegeville, Minnesota, 1992.

Nau, Arlo J. *Practically Poetry.* Privately published. Phoenix, AZ., 1994.

Orton, David E. *The Understanding Scribe.* Sheffield Academic Press, Sheffield, 1989.

Overman, J. Andrew *Matthew's Gospel and Formative Judaism, The Social World of the Matthean Community.* Fortress Press, Minneapolis 1990.

Perkins, Pheme *"Gnostic Christologies and the New Testament."* Catholic Biblical Quarterly, 43 (1981) 590-606.

Pfatteicher, Philip H. *Festivals and Commemorations.* Augsburg Publishing House, Minneapolis, 1980.

Philostratus. *The Life of Apollonius of Tyana, Vol. 1.* Trans. F.C. Conybeare. Loeb Classical Library; Harvard University Press, Cambridge, Mass., 1912.

Pilch, John J. and Bruce J. Malina, Eds. *Biblical Social Values and Their Meaning: A Handbook.* Hendrickson Publishers, Peabody, Massachusetts, 1993.

Powell, Mark Allan. *"Do and Keep What Moses Says,"* Journal of Biblical Literature, Vol.114, 3, (1995) pp. 419-435.

Powell, Mark Allen. *God With Us. A Pastoral Theology of Matthew's Gospel.* Fortress Press, Minneapolis, 1995.

Przbylski, Benno. *Righteousness in Matthew and His World of Thought.* Cambridge University Press, London, New York, 1980.

Quintilianus, Marcus Fabius. *Institutio Oratoria.* 4 vols. Loeb Classical Library. Harvard University Press, Cambridge, 1920-22.

Richardson, Alan, ed. *A Theological Wordbook of the Bible.* The Macmillan Company, New York, 1950.

Runciman, Steven. *The Great Church in Captivity, A Study of the Patriarchate of Constantinople from the Eve of the Turkish Conquest to the Greek War of Independence.* Cambridge University Press, Cambridge, Enaland, 1968, 1995.

Saldarini, Anthony J. *Matthew's Christian-Jewish Community.* University of Chicago Press, Chicago and London, 1994.

Schoedel, Wm. R. *Ignatius of Antioch.* Hermenia Commentariy Fortress Press, Philadelphia, 1985.

Scott, Bernard Brandon. *"The King's Accounting: Matthew 18:23-34,"* Journal of Biblical Literature, 104, 3, (September 1985) 429-442.

Senior, Donald. *"The Death of Jesus and the Resurrection of the Holy Ones."* Catholic Biblical Quarterly, 38 (1976) 312-329.

Senior, Donald. *The Passion Narrative According to Matthew: A Redactional Study.* Leuven University, Leuven, 1975.

Shuler, Philip L. *A Genre for the Gospels. The Biographical Character of Matthew.* Fortress Press, Philadelphia, 1982.

Smart, James E. *The Strange Silence of the Bible in the Church.* Westminster Press, Philadelphia, 1974.

Stambaugh, John E. and David L. Balch, eds. *The New Testament in Its Social Environment.* Westminster Press, Philadelphia, 1986.

Stanton, Graham N. *A Gospel for a New People: Studies in Matthew.* T & T Clark, Edinburgh, 1992.

Stanton, Graham N., ed. *The Interpretation of Matthew, 2nd ed.* T&T Clark, Edinburgh,1995.

Stein, R.H. *Difficult Sayings in the Gospels. Jesus' Use of Overstatement and Hyperbole.* Baker Publishing House, 1985.

Stendahl, Krister. *The School of St. Matthew, and Its Use of the Old Testament.* CWK Gleerup, Lund, n.d.

Stock, Augustine. *The Method and Message of Matthew.* A Michael Glazier Book. The Liturgical Press, Collegeville, Minnesota, 1994.

Strecker, Georg. *Der Weg der Gerechtigkeit. Untersuchung zur Theologie des Matthäus.* Vandenhoeck & Ruprecht, Göttingen, 1971.

Suetonius. *The Lives of the Caesars, Vol. II.* Trans. J.C. Rolfe. Loeb Classical Library; Harvard University Press, Cambridge, Mass., 1914.

Tacitus, P. Cornelius. *The Annals* and *The Histories.* Trans. Alfred John Church, William Jackson Brodribb. Great Books of the Western World. Encyclopedia Britannica, Inc., Chicago, 1952.

Tagawa, Kenzo. *"People and Community in the Gospel of Matthew."* New Testament Studies, 16, 2 (1970) 149-162.

Taylor, Nicholas *Paul, Antioch and Jerusalem; A Study of Relationships and Authority in Earliest Christianity.* Journal for the Study of the New Testament, Supplement Series 66. Sheffield Press, 1992.

Telushkin, Joseph. *Jewish Literacy: The Most Important Things to Know About the Jewish Religion, Its People, and Its History.* William Morrow and Company, New York, 1991.

Tenney, Merrill C. *New Testament Times.* William B. Eerdmans Publishing Company, Grand Rapids, 1965.

Tisera, Guido, *Universalism according to the Gospel of Matthew;* Peter Lang, Frankfurt am Main, Berlin, Bern, New York, Paris, Wien, 1993.

Theissen, Gerd *The Gospels in Context: Social and Political History in the Synoptic Tradition.* Trans. Linda M. Maloney; Fortress Press, Minneapolis, 1991.

Thompson, Wm. G. *Matthew's Advice to a Divided Community, Mt. 17:22-18:35.* Analecta Biblica. Biblical Institute Press, Rome, 1970.

Thompson, Wm. G. *"Reflections on the Composition of Mt. 8:1-9:34."* Catholic Biblical Quarterly, 33 (1971).

Thompson, Wm. G. *"An Historical Perspective in the Gospel of Matthew."* Journal of Biblical Literature, 93, 2 (1974) 243-262.

Thompson Wm. G. and E. LaVeriere. *"New Testament Communities in Transition."* Theological Studies, 37 (1976) 567-597.

Tillborg, Sjef von. *The Jewish Leaders in Matthew.* E.J. Brill, Leiden, 1972.

Walker, Rolf. *Die Heilsgeschichte im ersten Evangelium."* Vandenhoeck & Ruprecht, Göttingen, 1967.

Watson, Duane F., Ed. *Persuasive Artistry: Studies in New Testament Rhetoric in Honor of George A. Kennedy.* Journal for the Study of the New Testament, Supplement Series 50, Sheffield Academic Press, 1991.

White, R.E.O. *The Mind of Matthew, Unique Insights for Living Today.* Westminster Press, Philadelphia, 1979.